漫画

DREAMLAND JAPAN

WRITINGS ON MODERN MANGA

Frederik L. Schodt

Stone Bridge Press • Berkeley, California

Published by
Stone Bridge Press, P.O. Box 8208, Berkeley, CA 94707
510-524-8732 • sbp@stonebridge.com • www.stonebridge.com

This 3rd printing includes updates as of 2002 for sources and contacts in the Appendix: Manga in English.

Cover design by Raymond Larrett
incorporating an illustration by Yoshikazu Ebisu.

Text design by Peter Goodman.

Printed in the United States of America.

10 9 8 7 6 5 4
2007 2006 2005

LIBRARY OF CONGRESS CATALOGING-IN-PUBLICATION DATA

Schodt, Frederik L.
Dreamland Japan: writings on modern manga / Frederik L. Schodt.
p. cm.
Includes index.
ISBN 1-880656-23-X (paper).
1. Comic books, strips, etc.—Japan—History and criticism.
I. Title.
PN6790.J3S285 1996
741.5'952—dc20 96-11375
CIP

Dedicated to the memory of Kakuyū (aka Toba), A.D. 1053–1140

目
次

CONTENTS

前書き

PREFACE

ONCE UPON A TIME, IN THE DISTANT DAYS OF 1983, I WROTE A book titled *Manga! Manga! The World of Japanese Comics*. It never sold many copies, but it is now said to be something of a cult classic; it even has a Japanese bistro named after it in Berkeley, California. Certainly, when it first appeared most people had never heard of Japanese comics. Japan was the land of successful management or meditation techniques, or of beautiful arts and crafts. If the Japanese word for comics—"manga" (pronounced "mahngha")—evoked any sort of association at all in the average English-speaking brain, it was probably mixed in with mental images of a rare metal or something that one does at an Italian restaurant.

Much has changed since 1983. "Manga" and its cousin, "anime" (Japanese for animation, pronounced "ahneemay," sometimes also referred to as "Japanimation"), are firmly established in the lexicon of young fans of comics and animation; in due time both words will undoubtedly be listed in the standard English dictionary along with other Japanese imports like "hari-kari" and "karaoke." Manga and anime works are now widely available in translated form, multiple monthly English-language magazines cover both industries, and there are even conventions for non-Japanese fans held around the world several times a year. And manga themselves have changed. The industry has grown larger and fatter, and a whole new generation of younger artists has come to the fore with innovations in both style and content.

I therefore am often asked, "When are you going to

update *Manga! Manga!*?" As the years go by, this has become an increasingly painful question. The original Japanese publisher once asked me to do a revision, but for reasons only it knows changed its mind and at present, at least, is not amenable to the idea. At the end of the 1980s, a friend and I did most of the work for a completely different book on manga, only to have the New York publisher temporarily self-disintegrate in one of the corporate shake-ups that periodically steamroll through the industry.

But enough of that.

* * * * *

Dreamland Japan is not a revision of *Manga! Manga!* but a sequel of sorts. Like an architectural structure inspired by a predecessor, it builds upon and occasionally references the earlier work, but it isn't necessary to have seen the original to enjoy it (although doing so may make it easier to understand). *Manga! Manga!* is still in print and still a comprehensive introduction to the manga field in Japan, with many pages devoted to a historical overview. Readers of this book whose curiosity is piqued will thus find many of the answers to their questions therein.

Dreamland Japan is the product of observing and writing about the manga industry in Japan over the last sixteen years. It is designed in a sort of "Whitman's Sampler" of commentary and criticism, and it can be read in small morsels or (although not necessarily best for the digestion) at one sitting; either way, upon completion the whole will, I hope, be far greater than the sum of the parts. Some of the material has appeared at one time or another in different formats or other places, and I have rewritten and rearranged it here. A few readers may recognize sections from articles written for the Atlanta-based magazine *Mangajin* or the San Francisco–based *Animerica*. Some of the material is also derived from a monthly column I have written for nearly seven years in a Tokyo English-language newspaper called the *Mainichi Daily News*. This recycling of the newspaper column is not as shameless as it might first appear, however, for one characteristic of the *Mainichi Daily News* is that, despite the valiant efforts of the hard-working editors, it is not very widely read in Japan or anywhere else. For me, this has had advantages, as it has allowed me to experiment with and develop many of the themes that I wanted to later incorporate in this book.

* * * * *

Before plunging ahead, I need to go over a few housekeeping details:

Japanese comics are normally laid out in a mirror image of their English-language counterparts: the front cover is what would be the "back cover" of an American comic; the pages are turned from left-to-right instead of right-to-left; panels on a page start at the top right and are usually read from the top right across and down to the bottom left of the page; and the dialog or text in each word balloon is usually laid-out vertically, read from the far right line to the left. All manga illustrations in this book preserve the original Japanese order except where noted. Illustrations from manga translated and published in English, however, have already been arranged in English-language comics format. All photographs are by the author.

Unless otherwise noted, an exchange rate of ¥100 to the dollar is used.

In Japan, people's names are usually listed with the family name first and the given name last. Certain academic types in the English-speaking world are rather finicky about this convention and insist on preserving it even in English texts; not to do so they consider a form of cultural imperialism. This book is for the general public, however, so in the interests of clarity I have listed Japanese names with first names first, and last names last, the way they're supposed to be in English. Also, when Japanese words are transliterated into English, it is customary to romanize them according to specific rules. In almost all situations I have adhered to these rules, with the exception of manga magazine and story titles. Since many Japanese titles use English words, either phoneticized or even written in the

English alphabet, for the sake of simplicity I have generally written these English words using their standard English spellings, rather than try to phoneticize them *and* include a translation. Thus the Japanese borrowed word *komikku* may be rendered simply as "comic" in an otherwise Japanese-language context, rather than as "*komikku* ('comic')." "Long signs" over vowels—as in ō (pronounced "oh" as in "go") and ū ("oo" as in "moon")—indicate that the sound of the vowel is sustained.

Fans of Japanese manga (even more than academics) can be a rather persnickety and unforgiving lot, so before the spears are lobbed some words about what this book is about—and what it is not about—are in order.

First, this book is about manga, and not anime. Most non-Japanese today learn about manga after being exposed to anime. Even if in Japanese, the animation is usually more accessible, for unlike untranslated, printed manga, anime does not require reading the Japanese language or learning the sometimes unique conventions of printed Japanese comics. But while the anime is wonderful in its own right, it is derived from manga culture and often based on original manga works, and as such it is often a watered-down version of the original. Furthermore, anime are produced by teams for the broadest possible audience, while manga—usually created by individual artists—are more direct and personal. I am more interested in the personal. Also, for the record, although the word "manga" has some ambiguity to it and can at times mean "cartoons," "comic strips," "comic books," and even (occasionally) "animation," I use it in the modern Japanese sense of "printed comics," and I never write it with an "s" on the end. I treat it exactly like the word "sheep," which can be either plural or singular depending on the context.

Second, the manga that I discuss in this book are almost all what are called "story manga" in Japan. These are the narrative manga—the unique sequential art form, or "comics"—developed in Japan in the postwar period, with raga-like stories that may continue for thousands of pages. I have not included single-panel cartoons, political cartoons, or other genres, mainly because I think the "story manga" format is what makes Japanese comics so different from those in other countries and hence more interesting.

Third, and finally, fans of manga should not expect to see many of their favorite works here. There are no extended commentaries on *Ranma 1/2*, *Akira*, or *Pretty Soldier Sailor Moon*. These works have become so famous that they are readily available outside of Japan in several languages, either as translated comic books or dubbed and subbed animation. Readers can therefore form their own opinions. My focus, instead, is on manga and recent trends in manga that most people outside of Japan (and many inside Japan) have never heard of and probably never will. Since, for me, manga are also a window on another world, the works that I read tend not to be what is popular, but what I personally find interesting and unusual. This is, therefore, a personal book, and I only hope that readers find the material as interesting as I do.

* * * * *

Books are usually written by one person with the cooperation of many, and *Dreamland Japan* is no exception. Profuse thanks are offered to all who helped. I have talked with dozens of artists and industry people over the years, but special thanks are due to those who gave formal interviews and exceptional informational support between 1989 and 1996. I also apologize to any artists who may be disappointed because they either are, or are not, featured herein.

Artists: Sergio Aragones, Yoshikazu Ebisu, Will Eisner, Fujiko Fujio Ⓐ, Fujiko F. Fujio, Kiyoshi Gotō, Kazuichi Hanawa, Michio Hisaichi, Shingo Iguchi, Takashi Ishii, Arvell Jones, Eimei Kitano, Steve Leialoha, Suehiro Maruo, Tōru Minegishi, Shigeru Mizuki, Nobuyuki Morimoto, Hiromi Morishita, Miruku Morizono, Akira Narita, Kōji Narita, Reiko Okano, Richard and Wendy Pini, Monkey Punch, Trina Robbins, Jerry Robinson, Brian Stelfreeze, Hinako Sugiura, Shigeru Tamura, Buichi Terasawa, Murasaki Yamada, Teruhiko Yumura.

Editors and industry people: Takashi Akiyama, Hisashi Dōmoto, Satoru Fujii, Akira Fujita, Yoshio Irie, Junco Itō, Masahiro Katayama, Katsuichi Katō, Osamu Kawakami, Mary Kennard, Yoshiyuki Kurihara, Kazuhiko Kurokawa, Tetsuya Kurosawa, Fred Ladd, Takayuki Matsutani and the folks at Tezuka Productions, Michiyuki Miyaji, Kan Miyoshi, Masafumi Mizuno, Katsuichi Nagai, Mitsuru Okazaki, Sadao Ōtomo, Toshihiko Sagawa, Ryō Saitani, Toshiharu Sasaki, Vaughan Simmons, Toren Smith, Akira Suei, Keiko Tamura, Shūji Yatabe, Yoshihiro and Eiko Yonezawa.

Critics and various experts: Jay Fubler Harvey, Tomofusa Kure, Steve Pearl, Natsuo Sekikawa, Chris Swett.

For general and all-round assistance a tip of the hat is due to: Jonathan Clements; Douglas Dlin; Jō and Nanae Inoue; Helen McCarthy; Miyoko and Ami Mizuno; Hiromichi Moteki; Keiko Tokioka; the folks at *Mangajin*, the *Mainichi Daily News,* Studio Proteus, and Viz (thanks, Seiji and Kumi). Eddie and Margie Schodt, Fred Patten, and Leonard Rifas served as my official beta-version readers, and Leonard also helped create the graphs. For reading and commenting on Chapter 7, thanks also to Satoru Fujii, Alan Gleason, Trish Ledoux, and Toren Smith.

A special word of thanks is also due to all those in Japan and elsewhere who provided permissions for illustrations; to everyone at Stone Bridge Press, especially Peter Goodman, my editor and publisher and friend who believed in this book and tolerated my delays; to Leonard Koren, who helped in the genesis of several of the key ideas herein; to Raymond Larrett, who designed the perfect cover; to Yoshikazu Ebisu, who provided the explosive illustration; and to Misao, for her wonderful spirit.

FREDERIK L. SCHODT
San Francisco

Note: Much-beloved artist Fujiko F. Fujio passed away on September 23, 1996, shortly after this book was first published.

漫画

1

ENTER THE ID

イッドを覗く

IN 1995, FORMER JAPANESE PRIME MINISTER KIICHI MIYAZAWA began serializing a column of his opinions, not in a newspaper or newsmagazine, but in the manga magazine *Big Comic Spirits*. A respected seventy-five-year-old politician and thinker, Miyazawa probably rarely reads comics,* but the reason he chose a manga magazine to air his views is clear. *Big Comic Spirits* is read by nearly 1.4 million young salarymen and potential voters each week. In today's Japan, manga magazines are one of the most effective ways to reach a mass audience and influence public opinion.

Japan is the first nation in the world to accord "comic books"—originally a "humorous" form of entertainment mainly for young people—nearly the same social status as novels and films. Indeed, Japan is awash in manga. According to the Research Institute for Publications, of all the books and magazines actually sold in Japan in 1995 (minus returns, in other words), manga comprised nearly *40 percent* of the total.

Such industry statistics are indeed impressive, even frightening, but they hardly represent the entire picture or the true number of manga being read in Japan. There were 2.3 billion manga books and magazines produced in 1995, and nearly 1.9 billion actually sold, or over 15 for every man, woman, and child in Japan. Given the wild currency fluctuations of that year, the value of all comics

* Not so Ryūtarō Hashimoto, the youthful prime minister in 1996. His wife was widely quoted as saying that at home on quiet evenings, the couple liked to read manga.

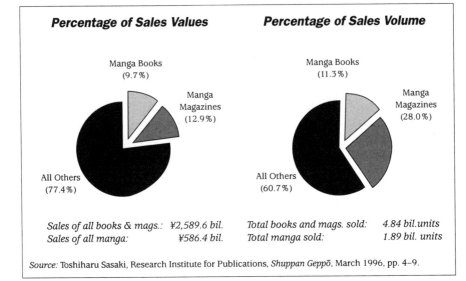

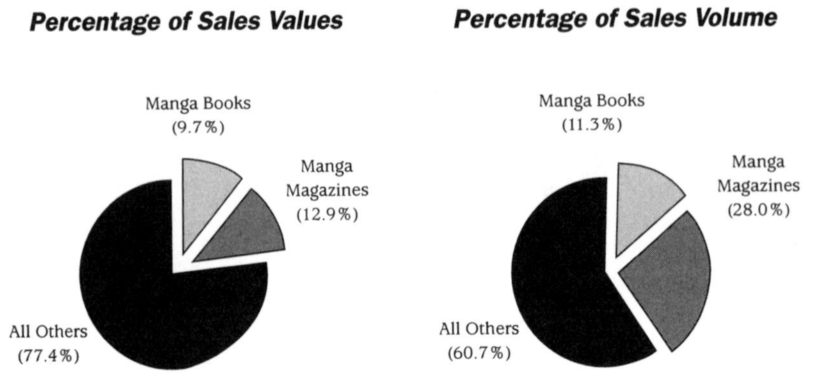

Sales of all books & mags.:	*¥2,589.6 bil.*	*Total books and mags. sold:*	*4.84 bil.units*
Sales of all manga:	*¥586.4 bil.*	*Total manga sold:*	*1.89 bil. units*

Source: Toshiharu Sasaki, Research Institute for Publications, *Shuppan Geppō*, March 1996, pp. 4–9.

Manga share of all published books and magazines in Japan, 1995.

produced ranged from U.S.$7–9 billion (a sum twice the GDP of Iceland), while those actually sold were worth $6–7 billion—an annual expenditure of over $50 for every person in Japan. Yet this does not include the millions of *dōjinshi*, or amateur manga publications, that do not circulate in regular distribution channels. Nor does it reflect the fact that non-manga magazines for adults, which used to be all text and pictures, now devote more and more pages to serialized manga stories. Finally, it does not take into account the popular practice of *mawashi-yomi*, of one manga being passed around and read by many people.

Statistics also do not indicate the huge influence manga have on Japanese society. Manga today are a type of "meta media" at the core of a giant fantasy machine. A production cycle typically begins with a story serialized in a weekly, biweekly, monthly, bimonthly, or quarterly magazine. The story, if successful, is then compiled into a series of paperbacks and deluxe hardback books, then produced as an animated series for television, and then made into a theatrical feature. For a particularly popular or long-running series, the cycle may be repeated several times. One manga story thus becomes fuel not just for the world's largest animation industry, but for a burgeoning business in manga-inspired music CDs, character-licensed toys, stationery, video games, operas, television dramas, live-action films, and even manga-inspired novels.

At Japan's largest and most prestigious publishers it is no secret that sales of manga magazines and books now subsidize a declining commitment to serious literature. Indeed, since manga are read by nearly all ages and classes of people today, references to them permeate Japanese intellectual life at the highest levels, and they are increasingly influencing serious art and literature. It is no exaggeration to say that one cannot understand modern Japan today without having some understanding of the role that manga play in society.

What Are Manga?

マンガとは何か

A LITTLE BACKGROUND

What are manga, exactly, and where did they come from? In a nutshell, the modern Japanese manga is a synthesis: a long Japanese tradition of art that entertains has taken on a physical form imported from the West.

* * * * *

In late 1994 I accompanied several well-known American comics artists to Japan for discussions with their Japanese counterparts. Will Eisner, the pioneer and reigning dean of American comic books, was along, and he was clearly shocked and puzzled at how popular comics are in Japan. After all, he himself had struggled long and hard to gain more recognition for comics in his own country. Yet when he took a long look at a display of 19th-century illustrated humor books in the Edo-Tokyo Museum, his face lit up in a satori-like realization of why Japanese so love comics: They always have.

Japanese people have had a long love affair with art (especially monochrome line drawings) that is fantastic, humorous, erotic, and sometimes violent. One of the most famous examples is the hilarious *Chōjūgiga*, or "Animal Scrolls," a 12th-century satire on the clergy and nobility, said to be by a Buddhist priest named Toba. Today's manga magazines and books, however, also have direct links to two types of entertaining picture books from the 18th and early 19th centuries—*toba-e* ("Toba pictures," after the author of the "Animal Scrolls") and *kibyōshi*, or "yellow-jacket books." These were mass produced using woodblock printing and a division of labor not unlike the production system used by manga artists and their assistants today. Often issued in a series, again like today's manga, they were beloved by townspeople in cities such as Osaka and Edo (today's Tokyo). In a very real sense, they were the world's first comic books.

The physical form of modern manga—the sequential panels with word balloons arranged on a page to tell a story—came from the United States at the turn of the century, when American newspaper comic strips like George McManus's *Bringing Up Father* were imported. But unlike the United States, where slim magazines called "comic books" were first compiled in the 1930s from "comic strips" in newspapers, in prewar Japan the first real "comic books" for children were hardback books compiled from "comic strips" serialized in fat, illustrated monthly magazines for boys and girls. This pattern continues today in Japan; individual manga stories are usually first serialized along with many other stories in omnibus-style manga magazines and then compiled into their own paperback and hardback books.

WHAT MAKES JAPANESE MANGA DIFFERENT FROM OTHER COMICS?

The two predominant and most distinctive forms of comics in the world today are those of America and Japan; minor variations on both are found in Europe, Latin America, and Asia. Although they have an essentially similar format, Japanese and American comics have developed into two very different art forms. Other than the fact that manga are read "backward" because of the way the Japanese language is written, the most striking difference is size. American comic books are usually between 30 and 50 pages long, contain one serialized story, and are published monthly. But manga magazines, many of which are issued *weekly*, often have 400 pages and contain twenty serialized and concluding stories (some magazines have 1,000 pages and over forty stories); when an individual story is compiled into a series of paperbacks it may take up fifty or more volumes of over 250 pages each.

Prices of manga are also extraordinarily low, even given the dollar's gutted value versus the yen in late 1995. Where a typical 32-page U.S. comic book (with many ads) cost over $2, a 400-page manga magazine rarely cost more than $3–4. On a per-page basis, therefore, the manga was six times cheaper than the U.S. comic book, a miracle made possible by the economies of scale Japanese publishers enjoy and by the use of low-quality recycled paper and mainly monochrome printing.

Manga magazines are not intended to last long, or even to be kept. Most are tossed in the trash can after a quick read, or recycled. Stories that are popular, however, are preserved by being compiled into paperback and hardback editions; most of the best comics in Japan—even those from forty years ago—are available in such permanent editions at a very reasonable price. As a result, Japan has largely been free of the disease from which American comics suffer: speculation. Collectors dominate the American mainstream comics market, and they are more likely to poly-bag their purchases and place them in a drawer than read them, thus driving up the price of both old and new comics. In 1995, one collector paid $137,500 for a copy of *Action Comics* No. 1, which first introduced Superman. As Toren Smith, a packager of Japanese comics in the U.S., notes, alluding to a company that produces coins especially for the collectors market, "many American comic book publishers have become the equivalent of the Franklin mint."

Unlike mainstream American and European comics, which are richly colored, most manga are monochrome, except for the cover and a few inside pages. But this is no handicap when it comes to artistic expression. On the contrary, some manga artists have elevated line drawing to new aesthetic heights and developed new conventions

Cinematic effects, 1949. Panels from a page in Osamu Tezuka's* Metropolis, *rearranged in left-to-right order to illustrate progression.

to convey depth and speed with lines and shading. Using the "less-is-more" philosophy of traditional Japanese brush painting, many artists have learned to convey subtle emotions with a minimum of effort; an arched eyebrow, a downturned face, or a hand scratching the back of the head can all speak paragraphs. And since manga today are increasingly mass produced, artists can avail themselves of many new tools for quickly detailing monochrome backgrounds. The copy machine, for example, is often used by artists at high-contrast to incorporate photographs into backgrounds (in recent years some photographers have filed claims against artists for "appropriating" their images in this fashion). Another modern-day tool is "screen tones"—ready-to-use, commercially available patterned sheets that can be applied on a page to instantly create shadings and texture. Artists around the world use screen tones, but Japanese artists have access to such a variety that their overseas counterparts can only drool with envy. There are even screen tones for ready-made backgrounds of city- and seascapes. For those who prefer to draw by hand, there are special manga "background catalogs" with carefully rendered line drawings (available for copying) of the interiors of school classrooms, office rooms, train stations, restaurants, and other popular settings.

Still, many manga are quite poorly drawn by American and European standards. At the meetings held in 1994 between several noted American and Japanese comics artists, the Japanese boasted of the superiority of their form of comics—until it came to artwork, at which

point they all looked rather sheepish and unanimously agreed that they could never match the draftsmanship of their Western counterparts.

The real hallmark of manga is storytelling and character development. After World War II, a single artist—Osamu Tezuka—helped revolutionize the art of comics in Japan by decompressing story lines. Influenced by American animation in particular, instead of using ten or twenty pages to tell a story as had been common before, Tezuka began drawing novelistic manga that were hundreds, even thousands of pages long, and he incorporated different perspectives and visual effects—what came to be called "cinematic techniques." Other artists in America, such as Will Eisner, had employed cameralike effects a decade earlier, but combining this technique with the decompression of story lines was new.

The result was a form of comics that has far fewer words than its American or European counterpart and that uses far more frames and pages to depict an action or a thought. If an American comic book might use a single panel with word balloons and narration to show how Superman once rescued Lois Lane in the past, the Japanese version might use ten pages and no words. (Of course, the monochrome printing, cheap paper, and the enormous economies of scale enjoyed by Japanese industry also make it economically *possible* for artists to do this.)

Many American artists have been heavily influenced by Japanese manga in recent years, so that some of the differences between the two art forms have begun to erode. But if one were to make a gross generalization, it would be that until recently many mainstream American comics still resembled illustrated narratives, whereas Japanese manga were a visualized narrative with a few words tossed in for effect.

The cinematic style enables manga artists to develop their story lines and characters with more complexity and psychological and emotional depth. Like good film directors, they can focus reader attention on the minutia of daily life—on scenes of leaves falling from a tree, or steam rising from a bowl of hot noodles, or even the pregnant pauses in a conversation—and evoke associations and memories that are deeply moving. Japanese comics are perhaps unique in the world in that it is not unusual to hear fans talk about weeping over favorite scenes.

The cinematic style also allows manga to be far more iconographic than comics in America and Europe. Individual illustrations don't have to be particularly well-executed as long as they fulfill their basic role of conveying enough information to maintain the flow of the story. And why should they be? A young American or European fan of comics may spend minutes admiring the artwork on each page of his or her favorite comic, but not the Japanese manga fan. As I wrote in 1983, to the amazement of many in the U.S. comics industry, a 320-page manga magazine is often read in twenty minutes, at a speed of 3.75 seconds per page. In this context, manga are merely another "language," and the panels and pages are but another type of "words" adhering to a unique grammar. Japanese say that reading manga is almost like reading Japanese itself. This makes sense, for manga pictures are not entirely unlike Japanese ideograms, which are themselves sometimes a type of "cartoon," or a streamlined visual representation of reality.

Japanese manga offer far more visual diversity than mainstream American comics, which are still shackled by the Greek tradition of depicting the human form and still reveal an obsession with muscled males and full-figured females. Only in American "underground comics" or "independents" can one find anything approaching the eccentricity of art styles that exists in Japan—where humans may be depicted in both realistic and nonrealis-

Cinematic effects, 1980. Tetsuji Hashimoto's Itsumo Kimi ga Ita *("You Were Always There").*

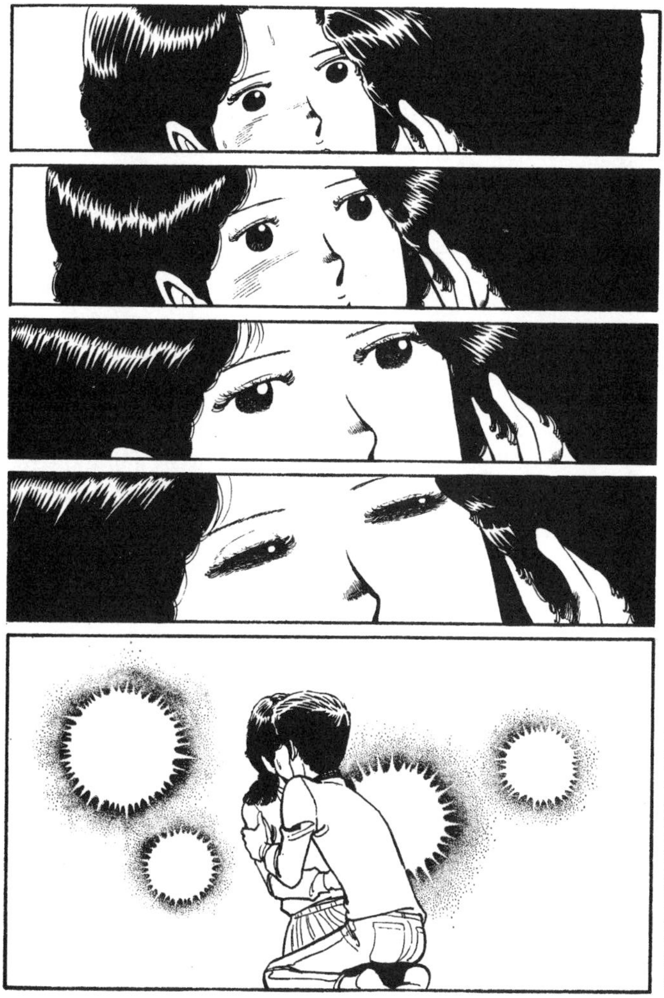

tic styles in the same story, with both "cartoony" and "serious" backgrounds.

The diversity of manga extends to subject matter. American and European comics long ago began dealing with very serious themes, thus making the word "comic book" a gross misnomer (leading some to use the term "graphic novel" instead). Nonetheless, despite many fine experiments, the bulk of American material is still for young males and of the superhero ilk. In Japan, however, there are stories about nearly every imaginable subject.

There are manga that rival the best in literature. There are soft-core and hard-core porn tales for both men and women. There are stories about the problems of hierarchical relationships in boring office jobs or about the spiritual rewards of selling discount cameras in Tokyo's Shinjuku district. A true mass medium, manga provide something for both genders, for nearly every age group, and for nearly any taste.

Ultimately, however, the real triumph of Japanese manga lies in their celebration of the ordinary. As American comic artist Brian Stelfreeze once commented to me, "Comics in the United States have become such a caricature. You have to have incredible people doing incredible things, but in Japan it seems like the most popular comics are the comics of normal people doing normal things."

Yet along with this celebration of the ordinary is the bone-crushing reality that the vast majority of manga border on trash. Even the good stories tend to run out of energy after a while. The pressures of mass production on artists, and the greed of publishers who wish to milk their cash cows dry, often result in watered-down stories being serialized far too long.

WHAT DISTINGUISHES MANGA FROM OTHER MEDIA?

In the marketplace manga are treated almost the same as any other medium in Japan, but artistically they still carry the stigma of having once been an inexpensive form of entertainment for children. They are not taken *quite* as seriously. Some manga artists embark on their creative journeys with hopes of becoming the Tolstoy or Kawabata of manga, but most don't. Most start out wishing merely to entertain their audiences, and themselves, and possibly become rich. In the process they face far less scrutiny than serious novelists or filmmakers—"artists" in other media. (There are manga critics in Japan, but perhaps because the public still thinks of manga as a disposable commodity, nearly all of the critics support themselves with other jobs.) Lack of scrutiny has led to relentless pandering to the lowbrow tastes of readers and a more than occasional glorification of sex and violence. Another result, however, is an unselfconscious freedom of expression and a refreshing creativity.

Manga are much easier to create than other forms of entertainment. Writers usually need education along with language skills. Filmmakers need social skills, enormous amounts of money, and a small army of production people. Successful manga artists may form a company and hire over a dozen assistants, a manager, a photographer, and a chauffeur, but the entry-level requirements for the profession consist mainly of good ideas, a certain degree of physical and intellectual stamina, and pens, pencils, and paper. It isn't necessary to be a particularly good artist.

As a medium of expression, manga thus exist in a niche somewhere between film, records, novels, and television. Manga are usually low-calorie, light entertainment—something to read in a free moment before work or cracking the books to prepare for an exam, or while riding a train home, getting a permanent at the beauty parlor, slurping a bowl of noodles, or waiting for a friend in a coffee shop. They are highly portable, and—not to be overlooked in today's crowded Japan—they provide a silent activity that doesn't bother others.

Why Read Manga?

なぜマンガを読むべきか

AN UNVARNISHED REALITY

For a translator, or an interpreter, or any nonnative speaker who aspires to true fluency in spoken Japanese, reading manga is one of the best ways to keep up with the many changes that are constantly occurring in the Japanese language. The language in manga is alive and closer to the "street" than one finds in other printed media, and it is a source of many new expressions. Because of their visual nature, manga can also be an excellent language-learning resource for beginning students of Japanese. In what is surely one of the most interesting experiments in American publishing in recent years, in 1990 Vaughn

Simmons, an American in Atlanta, Georgia, took this idea to its logical conclusion and began publishing *Mangajin*, a magazine that uses manga with English explanations to teach Japanese language and culture; when readers tire of struggling with unfamiliar *kanji* characters, they can relax and enjoy the English explanations or the pictures.

But there is an even more important reason to read manga. One of the most confusing aspects of Japanese society for foreigners is the dichotomy that exists in public discourse between *tatemae*, or "surface images and intentions," and *honne*, or "true feelings and intentions." This custom of tailoring one's statements or actions to the situation exists in nearly all societies, but in ultra-crowded Japan, especially, it helps people harmonize with others and compartmentalize their public and private selves. It is also one of the main reasons Japanese people constantly feel they are "misunderstood" by foreigners, and—conversely—that foreigners often find Japanese people somewhat "inscrutable."

Reading manga does not necessarily make Japan more "scrutable," but it definitely takes the lid off many otherwise opaque aspects of its society. In the beginning, most non-Japanese (and even the few Japanese who don't normally read comics) find manga confusing. No matter how well translated, many are still very "Japanese" in story, visual style, and pacing. Pictures are intrinsically linked with verbal jokes and even puns. Sometimes characters seem to have nothing but dots in their word balloons, or to be gazing incessantly at horizons or making poignant gestures. Lecherous male characters suddenly develop nosebleeds. Plots seem to proceed in a rather roundabout way. Why don't they just get to the point? The answer, of course, is that manga are written and drawn by artists thinking in Japanese, not English, so it can take a non-Japanese a little more work and a little more patience to read them, even in translated form. A new visual and written vocabulary must be learned. Besides, manga are hardly a direct representation of reality. Most stories—even if they depict normal people doing normal things, or impart hard information on history or the tax code—at their core are pure, often outrageous fantasy.

But once the new "vocabulary" and "grammar" have been learned, it soon becomes clear that manga represent an extremely unfiltered view of the inner workings of their creators' minds. This is because manga are relatively free of the massive editing and "committee"-style production used in other media like film, magazines, and television. Even in American mainstream comics, the norm is to have a stable of artists, letterers, inkers, and scenario writers all under the control of the publisher. In Japan, a single artist might employ many assistants and act as a sort of "director," but he or she is usually at the core of the production process and retains control over the rights to the material created. That artists are not necessarily highly educated and deal frequently in plain subject matter only heightens the sense that manga offer the reader an extremely raw and personal view of the world.

Thus, of the more than 2 billion manga produced each year, the vast majority have a dreamlike quality. They speak to people's hopes, and fears. They are where stressed-out modern urbanites daily work out their neuroses and their frustrations. Viewed in their totality, the phenomenal number of stories produced is like the constant chatter of the collective unconscious—an articulation of the dream world. Reading manga is like peering into the unvarnished, unretouched reality of the Japanese mind.

* * * * *

Those who think that seeing beyond the surface or *tatemae* level of Japanese culture has relevance only to Japanophiles or language students probably don't realize just how much influence Japan is exerting over our daily lives today, or how deep that influence goes. Manga and anime, in particular, have permeated into the bastion of American civilization known as "pop culture" and have slowly wormed their way into the collective consciousness of the English-speaking world. Subtle and not-so-subtle references to both manga and anime appear with increasing frequency in major Hollywood films, in rock music videos, and in the work of artists. They may even be affecting our taste in colors. As the *New York Times* noted in an October 3, 1995 article, prominent fashion designers such as Jean-Paul Gaultier are increasingly incorporating new, exotic tones such as those found on manga magazine covers. Our children, for that matter, are growing up watching more and more of what we think is domestically produced TV animation but which is actually repackaged Japanese anime with manga roots. Whether in the Americas, Europe, Asia, or Australia, it would behoove us all, therefore, to learn more about the thought processes behind these works. Why was *Astro Boy* so different from other shows on television in the 1960s? What was the hidden nationalistic theme in *Star Blazers*? Who thought up the transforming robot idea? Why did the female characters in the 1995 *Sailor Moon* series have such big eyes? Learning about manga, and Japanese culture through manga, can provide the answers.

For those who love comics, there is also another reason to read manga, and that is simply to see what can be done with the medium. Japan is the first nation to give the "comic book" format such legitimacy and to test its potential on such a grand scale. Manga are an experiment in progress, and for anyone who has the slightest interest in comics, in new media, in new ways of transmitting information, and in literacy, Japan is a fascinating case study. How far will Japan be able to go in using manga to transmit hard information? How easily will this new medium, once mainly for children, coexist with other forms of information? Will manga replace text-based communication? At this point, only time will tell.

Finally, the best reason of all to read manga is the simplest, and it has nothing to do with learning about Japan or its language or any other sociological gobbledygook. Manga are fabulous entertainment!

2 MODERN MANGA AT THE END OF THE MILLENNIUM

世紀末現象としてのマンガ

IN THE LATE 19TH CENTURY IT WAS FASHIONABLE FOR WESTERNERS to visit Japan and remark on what an "odd" place it was. Percival Lowell, who later became a famous astronomer and propagandist for the idea of life on Mars, did just this in an 1888 book called *The Soul of the Far East*, noting that "we seem, as we gaze at them, to be viewing our own humanity in some mirth-provoking mirror of the mind,—a mirror that shows us our own familiar thoughts, but all turned wrong side out." Fortunately (or unfortunately, as the case may be), Lowell didn't have manga to examine. Like many things in Japanese culture, comics in Japan are both utterly similar to and utterly different from their counterparts in the West. Yet it is precisely where the vectors of "similar" and "different" intersect that there is so much to learn.

What's in a Word?

漫画、まんが、マンガ、コミックス

YOU SAY MANGA, I SAY KOMIKKUSU

Almost everyone in Japan refers to comics as "manga," but the English-derived word *komikkusu* (and even "comics" itself") is frequently used in magazine titles and by industry and media people trying to sound sophisticated. A representative of the Research Institute for Publications, which tracks data on the publishing world in Japan and which *always* uses *komikkusu* instead of "manga" in its publications, told me that "manga" had long had a somewhat "unrefined" or "unsophisticated" image and had thus fallen out of favor. But in the near future, he predicted, it would probably become popular again, for magazine editors were already beginning to think that perhaps there had been nothing wrong with it after all.

So, just like their counterparts in the English-speaking world, Japanese people have floundered about trying to find the right term to describe the sequential picture-panels that tell a story. In America, words used include "cartoons," "comic books," "funny books," and "graphic novels," but most people just say "comics"—a true misnomer for an oft-serious medium and a word also used for people who tell jokes for a living. In Japan, simple cartoons have in the past variously been referred to as *toba-e* ("Toba pictures," named after the monk Toba, who reportedly drew some of the earliest humorous scrolls), *giga* ("playful pictures"), and *ponchi-e* ("punch" pictures, after the British "Punch and Judy" and after *Punch* magazine). The word "manga" was coined in 1814 by the woodblock artist Hokusai, apparently to mean something like "whimsical sketches," but it did not come into wide use to describe sequential art and what we now think of as "comics" until the 20th century. Even then it seems to have been applied quite arbitrarily. It was originally written with the two *kanji* characters *man* 漫 (which means "involuntary" or "in spite of oneself," with a secondary nuance of "morally corrupt") and *ga* 画 (which means "pictures"). Technically, "manga" can today mean "caricature," "cartoon," "comic strip," "comic book," and sometimes even "animation," although younger generations invariably use "anime" for the last in the list.

In its vagueness, *manga* is therefore similar to the English "cartoon." In its implication of something humorous or less than serious, it is similar to "comics." Understandably, many people would rather refer to their favorite medium with a more precise word, one that might also confer more legitimacy on it. One substitute occasionally encountered in Japan today is thus *gekiga* ("dramatic pictures," equivalent to "graphic novels"). The other is the above-mentioned *komikkusu*, an example of how foreign and especially English words are often used in Japan in place of perfectly good native ones, if for no other reason than that they tend to convey an air of newness and sophistication; often their very opacity provides an additional cachet. That the use of *komikkusu* creates an international Moebius strip of semantic confusion goes entirely unnoticed. Worse yet, in many circles in Japan, *komikkusu* specifically means manga books, and not magazines, which are called *komikku-shi* or *manga-zasshi*.

Even among industry people in Japan who might use the term *komikkusu* to sound sophisticated, when talk turns to comics overseas they will frequently revert to saying "manga" to differentiate the Japanese species from its American counterpart. American comics are referred to simply as *komikkusu,* or *ame-komi,* a catchy contraction for *Amerikan komikkusu*. Meanwhile, in the English-speaking world, after a smooth initial introduction, confusion around the word "manga" has been amplified. In the mid-nineties, the London-based firm Manga Entertainment was widely perceived to have attempted to trademark the word "manga" along with its logo, and it persisted in using "manga" to refer to the translated Japanese animation videos it marketed (to differentiate its animation videos from its translated Japanese comics, it referred to the latter in publicity brochures using the awkward redundancy "manga comics"). As of 1995, many fans in Europe were therefore using the word "manga" to refer to Japanese animation, while fans in the Americas used it exclusively to refer to Japanese comics.

For all its flaws and imperfections, the word "manga" will continue to offer many design benefits to illustrators and typesetters. The beautiful complexity of the Japanese writing system makes it possible to write it horizontally from left to right (right to left before World War II) or vertically. In addition to being presented as 漫画 using Sino-Japanese ideograms (*kanji*), it can be rendered as まんが with a lovely cursive phonetic script called *hiragana*, as マンガ with an angular phonetic script called *katakana* (usually reserved for foreign words or special effects), and as "MANGA," using the roman alphabet.

The *Dōjinshi* World

同人誌の世界

SUPER COMIC CITY

I felt like Alice going through the looking glass when I experienced my first manga fan convention in the spring of 1994. The trappings of American comic book conventions were there—hordes of fans, booths with people selling comics, and occasional costumes—but nearly everything else was topsy-turvy.

The convention was called Super Comic City 3, and it was held at Tokyo's huge Harumi Trade Center on April 4 and 5. The Tokyo fair is the biggest of a series of Comic City conventions that the sponsor—a for-profit event planning and publishing firm—stages in major Japanese cities throughout the year. It took up five giant exhibition halls and lasted two days. I might have become lost if it hadn't been for my able guides, Kan Miyoshi and Mary Kennard, editors from a Japanese publisher and experts on the world of manga conventions.

American comic book conventions are overwhelmingly attended by males, many middle-aged and some potbellied and tattooed. At Super Comic City, however, I had the slightly disorienting but by no means unpleasant experience of being surrounded by tens of thousands of virginal females in their late teens and early twenties. They appeared to make up at least 90 percent of the attendees; most were well-dressed, some even wearing frills and fragrances. But appearances can be deceiving. In the recent past, some of these conventions have been targeted by the police and the media due to the presence on site of some rather racy material; later in 1994, for example, a Comic City convention was shut down after a warning by the police. Fans, understandably, are a little sensitive. Mr. Miyoshi cautioned me about taking close-up photographs. "Many of the kids," he said, "don't want their parents or teachers to know they're here. . . . "

A large American comic book convention might have scores of dealers' booths, but inside the vast halls of Harumi there were nearly *18,000* booths. The U.S. comic

A sea of fans milling around long rows of dealers' tables, inside one of six giant halls at Super Comic City. May 1994.

book market is dominated by male collectors, and dealers usually sell back issues of commercial comics of the male superhero variety. The real buyers (who are mostly adults) often treat their purchases as investments and, rather than read the comics, carefully slip them into plastic bags, hoping they will one day appreciate and be worth thousands of dollars. At Super Comic City conventions, however, the comics being sold are all *dōjinshi*, or "fanzines," created by fans for fans and designed to be read, not collected. The creators are usually members of what are called *saakuru,* or "circles"—groups of like-minded amateurs who collaborate to create and publish their works. There are said to be over 50,000 manga circles in Japan today.

The *dōjinshi* sold at the conventions consist of a variety of genres, including *orijinaru* (original works), *aniparo* (parodies of popular animation shows), *ju-ne mono* (serious stories of love between gay males, of the sort pioneered by *Ju-ne* magazine), and *ya-o-i* (from the phrase *YAma-nashi, Ochi-nashi, Imi-nashi*, meaning "no climax, no punchline, no meaning"; playful stories of a nonsensical sort, often taking male characters from popular animation series and depicting them in gay relationships). For males the most popular genres are probably *bishōjo* ("beautiful young girls") and *rorikon* ("Lolita complex"). Some of the latter material would be regarded as kiddie porn in North America. Most *dōjinshi* are manga, but not all. Some are novels with manga-like themes. There are also circles at conventions that market manga-style video games.

The level of organization at Super Comic City 3 was awe-inspiring, illustrating that the *dōjinshi* subculture has become an industry unto itself. Amateurs pool their funds and issue small printruns of their books (ranging from 100 to 6,000 copies) at a level of quality that rivals the mainstream manga industry. Hardbound books with lavish color covers and offset printing are not uncommon. There are thus a wide variety of businesses present at the conventions that specifically support the *dōjinshi* market, including representatives of printing companies and art supply firms. For tired fans with an armload of purchases, delivery companies have trucks and employees standing by outside the halls, waiting to package up the books and deliver them to your home.

To help fans find specific artists and their works more easily in the vastness of Harumi's halls, the convention sponsors issue a 380-page catalog. In addition to maps and ads for suppliers and printers, it is filled with postage-stamp-sized illustrations of the work done by each of the thousands of circles. Since printruns are limited, *dōjinshi* manga sell on a first come, first served basis. Popular ones are quickly snapped up, so fans wait patiently in long lines to purchase books by leading artists. If the lines are too long and snake so far around the halls that it is difficult to see which artist they lead to, the last person in line is expected to hold a placard indicating where it goes. Waiting in lines is time-consuming, so savvy attendees like Mary Kennard—who is one of the few Americans working in this industry in Japan and often buys samples of the best *dōjinshi* for her company—go to the show with a group of friends; before entering the halls they formulate a plan of attack that allows them to cover as many booths as possible in the shortest possible time.

As I wandered around the floors of the convention halls, I was struck by the general mood—it seemed so feminine and genteel. But here and there were pockets of

Part of a page in the Super Comic City convention guide. May 1994.

people of a noticeably different disposition. In front of the booths of popular artists of the provocative Lolita-complex genre, noisy crowds of young males rudely jostled each other in line, their sweaty bodies steaming up the air. Elsewhere, males roamed the halls in organized high-tech purchasing gangs. Like packs of predators, they coordinated their movements with wireless headsets and microphones.

Super Comic City is but one of many large manga conventions held throughout the year in Japan today. A single convention may draw over 200,000 fans, making it a sort of manga Woodstock. A world unto itself, the manga convention has become a forum for direct, unselfconscious communication between readers and creators, free from the constraints and pressures of commercialism.

KOMIKETTO

The mother of all manga conventions in Japan is not Super Comic City, but an event with the more prosaic name of "Komike" or "Komiketto," short for "Comic Market." Held twice a year in Tokyo in December and August, Komiketto is a nonprofit event organized by fans for fans. Unlike Super Comic City, which was formed in the mid-eighties and has a heavy concentration of female fans of the *ya-o-i* genre, Komiketto has been around since December 1975 and has an attendance that is about 40 percent male.

According to Yoshihiro Yonezawa, president of the Komiketto organization and one of its founding fathers, Komiketto grew out of science-fiction fandom that for its part had been heavily influenced by sci-fi fandom and conventions in the United States. Now a noted manga critic, Yonezawa says that in the early seventies there were far fewer manga magazines in Japan and it was much harder to get anything other than very mainstream works published. In hopes of expanding and developing the medium to its full potential, he and some colleagues formed a coterie magazine of manga criticism. "To carry out the changes we wanted to see in the real world," he notes, "we started Komiketto."

The first Komiketto began with around 600 participants. In 1995 the three-day summer event drew nearly 300,000 people to the Harumi Trade Center grounds and featured over 60,000 sellers of *dōjinshi*. Traditionally two days long, in 1995 an extra day was added to cope with demand. The first day focused on anime-related, primarily female works; the second day featured original works, science fiction, music, etc.; and the last day was devoted mainly to male-oriented works and games. The so-called Planning and Preparation Committee was made up of a registered staff of 1,200 volunteers—among them Christopher Swett, a manga-loving officer in the U.S. Navy stationed in Japan. A fan of Japanese manga and animation ever since he saw Osamu Tezuka's *Astro Boy* on American television, Swett had in the past put together his own *dōjinshi* and sold it at Komiketto. His first book was around 100 pages long and contained the work of nearly twenty artist friends; he printed 300 copies, priced them at $5.00 each, and sold 178 copies at Komiketto in six hours, for a loss.

Why are *dōjinshi* and *dōjinshi* conventions so popular in Japan? When I asked this of Yonezawa and his wife, Eiko, in the fall of 1994, she stressed, above all, that the conventions are fun and that there is a secret thrill of attending a convention and knowing one's favorite manga magazines and books are sold only there. Mr. Yonezawa stressed the ease and the fun of creation. "*Dōjinshi* are something even amateurs can do," he said, "and they don't require much in the way of professional technique. It's maybe like rock and roll in the United States, because it doesn't require education and it's something young people can easily do on their own with just paper and pens. *Dōjinshi* also give instant results, unlike filmmaking, or even drawing commercial manga."

Both Yonezawa and his wife began drawing cartoons in the first grade by imitating their favorite characters. Today their children are following in their footsteps. So many young Japanese are equipped to create *dōjinshi* these days that by third grade they may bind their drawings into little books with staples and compete with their friends. Manga study clubs are common in elementary schools, as well as in junior high and high schools and universities. One reason so many people draw manga in Japan may have to do with the exam-oriented, academic pressure-cooker environment of modern Japan. "Manga," Yonezawa says, "are one of the few things young people aren't forced to do by their teachers, so it's a genre of expression they actively *want* to participate in."

Why are there so many more young women than men creating *dōjinshi* and attending conventions? The academic environment may again be a factor. "Most of the males," Yonezawa says, "tend to be older and are college students, because in the Japanese system, after being under extraordinary pressure for years to study for their entrance exams, this is when they finally have some free time." Females—apparently not under the same pressures as their male counterparts—start participating in the *dōjinshi* scene as teens in junior high and high school. "That's when they are the most 'free,'" Yonezawa explains, also noting that "Girls tend to avoid going to the conventions alone, and usually drag along two or three friends, even if the friends really aren't that into it."

One factor in *dōjinshi* popularity is probably not exportable. As Mary Kennard notes, "The proliferation of *dōjinshi* owes a lot to the rather relaxed ideas of copyright in Japan. In the States, some fanzines (notably those based on the *Star Wars* universe) were threatened with extreme penalties if they continued to publish."

Chris Swett further explains: "There's something that fans get out of reading books written by other fans that they don't get from their regular, weekly manga. [With parodies,] they can take their favorite characters and put them in ridiculous situations, bend stories around, and do things that the original artists don't have the freedom to do. Considering how much more freedom Japanese artists have than American artists, that's saying something. . . . In America we don't have a gray area in our copyright laws that allows this sort of fan art. It's not the way the copyright laws are written, but the way they're enforced. Copyright holders in the United States have to protect their trademark or it becomes public domain. That's not the case in Japan, so artists and publishers can afford to tolerate these homages. It doesn't mean they like it, but they don't want to do anything to alienate their customer base. The manga publishers benefit from happy fans, and some even send scouts to *dōjinshi* markets to find aspiring artists."

The overwhelming size of the *dōjinshi* market has caused the border between it and the commercial manga market to blur. At Komiketto, to preserve the amateur, fan-oriented nature of the conventions, businesses and companies are not allowed to participate, and the sponsors are set up as a nonprofit organization. But since a few *dōjinshi* manga artists can sell up to 6,000 copies of a book at over ¥600 each, there are nonetheless some "professionals" in the so-called amateur markets. Also, several of today's popular mainstream stars, such as Rumiko Takahashi, Hisaichi Ishii, or the women's group CLAMP, either once worked in, or emerged from, the *dōjinshi* market.

It would be hard for mainstream publishers—who are businesses, after all—*not* to notice the *dōjinshi* phenomenon. The amount of money that changes hands in two days at a convention is awe-inspiring. In the September 3, 1991 issue of Japan's *Aera* magazine, reporters estimated that at the Komiketto convention that year fans spent over ¥3 billion ($30 million) in forty-eight hours. And that doesn't even take into account the admission fees of $10 paid by more than 200,000 people.

Otaku

オタク

HONORABLE FANS

I couldn't avoid a chuckle when I saw the word *otaku* written in Japanese with no English explanation on the cover of the premiere issue of *Wired* magazine in 1993. The English language has absorbed many Japanese words in recent years. "Manga" and "anime" are slowly creeping into the average American's lexicon. But *otaku*, while apparently about to join the ranks of these other esteemed imports, has a far more complicated background.

Among English-speaking fans of Japanese animation and manga, *otaku* has been used for some time to mean a hardcore aficionado. At one of the early Japanese manga and anime conventions held in America at the beginning of the 1990s, some young Americans were walking around with the word *otaku* boldly written on black leather jackets and T-shirts as a badge of pride. By 1994 there was even an anime-related convention held in the U.S. called "Otakon."

Ironically, the particular usage of *otaku* now seen in the United States has a short history in Japan. *Otaku* was originally written as *o-taku*, with the honorific phonetic character *o-* preceding the Chinese character for "house." It could therefore mean "your house" or "your home," but it was (and still is) most commonly used as one of the multitude of words in the Japanese honorific hierarchy for "you," especially when addressing someone with whom you are not overly familiar and wish to be very polite.

At the beginning of the 1980s, young male manga and anime fans started addressing each other with this honorific. Exactly why they did so is not altogether clear, since young males in Japan have traditionally addressed members of their peer group with far rougher sounding personal pronouns. But the new usage coincided with an explosion in the popularity of manga and anime and with the increased visibility of hardcore fans who until then were called *mania*—a "Japlish" concoction derived from the English "maniac" (just as the similar "fan" is a contraction of "fanatic)"

Essayist Akio Nakamori claims to be the first person in Japan to have begun referring to manga-anime fans as *otaku*. In June 1983 he began writing a column titled *Otaku no Kenkyū*, or "Studies in Otaku" in *Manga Burikko* (a porno manga magazine of the Lolita-complex ilk for horny young males). In it he recounted his impressions of his first visit to a Komiketto convention: " [The fans] all seemed so odd . . . the sort in every school class; the ones hopeless at sports, who hole up in the classroom during break . . . either so scrawny they look like they're malnourished or like giggling fat white pigs with silver-framed glasses with the sides jammed into their heads . . . the friendless type . . . and ten thousand of them came crawling out of nowhere."

Then, after describing how the traditional term *mania*, or "enthusiastic fans," didn't really fit these young people's image, he went on to announce, that "since there doesn't seem to be a proper term to address this phenomenon, we've decided to christen them *otaku*, and henceforth refer to them as such."

Nakamori's column was soon canceled (probably because the editors felt he was insulting the readers, many of whom might have fit the category he described), but the appellation stuck. In fact, the mass media jumped on it, as only the herdlike Japanese mass media can. Nakamori later confessed to mixed feelings about the phenomenon he had unleashed, but he needn't have felt too guilty. He only gave the trend a name. Many other people in the media had also begun to notice what seemed to be a new phenomenon, of a huge population of young people obsessed with manga or anime or other hobbies—of socially inept young males, in particular, seeking refuge in a fantasy-world.

MANGA MADNESS

If it hadn't been for the Miyazaki incident in the late 1980s, *otaku* might have become just another variant on the term *mania*. It might simply have resembled "fanboy," a pejorative term often heard at American pop-media conventions that connotes a somewhat emotionally immature male overly obsessed with his hobby—the type that howls in protest when a publisher changes the color of his favorite superhero's belt buckle. It might simply have resembled "geek" or "nerd." At worst, it would simply have been another in a long line of derogatory terms (like *shinjinrui*, or "new humans") that the Japanese media periodically use to ridicule materialistic and effete younger generations.

Tsutomu Miyazaki was a disturbed twenty-seven-year-old man who kidnapped and killed four girls of pre-school age in 1988 and 1989, delivering the remains of one of his victims to her family using the pseudonym "Yūko Imada," reportedly the name of a favorite female comic book or anime character. When Miyazaki was finally apprehended, his apartment was found to contain nearly 6,000 videos, including "splatter" and "horror" films and many animation videos of the *rorikon* porno ilk, as well as similar fanzines and manga. He was the manifestation of the manga and animation industries' worst nightmare: a fan incapable of distinguishing between fantasy and reality, obsessed with the darkest and most degenerate genre of material—kiddie porn. Even more horrifying for the *dōjinshi* market, Miyazaki had also reportedly sold manga of his own creation at Komiketto.

Since Miyazaki's crime was particularly horrible and had occurred in a nation that prides itself on being almost crime-free, the media went into a feeding frenzy, establishing a perfect syllogism in the public mind—that *otaku* are people obsessed with manga and animation; that Miyazaki was an *otaku*; and that all *otaku* are therefore like Miyazaki. A flood of reports on *otaku* and the *otaku-zoku* ("otaku tribe") soon appeared in the media, creating the impression of a manga and anime fan community inhabited by socially deranged and autistic wackos.

It is hard to imagine any single Japanese word that has been so discussed and so mutilated in such a short period of time. From an honorific used in polite conversation, *otaku* soon came to also represent mostly young males who could no longer effectively relate to real world people (especially women) and thus bury themselves in pornographic manga and animation and masturbatory fantasies, and harbor dangerous sexual proclivities and fetishes; in short, people who might be mentally ill and perhaps even a threat to society.

Eventually, as often happens, *otaku* were partially saved by the excesses of the media itself. Some commentators protested that *otaku* was a discriminatory term and that the media were engaged in "*otaku*-bashing." *Otaku* became so popular and broad a term that by the mid-nineties it was being applied to nearly anyone with an obsessive hobby, whether it was taking photographs or collecting stamps. Many *otaku* also began referring to themselves as such, just as American hippies in the late 1960s turned an insult on its head and proudly proclaimed themselves "freaks." *Otaku* was even turned into an adjective, *otakii*, used to teasingly describe any introverted, obsessive tendencies.

The Miyazaki incident was not the only time *otaku* and manga were morbidly linked. In early 1995, Japan was stunned by anonymous nerve gas attacks in Tokyo subways that caused several deaths and hospitalized hundreds. Aum Shinrikyō ("Sublime Truth" sect)—an apocalyptic Buddhist-Hindu cult led by a charismatic but visually unappealing character named Shōkō Asahara—became the prime suspect. As reporters for the weekly *Aera* magazine revealed in a series of articles on the sect in April, the sect members were publishing and using anime and manga as a proselytizing tool; worse, they seemed to be lifting many of their more outrageous ideas from them, too.

Cover to the June 30, 1995, edition of "By Weekly AUM Comic."

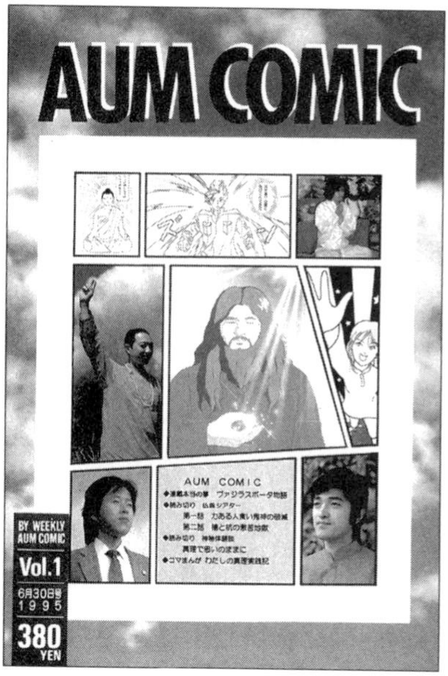

©1995 AUM SHINRIKYŌ

Asahara was known to have been a big fan of robot manga and animation as a child and to have dreamed of one day building a "robot empire." Several ideas and keywords in the group's ideology—references to "Armageddon," "earthquake bombs," and "cosmo-cleaners"—had their roots in popular anime and manga stories like *Uchū Senkan Yamato* ("Space Battleship Yamato," also known as *Star Blazers* in the U.S.), *Mirai Shōnen Konan* ("Conan, Future Boy"), *Genma Taisen* ("The Genma Wars"), and *Akira*. In a May 15 *Aera* article trying to explain how the sect was able to attract extremely intelligent and competent academics and scientists and make them believers in ludicrous theories (for example that the U.S. military had caused the 1995 Kobe earthquake with buried nuclear bombs or had spread sarin nerve gas over cult compounds with helicopters), sure enough, there was the dreaded *otaku* word again. Jinzaburō Takagi, a nuclear power expert explained it this way: "Graduate school, in particular, is a period when they were totally immersed *otaku*-style in a very narrow field. If they failed to discover the proper path to take, they probably sought salvation in religion."

Ultimately, any attempt to directly link manga, anime, *otaku*, religion, and crimes against humanity requires a considerable stretch of logic. More than anything, the whole brouhaha over otaku-hood and its dangers indicates just how much manga and anime have become a frame of reference for nearly the entire population; not just for traditional manga fans but for the well-adjusted and the maladjusted, for demagogues, priests, engineers, and social critics. In other cultures, people might allude to movies or novels or folklore to illustrate a point; scholars and religious people might blame the excesses of youth on the evil and corrupting influences of television or rock and roll, or even—as once was the case in America—on comic books. In Japan, it is increasingly manga and anime that are referred to by *all* segments of the population and that, in an extreme situation, are conveniently available to blame for an entire society's ills, and not just those of youth culture. As for the so-called *otaku*, they are surely more the offspring of their social environment than the product of reading too many manga.

Beginning in the 1980s, the newly wealthy Japanese population was encouraged by the government to work less and spend more time at leisure and hobbies (it is hard to imagine any other government ever making this suggestion). Children were growing up with unprecedented affluence and freedom of choice in a media-glutted society. Yet they were still being put through a factory-style educational system designed to churn out docile citizens and obedient company employees for a mass-production, heavy-industry-oriented society that had ceased to exist. Males, in particular, whose-workaholic fathers were rarely at home, were growing up spoiled by their mothers. In the claustrophobic confines of Japan's orderly cities, with intense pressures from "examination hell" at school, with physical and spiritual horizons seemingly so limited, who could blame these children for turning inward to a fantasy alternative, or for developing a *nijikon fetchi*, a "two dimensional fetish," for manga and animation?

As for the word *otaku*? In Japan, the association first established by the Miyazaki incident has never completely disappeared. Only when *otaku* was exported to the English-speaking world was it completely stripped of its negative connotations. France was not so lucky. In 1994, Jean-Jacques Beineix—the famous French director known for *Diva* and *Betty Blue*—made an exhaustive two-hour-and-forty-minute documentary on the so-called *otaku* phenomenon in Japan, focusing on young people with obsessive hobbies. The many French citizens who watched it probably still believe that Japan is filled with an entire generation of wackos.

Are Manga Dangerous?

マンガは危険？

A FREQUENTLY ASKED QUESTION

Americans who have visited Japan ask one question about manga over and over again: *Why are manga so violent and pornographic?* This is a loaded question, for it presumes that *all* manga are violent and pornographic. Nothing could be further from the truth. When I try to answer the question, however, I often find myself in the uncomfortable position of gamely trying to defend manga while distancing myself from the excesses of a wide-open medium. Knowing that the cultural perspectives of the questioners may limit their ability to understand, I reply as follows:

There are many offensive manga. (As liberal as I am in matters of art, even I have occasionally felt queasy over the content of some manga stories, and if I feel that way, I'm sure some others are ready to faint.) Fortunately, such works remain a minority. The vast majority of manga, even if they are basically trash with little educational value, are harmless entertainment. That stated, however, there are also some specific cultural factors that affect the perception non-Japanese have of manga and make them *seem* particularly violent and pornographic.

Every culture, whether Moslem, Christian, or Buddhist, has different norms of acceptability in the arts. Modern manga, although they look like American comic

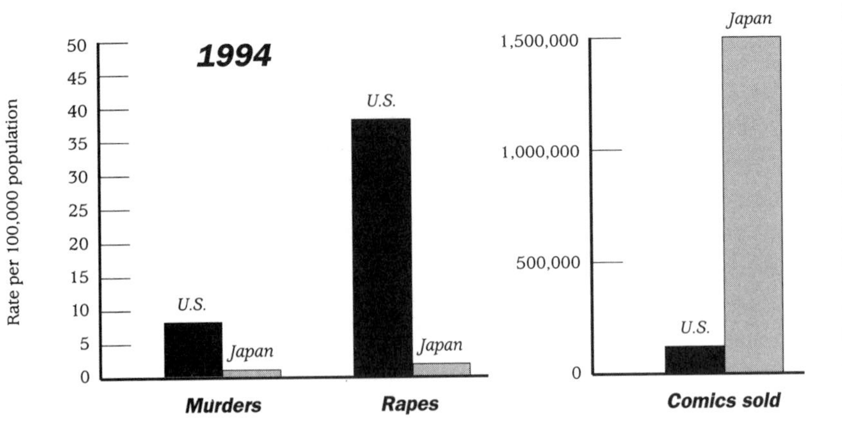

Sources: Crime statistics from Japan's 1996 *Hanzai Hakusho* ("White Paper on Crime") and the FBI's 1995 *Crime in the United States*. Manga and comics sales from Research Institute for Publications, *Shuppan Geppō*, March 1996, and from estimates in John Jackson Miller, "State of the Industry 1995: The Year Everything Changed," *Comics Buyer's Guide 1996 Annual*.

Comparison of murder and rape rates and comic book and manga sales per 100,000 population in Japan and America, 1994.

books, have inherited a centuries-old tradition of Japanese narrative art that entertains, that is humorous and bawdy, and that has a unique esthetic of visual violence. Manga are the direct descendants of popular art for the masses in the late Edo period (1600–1867), art in which exaggerated sexuality and stylized violence—scenes of samurai disemboweling themselves and blood spatters—were a standard feature.

Another point to remember is that no matter how erotic and violent manga are, they are not a direct reflection of Japanese society. If they were, Japan would resemble a violence-plagued 1980s Beirut or a sexually free-wheeling 1960s San Francisco. Despite a sexual revolution of sorts (and a huge sex industry), an increase in downtown shootouts, and nerve gas attacks on Tokyo subways, almost all statistics show that Japan remains one of the earth's better-behaved societies. Not only is the violent crime and sex crime rate far lower than that of the United States; in Japan itself both rates have dropped considerably during the very period that manga and anime were exploding in popularity. Or, in the words of U.S. comic artist Brian Stelfreeze on a 1994 trip to Tokyo, "With all the crowds of people, it feels incredibly safe. I think a mother could send her daughter out naked with a ¥100,000 bill taped to her back and know she'd be okay."

The gap between fantasy and reality in Japan is enormous, and for that very reason readers of manga may actually be better at making a distinction between the two than readers in other nations. To a high school student in Japan, the notion of getting hold of an AK-47 and mowing down the teachers in his school is clearly absurd, a fantasy. But to a high school student in Los Angeles it is a distinct possibility. He may know someone with an automatic weapon he can borrow, and he probably has heard news reports of people who have already done something similar to what he is imagining. The point here is that the inherent stability of modern Japanese society—in particular the stability of family life—may give people *more* leeway in their fantasy lives. And a vivid fantasy life may act to defuse some of the more primal impulses that occasionally come over all of us.

Akira Fukushima, a prominent psychiatrist and writer, has written an eloquent defense of manga titled *Manga to Nihonjin: "Yūgai" Komikku Bōkokuron o Kiru* ("Manga and the Japanese: Dissecting the Myth of 'Harmful Comics' Ruining the Nation"). In it, he persuasively uses statistics and survey results to argue that despite the barrage of sexual material they are exposed to, and despite public impressions to the contrary, young Japanese are highly repressed and late to develop sexually compared to their counterparts in other nations. He finds no evidence that exposure to sexual material results in increased sex crimes or activity at all. Indeed, he claims that (1) "the amount of sexual information that a people have access to is inversely proportional to the number of sex crimes in any country" and (2) "sexual information can substitute for actual sexual activity."

It might be premature to conclude that reading manga would in and of itself reduce the violent- and sex-crime rate in all countries, but there is a third and important point here. Many non-Japanese who perceive manga to be pornographic and violent are often

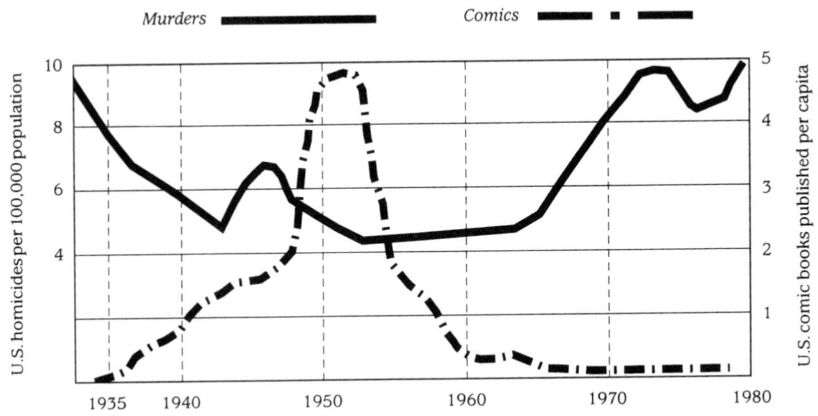

Sources: Homicide rate from *Historical Statistics of the United States: Colonial Times to 1970* and from *World Almanac*. Number of comic books from Ernst and Mary Gerber, *The Photo-Journal Guide to Comic Books*, vol. 1 (Minden, N.Y.: Gerber Publishing, 1989), p. a-9.

U.S. murder rate vs. sales of comic books. Caution: The only thing this graph demonstrates is that no direct correlation exists between comics and crime rates.

unaware of how biased their own perspective is. North Americans, for example, are often horrified by the contents of manga because they unconsciously compare them with American comic books. Yet what most American visitors to Japan fail to realize is that manga today are no longer a medium for children alone and that manga have become a mass medium of entertainment as common as novels or film. They also overlook the fact that until recently most American comic books were heavily censored. A draconian program of self-censorship was implemented in the United States comic book industry in the early fifties in response to political and social pressure. Comic books were nearly sanitized to death (circulations plummeted and have never recovered; precise figures are extremely difficult to come by, but based on information in the *Comics Buyer's Guide 1996 Annual* and an estimate from the *Wall Street Journal* in 1953, today's sales are less than a third of what they were then. In America comics came to be stigmatized as a shallow entertainment for children; instead of developing a symbiotic relationship with television and animation—as has happened in Japan—they were eclipsed.

It therefore makes more sense to compare manga with videotapes or popular novels. Any video rental store in the United States easily carries as much sex and violence as any manga shop in Japan. Similarly, if you could "visualize" the text in the steamy romance novels so many English-speaking women enjoy, you would probably produce stories strikingly similar to the racy romance manga that grown women in Japan often read.

Freedom of Speech vs. Regulation

「表現の自由」対「規制運動」

THE PTA FIGHTS BACK

Having thus defended manga, some strong criticism is also in store. Perhaps because manga began as children's entertainment and then exploded in the postwar period into a mass, mainstream medium for the entire population, the borderline between adult and children's material is less defined than in other media. It is surely a characteristic of Japanese manga, for example, that both elementary school children and office employees in their thirties can be seen reading the same weekly *Shōnen Jump* ("Boys' Jump") on the subways, even though the magazine is primarily for males around junior high school age. If one subscribes to the theory that adults should be allowed to read whatever they choose, but that children should not, it is from this borderline area that some truly disturbing trends have emerged, some of which transcend manga altogether.

In the late eighties, in particular, many of the traditional limits on content in manga began to collapse. Manga had until then observed explicit prohibitions against overt depictions of sexual intercourse and adult genitalia (derived from an interpretation of Article 175 of Japan's very vaguely worded obscenity laws) as well as a general, more implicit social consensus about what was proper and what was not. But when the guidelines disappeared, the "me-too" syndrome so often seen in Japanese media resulted in manga magazines vying with each other to pro-

Paperback cover to volume 3 of the problematic series* Angel, *the "Highschool Sexual Bad Boys and Girls Story" by U-JIN. First serialized in Shōgakukan's* Young Sunday, *a biweekly manga magazine for high school and college-age males.

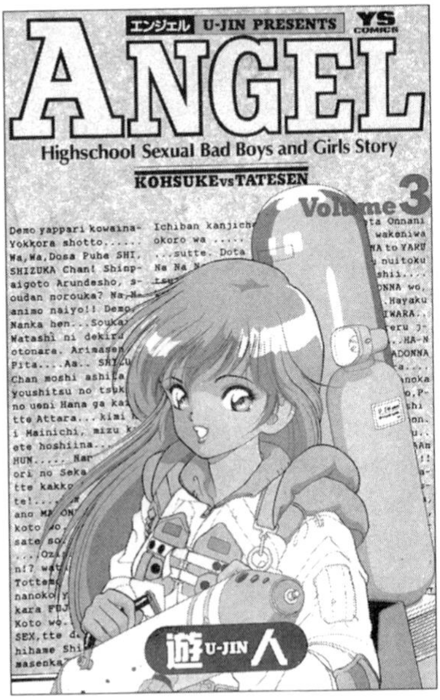

duce the most provocative stories possible. Works such as *Angel*, *Rapeman* (which seemed to condone violence against women), and *rorikon* ("Lolita complex") stories began to appear in mainstream magazines and in magazines designed for teenagers or younger children.

Japanese manga artists have traditionally played a cat-and-mouse game with the authorities over the issue of depicting nudity. For decades, the government prohibited any depiction of adult genitalia or pubic hair in all art, highbrow and otherwise, resulting in the knee-jerk censorship of serious foreign films, *Playboy*-type magazines, and reproductions of several famous 19th-century Japanese woodblock prints held by foreign museums. The specific prohibition against showing pubic hair, however, may have indirectly encouraged some clever erotic manga artists to draw prepubescent girls as sex objects, with ridiculously inflated breasts. Whatever the original motivation, in the 1980s traditional erotic manga for adult men (often referred to in the industry as *sanryū gekiga*, or "third-rate graphic novels") gradually gave way to erotic manga with a *rorikon* flavor. Instead of adult males doing very adult things to mature women (neighbor's wives, waitresses, office workers, buxom foreigners, that sort of thing), the sex objects became increasingly "cute"—and younger. That more and more women, who tended to draw characters in a "cuter" style anyway, were entering the erotic comic market certainly accelerated the phenomenon.

In a way, manga were merely reflecting a trend throughout Japan in the go-go economic years of the 1980s—a sort of *rorikon* virus that infected the whole society and still persists. "Cheeriness" and terminal "cutesy-ness" were "in." Cynicism, reflection, pessimism, introspection, seriousness, and anything "heavy" or depressing all fell out of favor in films, novels, and intellectual life. If in the West it was a madonna-whore (but nonetheless adult woman) image that fired men's sexual fantasies, in Japan the equivalent was a smiling junior high school virgin, clad in her "sailor suit" school uniform and holding a stuffed animal toy. And young women were eager to cater to this fantasy; many in their late twenties could be seen around town with their cute stuffed toy dolls and innocent looks and high-pitched voices. Their numbers spawned the term *burikko*—the sophisticated, experienced adult female who acts like an innocent little girl.

As noted above, there is no solid evidence that images in comic books directly affect behavior; if such a simple cause-and-effect were at work, millions of children in the United States would have jumped off high buildings after reading *Superman* comics. But since sexual desire is in real life so extraordinarily wrapped up in fantasy and irrational urges, one wonders how young adult males in Japan raised on *rorikon* material can relate to real-world adult females—without being terribly disappointed.

At the end of the 1980s, at the height of the contamination of manga and anime by the *rorikon* virus, the Tsutomu Miyazaki murders took place. Mainstream Japanese society and establishment leaders took a hard look at what many young Japanese youths—especially the media-saturated *otaku* generation—were reading, and they were horrified.

In the city of Tanabe, in Wakayama Prefecture, several housewives started a movement in favor of regulating manga that developed into the Association to Protect Children from Comic Books. One of the manga the women found particularly offensive was *Ikenai! Luna-sensei* ("Watch-out! Luna, the Teacher"). Serialized in a mainstream boy's magazine, it was about a beautiful tutor who comes to live in a young boy's house (its author, Junko Uemura, was not some dirty old man, but a young woman). In a later interview, Isako Nakao, founder of the children's-protection movement, described her reaction to one of the manga paperbacks she came across at the local bookstore in 1990: "It had a cute picture on the cover designed to appeal to children, but inside it was filled with the most blatantly sexual material—the sort of thing that should never be shown to children."

Nakao's movement resonated throughout Japan. Crackdowns on sex and violence in manga by the authorities occur at fairly regular intervals in Japan, but this time a powerful nationwide "movement to banish harmful manga" emerged, joined by housewives, PTAs, Japan's new feminist groups, and politicians. Tougher local ordinances against obscene manga material were passed by various prefectures throughout Japan. Arrests of publishers and store owners found to be selling obscene material increased dramatically. Even major publishers were targeted. Up until then, artists had rarely been arrested and the *dōjinshi* or amateur market had been left largely untouched. But on April 15, 1991, forty-five *dōjinshi*-related publishers, editors, and artists were arrested for possessing obscene material with the intent to sell. Extra trash bins emblazoned with the words *Minai, Yomanai, Yomasenai* ("Don't look at them, Don't read them, Don't let anyone read them") were set up throughout Japan in public places for good citizens to toss "harmful reading matter."

Then, on September 4, 1990, Japan's prestigious national paper, the *Asahi Shinbun*, ran an editorial titled "There Are Too Many Impoverished Manga." Quoting a Tokyo city government report that claimed over 50 percent of all manga had sex scenes and that at least 8 percent had scenes of masturbation, the editorial appealed to Japanese national self-respect, noting how even foreign visitors are shocked by Japan's manga and that "even in

America and Europe, where pornography is legal, there are probably few areas so blatantly deluged by 'sex' without regard to time or place." In a consensus-minded Japanese fashion, however, the *Asahi* added: "Of course, just because there are vulgar manga doesn't mean we should have regulation by laws and ordinances. Even if there are particularly problematic magazines, the problems should be solved through discussions and self-restraint on the part of the publishers."

The last thing the *Asahi* and the rest of the media establishment wanted to see was government censorship, and for a very good reason. Freedom of the press has existed in Japan only since the U.S.-authored postwar constitution guaranteed it in 1946. And it has been a precarious existence. For over 250 years during the Edo period (1600–1868), government control over political expression was absolute. For many artists, dabbling in erotic expression has always been far safer than dabbling in politics, yet still a good way to tweak the noses of the authorities. Even today, those engaged in producing erotic or pornographic material—whether manga or videos—often have a rather romantic image of themselves as rebels working against the establishment.

Nonetheless, after the initial crackdown, publishers recalled the most offensive works and began practicing what Japanese called *jishuku*, or "self-restraint," toning down the erotic level of stories for children and identifying some manga magazines and books as being "for adults only." Finally, after such relentless criticism, the pendulum slowly began to swing the other way. In 1992, some of the top artists in Japan—national heroes like Shōtarō Ishinomori and Machiko Satonaka—formed the Association to Protect Freedom of Expression in Comics to counter the pro-regulation movement.

In the *dōjinshi* world, sponsors like the Komiketto organization began to warn artists at conventions about what sort of material would cause a problem. Still, events had a certain Japanese twist to them. When local ordinances in Chiba Prefecture finally made it impossible to hold conventions there (the local authorities declared that *dōjinshi* with more than 20 percent nudity were "harm-

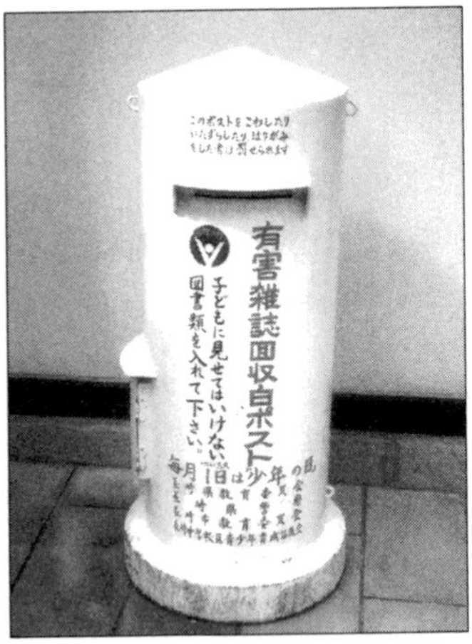

The place to dispose of "harmful magazines"—a receptacle in the shape of a mailbox (painted white instead of the usual red), with a stern warning on the top to anyone thinking of defacing or damaging it. Nagasaki City, 1993.

ful"), the conventions moved to Tokyo, where regulations are looser. As Yonezawa, the head of the Komiketto organization puts it, "*Dōjinshi* should not be drawn by grownups for children. They should be drawn by young people for young people. Since most artists and readers are around nineteen, at this age it's impossible not to talk about sexual motives and themes. The important thing is that manga be drawn by young people for young people; that a 'same-generationality' be preserved."

Ultimately, the great debate that occurred in Japan over freedom of speech versus regulation was long overdue and part of the natural democratic process. Manga are so entrenched in Japanese society today that there is unlikely to be an overreaction of the sort that occurred in the 1950s in the United States. A balance between the interests of the artists and the interests of the general public will probably result, and Japan, in its own way, will muddle toward a resolution of the obscenity debate. But no matter what happens, in the eyes of non-Japanese people manga will continue to appear terribly violent and pornographic.

By the end of 1994, the controversy already appeared to have peaked and resolved itself. Manga magazines with "adults only" marks were disappearing because stores refused to handle them—just as "X" ratings nearly disappeared from "serious" U.S. movies because they spelled doom in the distribution channels. The most offensive *rorikon* material was dropped from mainstream magazines for children (although if anything, erotic material in adult manga became even more graphic, especially with the final crumbling in 1993 of Japan's long-time prohibition against depicting pubic hair and sex organs). The charge of relentless debasement of women by men in erotic manga was offset by the fact that by 1995 some of the raciest material was in magazines not for men but for women (and drawn by women). Finally, live action videos and photography books had become so blatantly eroticized that they were a far greater concern to police and citizen's groups than static, monochrome manga.

As one artist friend of mine commented when I asked him about restrictions on manga, "Well, there was a big fuss about it for a while, but now everything seems pretty much the way it's always been."

Black and White Issues #1

白黒の世界 1

A SUBJECTIVE VIEW OF REALITY

In the late 19th century, writer Lafcadio Hearn went to live in Japan. Although he eventually became a Japanese citizen, his amazement over cultural differences never ceased. On March 6, 1894, he commented in a letter to a friend that "When I show beautiful European engravings of young girls or children to Japanese, what do they say? I have done it fifty times, and whenever I was able to get a criticism, it was always the same:—'The faces are nice, —all but the eyes: the eyes are too big, —the eyes are monstrous.' We judge by our conventions. The Orient judges by its own. Who is right?"

Times have changed dramatically. When most foreigners look at manga for the first time today and see characters with huge saucer eyes, lanky legs, and what appears to be blonde hair, they often want to know why there are so many "Caucasian" people in the stories. When told that most of these characters are not "Caucasians," but "Japanese," they are flabbergasted.

Comics are drawings, not photographs, and as such they present a subjective view of reality. This subjective view of reality is particularly apparent in depictions of self, for each culture tends to see itself in a unique, often idealized fashion that may change over time. Just as American and European comics do not depict people realistically (how many people really look like Superman?), neither do manga. Japanese people, however, may be a little more flexible than others in their self-perception.

Prior to the Meiji period, which began in 1868, Japanese artists usually drew themselves with small eyes and mouths and variable proportions; "Europeans" were drawn as huge hairy freaks with enormous schnozzles. With the introduction of Western art and esthetics after the arrival of Commodore Perry in 1853, however, the Japanese ideal began to shift toward the classic Greek model, what Japanese artists call the "eight-head physique": a human's height should be equivalent to eight lengths of the head. Faces also started to change. In popular prewar romance magazines for young women, illustrations by Jun'ichi Nakahara, for example, showed heroines with large dreamy eyes, in a style directly imported from the West.

Defeat in World War II caused a national loss of con-

Typical Japanese schoolgirls in **shōjo** ***manga. From Chiaki Yagi's "Merry-go-Round" in*** **Nakayoshi.**

fidence that clearly extended to Japan's self-image. Western ideals of beauty were not only accepted but pursued, often to a ludicrous degree (operations to remove the epicanthic fold of skin over the eye, which creates the graceful, curved look in Asian eyes, are still popular). Nowhere was this tendency more pronounced than in manga.

Early comics of the postwar period were heavily influenced by Osamu Tezuka's style of cartooning, which was in turn derived from American animation (see chapter 1). Tezuka drew large eyes, and when he began drawing for girls' romance comics he further exaggerated this tendency. Tezuka, and the other men and later women artists who followed him, found that a Caucasian look, with dewy, saucer-shaped eyes, was extremely popular among young readers and that the bigger the eyes, the easier it was to depict emotions. (The appeal of big eyes is, of course, not limited to Japan; look at the Keane paintings of wistful waifs with absurdly orblike eyes—windows on the soul—so popular in America in the sixties.) Eventually, depicting Japanese people with Caucasian features and large eyes became an established convention; readers internalized the images, and demanded them.

Since most Japanese comics are drawn in black and white, artists have generally differentiated between Japanese characters by shading the hair of some and not of others. To foreigners, this has the effect of making some Japanese look blonde. Fans know better, of course; they know the hair is really meant to be black, even when rendered in white. It is in girls' and women's comics, where the adoption of Western ideals of beauty has been much more thorough, that readers have adjusted to much more mind-boggling changes in self-image. Not only are Japanese females depicted like leggy New York fashion models, but on color covers of magazines, they are sometimes presented with clearly "blonde" hair and clearly "blue" eyes.

In the early eighties I commented on this phenomenon to Machiko Satonaka, a popular girls' comic artist. She noted that Japan has always been attracted to what it perceives as more advanced cultures than its own, and that in the Heian period (ca. 10th century) it was the Korean face that was regarded as the ideal, particularly by the imperial court. Adoption of the Caucasian model of beauty, she suggested, may have been a case of the grass appearing greener (or the hair lighter) on the other side of the fence. She added, however, that there was a trend toward smaller eyes in girls' comics and an appreciation of a more "Japanese" look.

Over ten years later, while the "Western" look remained very popular, there was indeed the growing "realism" that Satonaka had spoken of, especially in manga for adult women. Perhaps inspired by superstar Katsuhiro Ōtomo, who initially shocked readers by drawing Japanese people with a distinctly "Asian" look, many women artists such as Akimi Yoshida were drawing smaller eyes and more Japanese-looking faces. At the same time, in what is certainly a case of historical irony (if not a case of self-transformation through visualization), the real-life proportions and even the facial structures of young Japanese were indeed approaching the Western "ideal," largely as a result of improved diet and different lifestyles (ways of raising babies, increased use of chairs, etc.). According to a 1990 survey of children conducted by the Ministry of Education, the average height of thirteen-year-old boys had increased an astounding 17.6 centimeters, or 6.9 inches, since 1950.

When asked about the Japanese self-image in manga, many artists and readers assert that they have little "racial consciousness." While this is debatable, it is true that Japanese people have shown a remarkable flexibility in depicting themselves. Long before punk fashions influenced the art world, in color manga Japanese characters were sometimes drawn not only with blonde hair, but blue, pink, and even green hair.

This Westernized or internationalized depiction of Japanese characters has also provided the manga and anime industries with a distinct export advantage by making it easier for them to win acceptance in the United States and Europe. Many young American fans of Japanese TV shows such as *Astro Boy* in the sixties or *Robotech* in the eighties never even realized that some of their favorite characters were actually Japanese.

Black and White Issues #2

白黒の世界 2

A STEREOTYPED VIEW OF REALITY

In 1990, the Association to Stop Racism against Blacks initiated a campaign to stop the publishing of "racist" manga. This tiny Osaka organization—essentially consisting of Mr. Toshiji Arita, his wife, and his son—had previously been instrumental in getting the "Little Black Sambo" story removed from bookstores and in discouraging the use of racist imagery in advertising.

The Arita family took the hard-to-dispute position that Japanese media contain too many negative stereotypes of people of African descent. They complain that black people are too often portrayed as grass-skirted, bones-in-their-noses cannibals, servants, or jazz musicians, and that in manga they are often heavily caricatured, with rounded faces, fat bodies, big eyes, and thick lips.

Although the Aritas' goals were laudable, the family claimed to represent the diverse opinions of all blacks around the world and took an approach that was dogmatic and formulaic. First, their organization presented manga publishers with strident demands for retraction of what it deemed offending material. Then, it enlisted scores of religious and civil rights groups in the United States to deluge the publishers with letters. That the letter writers were outraged was understandable; but most could not read Japanese and had been shown isolated images taken out of context from long stories, even stories with a strong antidiscrimination theme.

To everyone's shock, one of the main targets of the campaign was Osamu Tezuka, the "God of Comics." Tezuka was beloved in Japan in large part because of his humanism and his compassion. To accuse him of being a racist was rather like accusing Mother Theresa of being a child molester.

What kinds of images were at issue in Tezuka's work? First, he sometimes inserted "cartoony" drawings of African natives in his stories as a form of "comic relief." Second, and more problematic, he sometimes drew Africans and African-Americans in a style lifted from American cartoons of the thirties and forties. His much-loved classic, *Jungle Emperor* (known to Americans as *Kimba, the White Lion*), is a case in point. Created in 1950, this is a romantic saga of beleaguered wild animals in Africa trying to learn to live in harmony (and an inspiration for Walt Disney's *The Lion King*). It is a sweet story, full of all the usual Tezuka charms, but as critics have noted, the depiction of the native population is probably influenced by early American Tarzan movies.

Several targeted artists in Japan redrew the offending images in their work. In the 1980s there was a brief boom in "cute," African cartoon characters—drawn in the spirit of the inflatable black Winkie dolls once popular in America. Akira Toriyama, who had drawn four little "cute" African natives in this style, obligingly went back and transformed them into "cute" cats.

If Tezuka were still alive, one suspects he would have been horrified by the criticism and immediately redrawn many of his illustrations. However, his publisher, Kōdansha, which issues a collection of the late artist's work that runs to over 300 volumes, was in no position to do this for him. Instead, it temporarily halted reprinting and decided, after a great deal of internal debate, to include a message to the readers. The message—a disclaimer—explains that some of the illustrations were drawn in a less-enlightened age and may be offensive to some readers, but that Tezuka himself was adamantly opposed to racism in all forms, as is the publisher. This approach was unlikely to satisfy all critics, but it was nonetheless a very progressive step, and one that U.S. publishers of classic novels attacked by religious and ethnic groups might do well to emulate.

The reaction of Japanese artists and fans to the campaign against racism was confused. Citizens of a relatively homogeneous nation (with only around 1 percent "minorities"), Japanese until recently rarely worried about other people's sensitivities. This did not mean that artists maliciously exploited racist imagery, but that the checks and balances that might exist in a multiracial society were absent. Most Japanese artists were simply

In Osamu Tezuka's* Phoenix, *a character in ancient Japan is being pursued through an overgrown area. As a gag, Tezuka draws the pursuers as riot police and includes an African native. Created in 1968, a time of great turmoil on university campuses.

unaware that some of the images of blacks they had appropriated were developed in the social context of discrimination, exploitation, and slavery.

In 1991 the review magazine *Comic Box* ran several feature articles on the antiracism campaign along with comments from readers and artists. Many expressed indignation at the dogmatic nature of the campaign and at the way some Japanese publishers had caved in to its demands. Manga artists particularly resented being told what is politically correct to draw or threatened with anything resembling censorship. In some genres of comics, moreover, the very purpose of cartooning is to distort, to poke fun, and to ridicule. In this visual world, *everyone*, including Japanese people, is drawn in what could be construed as an offensive style. Also, as several respondents pointed out, works created thirty or forty years ago are a reflection of their times. To ban them opens a Pandora's box. Should Shakespeare be banned for his depiction of Shylock? Should all Tarzan movies be banned? The American media, others noted, is itself filled with negative racial stereotypes. To make a point, some submitted drawings of Japanese people rendered with buckteeth, slant eyes, and cameras.

One of the inadvertent tragedies of the antiracism campaign was that it made some artists afraid to draw any black characters in their stories, even if they had been planning to include positive portrayals; why take the chance? On August 4, 1993, Yoshinori Kobayashi—one of the most outspoken and opinionated Japanese manga artists and author of the popular *Gōmanizumu no Sengen* ("A Declaration of Arrogant-ism")—created a very funny strip that reflected the unspoken feelings of many artists. In it, he railed against the pressure artists were receiving from editors not to draw black characters with kinky hair or fleshy lips. Ultimately, he said, everyone would be forced to draw blacks that looked like Michael Jackson.

The antiracism campaign may have sensitized the public and contributed to a general consciousness raising, but its ham-fisted approach clearly exacerbated Japanese paranoia about being unfairly criticized. It also ignored the many fine manga stories that oppose racism and are sympathetic to those of African descent, and it diverted attention from the fact that people of African descent are not the only ones stereotyped. In the topsy-turvy world of Japanese manga, although Japanese characters are frequently drawn with Caucasian features, when real Caucasians appear in manga they are sometimes shown as big hairy brutes. Chinese or Korean characters are frequently drawn with slant eyes and buckteeth, in much the same stereotyped fashion that Japanese were depicted by American propagandists in World War II.

Ultimately, the debate over "racism" in manga is but part of a larger discussion about balancing freedom of expression with responsibility, and it has its parallels in the "political correctness" controversy in the U.S. Manga artists are under increasing pressure from the public and from publishers to reign in not just their depictions of foreigners but Japanese minorities and the physically and mentally handicapped. And they are expected to tone down the eroticism and violence. Osamu Tezuka used to complain of not being able to draw characters with four fingers as American animators often do—in Japan it signifies "four legged beasts" and by extension the former outcaste (and still discriminated against) class that used to slaughter them—the *eta* or *burakumin*. Not surprisingly, independent-minded artists resent such externally imposed constraints, even if they would never dream of creating such demeaning portrayals themselves.

To the manga industry's credit, many artists, editors, and publishers have actively tried to learn what is acceptable and what is not in art, and to build bridges with offended communities. At the late Osamu Tezuka's company, for example, management has gone out of its way to establish a dialogue with African-American groups, such as JAFA (the Japan-African-American Friendship Association). As the president of Tezuka Productions, Takayuki Matsutani, wrote in a Fall 1992 edition of the magazine *Tsukuru* ("Create"), all too often the industry has merely tried to figure out how to avoid being criticized or attacked, rather than determine the root cause of the problematic depictions, whether they be racial or sexual.

While artists debate how to depict foreigners, Japanese society itself is undergoing major changes. The mental horizons of young Japanese have been expanded by foreign travel and real-time television imagery from around the world. Over the last few years there has been a visible increase in the number of foreigners in Japan and greater variety in their nationalities and occupations. At one time most *gaijin,* or "outsiders," in Japan were tourists, businesspeople, U.S. soldiers, or English teachers. Now, owing to the reluctance of effete young Japanese to do hard physical labor, there are many legal and illegal foreign workers in Japan; it is not unusual to encounter Iranians, Bangladeshis, Brazilians, Vietnamese, and Chinese working in factories, driving trucks, or washing dishes. Blacks, too, from Africa and America, can be found in a wider variety of occupations in Japan than ever before. There is even a surprising amount of intermarriage between Japanese and foreigners, including Filipinos, Thais, and Russians.

As a result, today one can find nearly any type of foreigner in Japanese comics. There are the occasional negative stereotypes, bound to offend some, but there are also sympathetic, intelligent portrayals. Basketball has achieved explosive popularity among young Japanese and some African-American athletes such as Magic Johnson and Michael Jordan have achieved hero status among Japanese youth. A few years ago, the influential boy's manga monthly *Jump* ran a popular series about the L.A.

Lakers that had been officially authorized by the NBA. In the adult weekly *Morning*, Kaiji Kawaguchi's *Silent Service*—an international thriller about a renegade Japanese sub battling the U.S. military—has had very positive depictions of African-American officials working in the highest ranks of American government (the author was undoubtedly influenced by Colin Powell's frequent appearance on television news). Many artists who create science fiction manga, like Masamune Shirow, also increasingly depict a future Japan that is a mixture of different races and cultures.

Since the mid-eighties, the Japanese government has been heavily promoting *kokusaika*, or the "internationalization" of Japan. The officials certainly never had manga in mind, but in manga it is occurring.

Do Manga Have a Future?

マンガに未来はあるか

GODZILLA GROWS OLD

For decades, Japan's mass media marveled over the stellar growth rates of the Godzilla-like manga industry. But on March 27, 1995, Japan's respected *Aera* newsmagazine ran an article that took a different tack. Provocatively titled "The Beginning of the Twilight of the Manga Industry," it noted that while manga had ballooned into a ¥550-billion market in the postwar period, "Even this champion of entertainment, which has exhibited such remarkable growth, has proven that it has limits. The giant industry is slowly being beset with troubles from within and without."

The main focus of the article was on slowing growth rates for specific genres. The Research Institute for Publications annually releases figures on manga publishing, and for the previous decade and longer these have been awe-inspiring numbers. In 1993, however, it was noted that while overall manga sales had grown 8 percent over the previous year, two important categories had slowed—manga for young boys, which had declined 0.4 percent, and manga for young adult men, which had dropped 0.7 percent two years in a row. In any other industry a performance record of this sort—after decades of hypergrowth—would probably be a good reason to break out the champagne, but the *Aera* article's note of impending doom showed just how conditioned the manga industry had become to its continued success. In 1996, industry fears practically turned to terror, for it was discovered that while overall dollar and unit sales of manga had increased in 1995, dollar sales as a percentage of all books and magazines had actually declined (0.5 percent). Most shocking, dollar sales of the hitherto always lucrative manga paperbacks had dropped 0.03 percent, leading the above-mentioned, normally staid Research Institute for Publications to run a feature in its March report titled "Limit Demonstrated to the Myth of Endless Growth!"

The *Aera* article gave as one reason for the decline a paucity in good stories, for which it largely blamed editors. This might seem odd in a genre where the artists and writers are supposed to be the creators, but in Japan manga editors have a major hand in story planning and execution, supplying ideas, shepherding authors (even acting as surrogate parent figures for the very young artists), and occasionally helping write the stories. *Aera*'s article claimed that in the larger publishing firms, editors were becoming cowardly organization men merely going through the motions rather than aggressive cocreators driven by a love of comics, as was true of many of the early, legendary editors. In children's manga the article noted a more disturbing trend—competition from video games. When a boy can get over thirty hours of enjoyment out of a video game, but finishes reading his manga magazine and tosses it in the trash can after twenty minutes, manga cease to have much of a price-performance advantage, even if they do cost ten times less than a video game.

Realistically, the areas in which manga can continue to grow are limited. When over 40 percent of all Japanese books and magazines are now in comic form, one has to wonder how many new genres can be developed. Certainly as the core generations of manga readers age there will be more and more manga created for older age groups; publishers excitedly talk of their future plans to make what they refer to as "silver" manga—magazines specifically for the senior citizen set. Overseas markets, of course, represent a still largely untapped gigantic new market. In my own 1983 book, *Manga! Manga!*, I wrote that "Japanese comics, like American rock and roll music, began as a limited form of entertainment for young people. Now both are ponderous industries in the mainstream of society." Today, more than ever, it is clear that the manga industry has entered a mature phase.

And with maturity comes an entirely different set of problems, not the least of which is quality. Most manga, as a pop-culture medium, have always been trash. In the early days, many artists and editors and publishers burned with the ambition to show the skeptical world at large that their beloved medium of expression had far greater potential than most people were willing to recognize. They were like young revolutionaries, boldly breaking down barriers in their path. But now they have come into power, and the corrupting influences of that power are starting to show.

The manga industry has become a little long in the tooth, a little plump around the waistline. Artists certainly don't have to be starving to create good work, but the potential earning power of artists today is staggering—in 1994 alone, Yoshihiro Togashi, author of the popular boys' manga *Yū-Yū Hakusho* ("The Yū-Yū Report on Apparitions"), is estimated to have made over $7 million. At the popular *Shōnen Magazine*, with sales of over 4 million copies per week, the editor-in-chief estimates that out of twenty artists around eight earn over a million dollars per year. One has to question what happens to the creative soul of a millionaire young artist when he or she is surrounded by sycophants, rides in a chauffeured car, and presides over an assembly line of hierarchically ranked manga assistants who obligingly carry out more and more of the drawing and scripting tasks.

Caught up in their success, many mainstream manga production companies start to look like factories engaged in mass production for the sake of mass production—victims of the same disease that afflicted much of the Japanese manufacturing economy in the late 20th century—an obsession with volume when the world demanded not "more," but "unique," "interesting," and "better." It is a revealing moment when the talk of highly successful manga artists at informal gatherings quickly turns to boasting about how many serializations they are simultaneously in charge of, how many copies their works are selling, and—inevitably in Japan—how they only need four or five hours of sleep a night.

The results are apparent, not only in boring stories but in a visual dissonance that afflicts many successful manga today—the result of dividing the labor of drawing among multiple assistants who use disparate styles when drawing backgrounds or even different characters. Corporatization is also a reason that many of the most interesting trends in Japanese comics come from outside the mainstream industry, from the *dōjinshi* world, from erotic comics, and from the underground. It was no surprise when *Comic Box*'s annual manga roundup edition in 1995 bore the title "Are Manga Finished?"

The problems of the manga industry involve much more than the struggle to produce interesting material, or even the growing competition from video games. Modern manga began as a children's medium, as a subculture, but manga are now read by adults of nearly all ages and are part of the cultural mainstream. Yet no matter how hard artists try to create "grown up" material, manga still

At the Seibu Ikebukuro rail station, a kiosk vendor looks anxiously at stacks of manga magazines. Most are a popular weekly designed for boys, and she will sell them all during rush hour, mainly to adult salarymen and college students.

betray their origins—in their continuing emphasis on "cuteness" and in the way the border between material for children and adults is still much more blurred than in other entertainment media.

Since Japan is the first nation on earth where comics have become a full-fledged medium of expression, one has to question what it means when adults get so much of their primary information from a medium of expression that is a form of caricature, that deliberately emphasizes deformation and exaggeration. Or when misguided publishers or cults or the government abuse the essence of manga, and perhaps take them a little *too* seriously. After all, the conventions for imparting hard information in the manga medium are not as well established as they are in film or prose; even if footnoted and done in documentary style, manga are still going to present reality with a greater degree of distortion. What will it mean when entire generations start living in a comic book reality, or when they have formed many of their impressions of other nations and peoples from manga?

As Japanese society itself becomes increasingly "manganized" it may make people happier, but it may also affect the intellectual core of the nation. In the 1980s the expression *keihaku tanshō* (written with the characters for "light-thin-short-small") was a popular phrase for describing not only national trends in consumer goods but what was perceived as "lightweight" intellectual activity. Is it just a coincidence that during this same period manga began to have a profound impact on other arts, including literature and film? Manga creative and production values may indeed underlie the "low-calorie" examples of literature and film that increasingly pass for serious intellectual efforts in the Japan of today.

The manga industry may fret about a slip in growth rates, but as manga mature into the mainstream of society, Japan itself faces much larger challenges. In the meantime, manga continue to diversify into more and more areas of society, and as a medium of expression, to continually transform. . . .

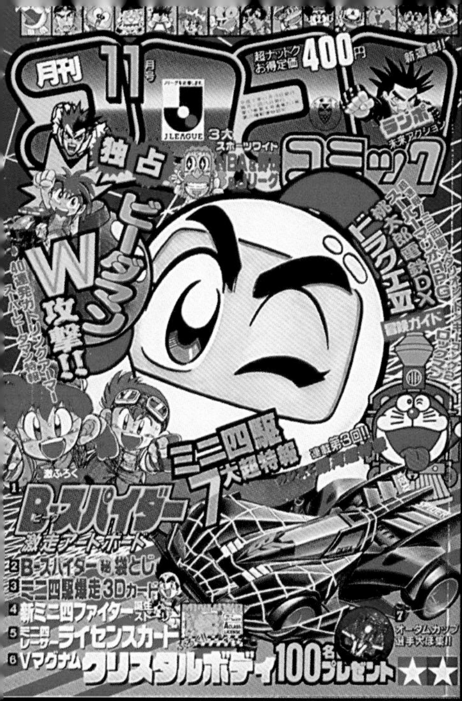

LEFT:
Korokoro Komikku (*"Coro-Coro Comic"*). *November 1995.*

BOTTOM LEFT:
Shūkan Shōnen Janpu (*"Weekly Boys' Jump"*). *May 29, 1995.*

BOTTOM RIGHT:
Nakayoshi (*"Pals"*). *May 1995.*

COVERS OF MANGA MAGAZINES DISCUSSED IN CHAPTER 3

RIGHT:

Biggu Komikku *("Big Comic"). July 25, 1994.*

BOTTOM LEFT:

Biggu Komikku Orijinaru *("Big Comic Original"). September 20, 1993.*

BOTTOM RIGHT:

Biggu Komikku Supirittsu *("Big Comic Spirits"). August 31, 1993.*

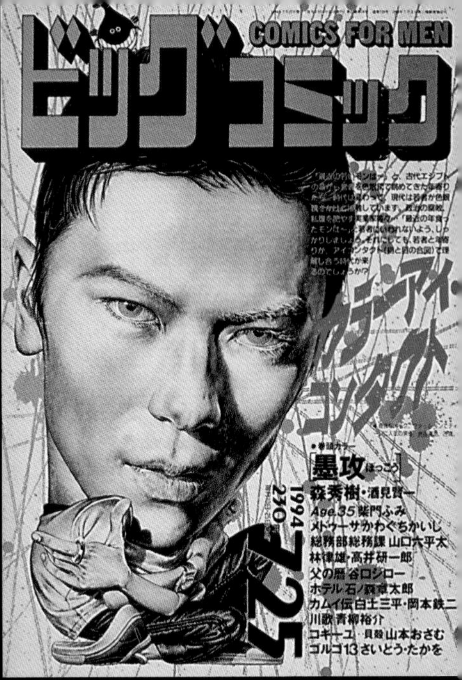

Biggu Komikku Superiōru (*"Big Comic Superior"*). *September 15, 1993.*

Biggu Gōrudo (*"Big Gold"*). *August 17, 1993.*

Shūkan Mōningu
("Weekly
Morning").
October 15,
1992.

Afutanūn
("Afternoon").
November 1992.

LEFT:

Kindai Mājan Orijinaru ***("Modern Mahjong Original"). May 13, 1994.***

BOTTOM LEFT:

Bessatsu Kindai Mājan ***("Modern Mahjong Supplement"). June 1994.***

BOTTOM RIGHT:

Kindai Mājan Gōrudo ***("Modern Mahjong Gold"). June 1994.***

Manga Pachinkā *(“Manga Pachinker”). November 27, 1994.*

Pachinkā Wārudo *(“Pachinker World”). June 2, 1994.*

RIGHT:
Konbatto Komikku (*"Combat Comic"*). *May 1995.*

BOTTOM LEFT:
June. *November 1994.*

BOTTOM RIGHT:
Comic Amour. *December 1994.*

Yanmama Komikku *("Yan Mama Comic"). October 1994.*

Garo. *October 1989.*

3

THE MANGA MAGAZINE SCENE

マンガ雑誌の世界

THE JAPANESE WORD FOR "MAGAZINE" IS *ZASSHI*. WRITTEN with 雑 *zatsu* ("rough," "rude," "coarse," and "miscellaneous"), and 誌 *shi* ("record," "document," or "magazine"), the word has a rather harsh sound to Japanese ears.

Manga magazines reflect the nuances of the word *zasshi* in more ways than one. They are extremely inexpensive and except for a few full color glossy pages at the beginning are usually printed on rough recycled paper (which may be tinted to hide traces of ink left over from a former incarnation). They consist of a miscellany of serialized and concluding stories. And they are eminently disposable, often abandoned in a trash can after a cursory read during the train ride home from work. In 1994, writing in the media magazine *Tsukuru*, manga critic Eiji Ōtsuka posed the question, "Why were manga able to surpass, even overwhelm, other media in postwar Japanese culture?" His answer: "Ultimately, the main reason must surely have been their utterly, almost hopelessly 'cheap' quality."

This "cheapness" is an outgrowth of the explosion in demand for inexpensive entertainment that occurred at the end of World War II, after years of deprivation. Children in particular craved manga, and publishers vied to satisfy them by increasing the number of pages devoted to comics in their magazines. In 1959, manga magazines finally assumed their modern format when one of Japan's largest publishers, Kōdansha, issued *Shūkan Shōnen Magazine* ("Weekly Boy's Magazine"). The first of several all-manga omnibus magazines for boys, it quick-

DATABOX

MANGA MAGAZINES IN JAPAN, 1995

CATEGORY	NUMBER OF TITLES	CIRCULATION (MILLIONS)
All Boys' & Girls'		
Boys'	23	662.26
Girls'	45	145.55
Subtotal:	**68**	**807.81**
All Adults		
Young men's (*seinen*)	37	551.40
Ladies'	52	103.09
4-panel	21	
Pachinko/ pachi-slo	8	
Tanbi mono	7	132.45
Golf	3	
Miscellaneous adult	69	
Subtotal	**197**	**786.94**
GRAND TOTAL	**265**	**1,594.75**

Source: Research Institute for Publications, *Shuppan Geppō*, March 1996, p. 9.

ly achieved a circulation of 1 million and a page count of nearly 300.

Today, manga magazines can be divided into two types: those that are folded and stapled, and those that have glued and squared backs. Beyond that, most have at least 200 pages, and some have 1,000. The vast majority use paper in the B5 (7" x 10") or A5 (5.8" x 8.2") size. Almost all target either males or females, but rarely both. The only magazines that consistently sell well to both genders are aimed at very small children, where gender differences are least emphasized in society. One of the main differences between manga magazines for adults and those for children is that the children's magazines have what is a godsend for foreigners learning Japanese—the *rubi*, or little pronunciation keys next to all the difficult *kanji* characters that children are still struggling to learn.

There were 265 manga magazines regularly published in 1995, in quarterly, monthly, bimonthly, biweekly, or weekly format, with circulations ranging from a few thousand to over 6 million per week. Three publishers—Shūeisha, Kōdansha, and Shōgakukan control the bulk of the market; the rest is fought over by dozens of other companies, many of whom appear and disappear along with their magazines.

The magazines introduced in this section have been chosen to illustrate the variety and scope of the Japanese manga industry. Some are typical and others are not. All, however, reflect the grassroots power of manga as a medium of expression, for it is in manga that artists first create the stories that go on to become books and fuel the giant industries of animation and merchandising.

CoroCoro Comic

「コロコロコミック」

AN ENTRY-LEVEL MANGA MAGAZINE FOR BOYS

To enter popular discount electronics stores in Japan is to experience sensory overload—neon-colored price placards hang everywhere, dissonant music blares from every direction, and dozens of video games play simultaneously on scores of computers. Reading the monthly manga magazine *CoroCoro* produces a similar sensation, especially if one is a middle-aged adult.

CoroCoro, published by the giant Shōgakukan, is designed for very young boys. It is as nearly as hyper as they are. Covers are a psychedelic explosion of assorted popular characters. Inside, page layouts convey an impression of unbounded energy (although it takes considerable energy to read them all). "Thick, inexpensive, and interesting!" (as *CoroCoro* sometimes bills itself), a typical issue retails for the bargain price of ¥400 yet contains 600–700 pages. Still, *CoroCoro* fits into little hands better than most manga magazines, for it is one of the first for boys printed in the A5 (5.8" x 8.2") "flattened brick" (as opposed to "telephone book") format. It can

Korokoro Komikku *("CoroCoro Comic"). March 1995.*

thus serve as a firm pillow or a relatively soft projectile; and unlike its name—an onomatopoeic word for "rolling"—it will definitely stay wherever it is put.

According to Kazuhiko Kurokawa, the editor-in-chief of *CoroCoro* when I spoke with him in 1994, readers range from third to sixth graders, with a smattering of junior high school boys. There are manga-like magazines in Japan for even younger readers, such as the popular and heavily illustrated semi-educational *gakunenshi*, or "school year magazines" (with titles like "First Grader," "Second Grader," etc.), and *Terebi* ("TV") publications. But these are like manga with "training wheels." Most young boys start reading true manga in either *CoroCoro* or its primary competitor, Kōdansha's *BonBon*. And *CoroCoro* reflects this in far more ways than its hyperkinetic design.

Most manga magazines in Japan have a loose slogan that reflects their editorial stance, and at *CoroCoro* it is *yūki* ("bravery"), *yūjō* ("friendship"), and *tōshi* ("fighting spirit"), as well as what Kurokawa refers to as *tokotonshugi*, which loosely translates as a "go for broke" attitude. Like most manga magazines, *CoroCoro* has a mix of serialized and concluding stories, including many sports stories. But as Kurokawa notes, one of the most important themes is humor. Thus nearly 60 percent of the stories are "gag" strips. Young elementary school boys, he also explains, still find it difficult to read the longer and more serious serialized manga (perhaps partly because their attention span is too short), and regular reader surveys consistently show they want their comics to be funny.

One of the magazine's mainstays is *Doraemon*, Fujiko F. Fujio's comical story of a robot cat who lives with a bumbling young elementary school boy. Practically an icon of Japanese popular culture at this point, *Doraemon*, a low-key and sweet story, was the original raison d'être for *CoroCoro*. It first appeared over twenty-five years ago in one of Shōgakukan's "school-year" magazines but proved so popular that it was featured in a separate quarterly, then bimonthly, and finally a monthly magazine that became *CoroCoro*. Anything with *Doraemon* on the cover still helps sell the magazine, especially when the annual *Doraemon* animated feature film is released each spring vacation.

Most stories in *CoroCoro* are far wilder than *Doraemon*. Gag stories, in particular, are filled with silly third-grader humor. In 1994, for example, Shinbo Nomura's *Babū Akachin* (which loosely translates to "Baboo Baby Wee-wee") starred a young tyke who could perform all sorts of stellar feats with his little penis. But there were also some gag stories with bite that even adults could enjoy, such as *Obotchama-kun* (roughly, "Little Lord Fauntleroy"), by Yoshinori Kobayashi, famous in more mature manga circles for his biting satires on Japanese society.

The most striking aspect of *CoroCoro* is not the quality of its stories; it is the number of tie-ins with other industries. As is common in the manga world, popular stories are compiled into paperback books, made into animated series, and heavily merchandised. Yet in *CoroCoro*—an indication of the degree to which TV and Nintendo video-game culture has saturated young Japanese minds—perhaps over 30 percent of the stories and characters are not original, but *derived* from animation and video games or from tie-ins with toy companies. In 1995 Capcom's popular *Street Fighter II* video game appeared

D
A
T
A
B
O
X

CoroCoro Comic

Publisher:	Shōgakukan
Date founded:	1977
Price:	¥400
Format:	A5, squareback, monthly
Avg. no. of pages:	700
Sale date:	15th of each month
Est. circulation:	750,000
Rubi pronunciation key:	yes

as a gag strip (along with ads for the animation film) and so did Nintendo's *Donkey Kong*. Other tie-in stories impart information on how to play the video games. In fact, to read *CoroCoro* requires considerable video game vocabulary; *Street Fighter II* and *Dragon Quest* are affectionately truncated as *Suto II* and *Dora Kue* respectively. English acronyms such as RPG ("Role-Playing Games") are sprinkled liberally throughout the text.

CoroCoro also has far more ads than other manga magazines. Most are for video games and toys and other Shōgakukan publications, but on the inside back cover, reminiscent of American comic books of forty years ago, there are even ads for boxing gloves, "Rambo-style knives," and military-style toy pellet guns. Reflecting the boom in soccer and the heavily commercialized J-League in Japan (which *CoroCoro* helps support), in 1994 and 1995 soccer-related merchandise was also heavily hawked. At one point the magazine even ran gag strips starring Ruy Ramos, the Brazilian star of the Kawasaki Verdy soccer team.

Publishing manga magazines for the younger set is not easy in Japan today. *CoroCoro* is one of the best sellers in its category, with a circulation many publishers would envy, but sales in 1994 were around 750,000 per month, down from a peak of 1.5 million. One of the biggest problems, Kurokawa notes, is finding good manga artists with staying power. Many artists feel intimidated by the small children's genre, believing they are too restricted in content and sophistication. Besides, few artists can create classics like *Doraemon*. Noting how high budgets in the movie industry attract some of the best creative minds in the United States, Kurokawa also laments, "Manga used to be a road to riches, but for this genre the video game market has become so big it is starting to siphon off the most talented people as scenario writers and designers."

Another problem is the modern lifestyles of little children. "Kids in today's Japan are far too busy," Kurokawa says, highly critical of his country's rat-race education system. "Between the after-school cram courses they have to attend and their other activities, it's hard for them to find time to read our magazine. . . . We know that we have to do something new as we approach the 21st century, and that if we stay the same we'll just get old."

Like other manga magazines in Japan, *CoroCoro* now fights back by adding *furoku*, or "freebie-supplements," and by occasionally boosting the number of pages. One September 1994 issue came with a writing pad with a J-league theme and a special *Doraemon* insert, yielding a total page count of 980. But such moves clearly aren't enough.

What seems like shameless commercialization—the large number of tie-ins with game and toy companies—is thus part of a survival strategy. Young children in Japan in the *CoroCoro* reader age group are spending more and more time playing video games and watching animation, and reportedly reading fewer manga. *CoroCoro* forms the first line of defense against this trend. What better way to combat the enemy than to join it?

Weekly Boys' Jump

「週刊少年ジャンプ」

THE MANGA MAGAZINE GODZILLA

Of all the manga magazines in Japan, *Shūkan Shōnen Jump* ("Weekly Boys' *Jump*") is the hardest to ignore. Huge stacks of it are piled in front of newsstands and kiosks for sale every Tuesday, and from there they are transported by hand to schools, offices, factories, coffeeshops, and homes throughout the land. On crowded commuter trains, it's not unusual to see a twelve-year-old elementary school student standing next to a thirty-year-old salaryman—both reading their own copies. There are advertisements for *Jump* on train station posters, on television, and on full pages of major newspapers. After Tuesday, copies of it can be found left on subway overhead racks, stuffed in trash cans, or piled up outside houses waiting to be collected for recycling.

Weekly Boys' Jump is not just the best-selling manga magazine in Japan; with a weekly circulation between 5 and 6 million, it is one of the best-selling weekly magazines of any type in the world (in the United States, with a population twice that of Japan, *Time* magazine's circulation is only around 4 million). But it is not just the circulation of *Jump* that is big. *Jump* is the size and shape of a large city's telephone book. Square-backed and bound with both staples and glue, it usually has around 428 pages.

In size and format, *Jump* is identical to other major weekly boys' manga magazines such as *Shōnen Magazine* and *Shōnen Sunday*. The typical cover is a full-color explosion of popular characters, names of artists, and titles of stories—a design only a tad less hyperactive and garish in mood than that of *CoroCoro* magazine. Inside, there are eight full-color slick-paper pages devoted to the opening section of the lead story and to ads for video games and muscle-building equipment. Then there are around thirty-two pages of the lead story and more ads, printed on rough recycled white paper with black and red ink to create an illusion of color. The rest of the magazine, which contains between seventeen and eighteen serialized or concluding stories, is all recycled rough paper printed in monochrome, with stories visually distinguished by different colored inks and paper tinted in different shades.

Until recently *Jump* put its competitors to shame: it vastly outsold them and had a return rate of around only 2 percent. Designed originally for late elementary and junior high school boys, *Jump* achieved a publishing miracle by selling to children as well as middle-aged businessmen, thus becoming the Godzilla of Japan's publishing world.

Shūkan Shōnen Janpu *("Weekly Boys' Jump"). November 20, 1995.*

©1995 SHŪEISHA

What was the secret of *Jump*'s success? The fat, weekly boys' manga format was pioneered by *Shōnen Magazine* and *Shōnen Sunday* in 1959; *Jump* did not appear until 1968. Shūeisha, however, became Japan's largest magazine publisher (issuing over 50 million manga and non-manga magazines per month, or more than one for every Japanese family), so it seems to have known what it was doing. Unable to attract some of the most popular manga artists, the company instead located newer, younger ones, helped them develop their own identity, and contracted with them so they would continue with the magazine, even if they later became successful. In effect, the magazine became their agent, also handling their licensing and merchandising.

In addition, *Weekly Boys' Jump* established a firm editorial policy that continues to this day. First, it conducted a survey of young readers, asking them to name (1) the word that warmed their hearts most, (2) the thing they felt most important, and (3) the thing that made them the happiest. The answers were *yūjō* (friendship), *doryoku* (effort, or perseverance), and *shōri* (winning, or victory). These three words then became the criteria for

D
A
T
A
B
O
X

Shūkan Shōnen Jump

Publisher:	Shūeisha
Date founded:	1968
Price:	¥190
Format:	B5, squareback, weekly
Avg. no. of pages:	428
Sale date:	every Tuesday
Est. circulation:	5,000,000–6,000,000
Rubi pronunciation key:	yes

selecting the stories, whether adventures or gags. As the editor-in-chief, Hiroyuki Gotō, commented in a June 12, 1990 article in the newsmagazine *Aera*, "Children know they're equal in terms of rights, but not ability. Out of ten children, perhaps one will excel in both sports and study, and one will have no interest in either. The remaining eight just want to do better in study or sports. . . . They are the ones we're targeting, and the three words reflect their positive, optimistic outlook. At *Shōnen Jump* we don't believe in the esthetics of defeat."

This has proved a phenomenally successful formula. A steady stream of hits—such as *Dr. Slump*, *Cat's Eye*, *Kinnikuman* ("Muscle Man"), *Slam Dunk*, and *Dragon Ball*—has poured forth from the magazine over the years, triggering national fads and generating millions of dollars in profit. The weekly *Jump* retails for an inexpensive ¥190 and probably just breaks even; the real profits are made from sales of paperback compilations of the serialized stories, animation rights, licensing of toys, and so on.

Stories serialized in *Jump* run the gamut from school campus love comedies to SF-violence-action thrillers, basketball adventures, baseball comedies, soccer tales, and assorted fantasy and gag strips. Occasionally, out of a sense of duty perhaps, the magazine even runs what is usually the kiss of death in comics—educational material; in the early 1990s it published a series of illustrated stories about scientists around the world who had won Nobel prizes.

The wide variety of stories helps ensure *Jump*'s popularity among a readership varied in both age and taste. Each issue, however, contains a reader-response card surveying preferences in stories, artists, and characters. If a story is not popular for ten weeks in a row, it is usually dropped. If successful, however, it may run for a very long time. Osamu Akimoto's enormously popular light comedy about a neighborhood cop, *Kochira Katsushika-ku Kameari Kōen-mae Hashutsujo* ("This is the Police Station in Front of Kameari Park in Katsushika Ward"), began serialization in 1976. By the end of 1995 it was approaching its 1,000th episode and had been compiled into more than 92 paperback volumes, for a total of over 18,000 pages.

Ironically, in 1995, the manga industry in Japan was abuzz with rumors about *Jump*'s slide from its exalted position in the industry hierarchy. Rival *Shōnen Magazine* was expanding, and for the first time in years *Jump*'s announced sales figures for its August special edition failed to increase; popular series such as *Dragon Ball* had ended, and competitors even whispered that actual sales had dropped from 6.3 million to 5.5 million. *Jump* responded by *reducing* its price from ¥200 to ¥190. But ultimately, all the speculation really revealed was that public expectations had become unrealistic—how can any magazine *grow* forever?

Once you find a winning formula, it's important to exploit it. *Weekly Boys' Jump* is now accompanied by *Young Jump*, a biweekly targeting an older audience of males; *Business Jump*, a biweekly "For Business Boys"; *Super Jump*, a biweekly for young adults; *Gekkan Shōnen Jump* ("Monthly Boys' *Jump*"), a 650-page monster magazine that has serialized, among other things, a manga version of Magic Johnson and the L.A. Lakers story, authorized by the NBA; and *V-Jump*, which targets the video game market. Finally, perhaps out of a sense of guilt over the way it has helped saturate young Japanese male minds with manga, in 1991 Shūeisha began publishing *Jump Novels*, a biannual manga-magazine-style publication featuring mainly text-based, manga-inspired stories, illustrated by manga artists.

Nakayoshi

「なかよし」

THE MEDIA-MIX

Publishing manga magazines is a cutthroat business. Profit margins are razor thin, competition is fierce, and it takes constant innovation to survive. Nowhere is this more true than in the high-volume children's manga market. *Nakayoshi*, a monthly for elementary and junior high school girls, uses a "media-mix" strategy.

One of the oldest and most famous manga magazines for young girls in Japan, *Nakayoshi* was first published by one of Japan's largest book publishers, Kōdansha, in 1954. It originally contained serialized novels, articles, and illustrated pieces, but in the postwar manga boom it soon became all-manga. As of 1995 it retailed for ¥400 yen and contained the usual mix of twelve or fifteen serializing and concluding manga stories, ranging from fantasy-adventure to romance and gag pieces. Some immensely popular works have been serialized in it over the years, including *Ribon no Kishi* ("Princess Knight") by Osamu Tezuka and *Candy Candy* by Yumiko Iigarashi. One of the big hits in the mid-nineties was Naoko Takeuchi's *Bishōjo Senshi Sailor Moon* ("Pretty Soldier Sailor Moon"). Circulations go up and down, but in 1995 *Nakayoshi* claimed a figure of nearly 2 million per month.

Yoshio Irie, the editor-in-chief, assumed his position in 1990 at the young age of thirty-four. A soft-spoken man with an aggressive vision, he felt the magazine was overemphasizing the stock girl-meets-boy/first-love type of stories and failing to exploit the real strengths of manga. He thus tried to introduce more fantasy-oriented stories, an example being the wildly popular *Sailor Moon*, which stars five young women who were warriors in previous lives. Irie's ultimate goal is to make *Nakayoshi* the largest-selling magazine in the young girls' genre and to overtake rival Shōgakukan's magazine *Ribbon*, which leads the pack.

"Our media-mix strategy" he told me, "includes uti-

Nakayoshi ***("Pals"). June 1994.***

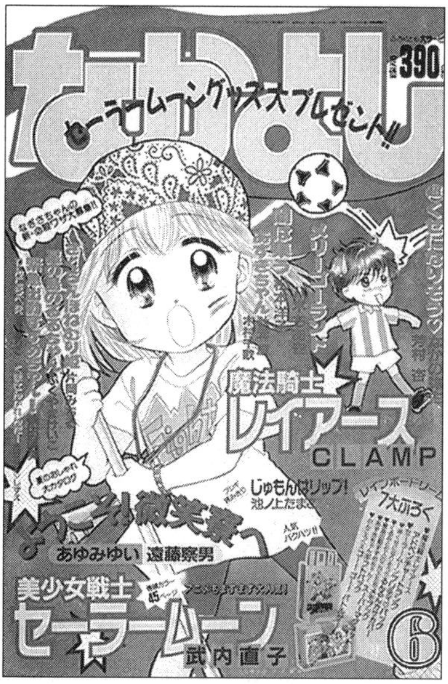

lizing not only the magazine, but television animation, character merchandising, and events." Traditionally, he explained, a manga story would be animated for television quite a while after it appeared in a magazine, and then merchandise would be created based on the characters. For *Sailor Moon*, however, the basic story was determined in editorial meetings nearly a year before publication, and a coordinated media offensive was developed. The animated series started up after the second episode of the written story. "Animation and toys usually have very different production schedules," Irie says, "with at least three or four months lead time required for television and six months for toys. Because we discussed schedules in advance, we were able to carefully coordinate them."

Peak sales seasons in this genre are February (new year), April (new school year), and September (summer vacation), so the *Sailor Moon* plot was designed to have exciting episodes hit at just these times, along with new characters or warriors and surprising revelations. The television animation show, furthermore, lagged the magazine story by only a month or two, and care was taken to

DATABOX

Nakayoshi	
Publisher:	Kōdansha
Date founded:	1954
Price:	¥400
Format:	B5, squareback, monthly
Avg. no. of pages:	448
Sale date:	3rd of each month
Est. circulation:	1,800,000
Rubi pronunciation key:	yes

make sure it did not overtake it. Merchandising was also coordinated, with sales of important items targeting summer vacation and Christmas.

Irie also used other techniques to expand market share, including targeting the *dōjinshi*, the huge amateur manga market that had previously been thought to offer only limited opportunities. One of the most popular stories running in *Nakayoshi* in 1995 was *Mahō Kishi Ray Earth* ("Magic Knight Rayearth"), by the enigmatic CLAMP, a team of four women who have a near-fanatical following in the *dōjinshi* market. "Our use of CLAMP for a story was a big shock to the industry, but it has helped us a great deal," Irie says.

More traditional methods were also used. Each *Nakayoshi* issue has a *furoku*—a supplement or "freebie"—attached, making the already huge monthly even more physically impressive. The June 1994 issue, for example, came with a *Sailor Moon* bag, a cardboard cutout carrying box with a *Rayearth* motif, a board game, a plastic umbrella cover for rainy days, and a decorative little plastic bag in which to put a gift for "papa." Readers who send in coupons are also entitled to unique little prizes, and since they need coupons from two consecutive magazines, they are enticed into buying the magazine regularly. This helps reduce the perennial problem (for publishers) of *mawashi-yomi*, wherein one purchaser shares the magazine with many friends. "With our prize system," Irie notes with satisfaction, "even two sisters will each buy their own copy of *Nakayoshi*. Sometimes we give out as many 700,000 prizes for free."

The media-mix strategy for manga marketing has paid off handsomely. *Nakayoshi*'s circulation increased over 1 million in the year 1992/93. At the end of 1995, thirteen paperback volumes compiled from the *Sailor Moon* series had sold nearly 1 million copies each; twenty volumes compiled from the animation series of *Sailor Moon* had sold around 300,000 each; and there were over ten types of video games on the market, each having sold between 200,000 and 300,000. In five years, total revenues from character merchandising exceeded ¥300 billion. By the end of 1995 the *Sailor Moon* manga books and the animation series had been exported to over twenty-three countries, including China, Brazil, Mexico, Australia, most of Europe, and North America. A truly global market had been opened up.

Another sign of success: among its 448+ pages, save for a few pages devoted to character-related merchandise, fake jewelry, and sanitary napkins, *Nakayoshi* has almost no ads. Nearly 100 percent of the magazine's revenues comes from actual sales. "And at ¥400 per copy," Irie adds, "we can afford few returns. Luckily, sales have usually been above 90 percent. In one period, we even reached 98 percent."

Irie will still have to struggle to reach the top of the manga heap, given the glut in manga magazines. "Recently," he says, "we've begun advertising *Nakayoshi* on television, to announce when the magazine will come out and to augment our media-mix policy."

Big Comics

「ビッグ」

YOU SAY MANGA, I SAY KOMIKKUSU

Manga magazines in Japan are often divided into four or five categories: *shōnen* ("boys"), *shōjo* ("girls"), *redisu* ("ladies"), *seijin* ("adult" as in "erotic manga for men"), and *seinen* ("young men"). *Seinen*, despite its youthful conno-

LEFT: **Biggu Komikku** ***("Big Comic"). May 25, 1995.*** *RIGHT:* **Biggu Komikku Orijinaru** ***("Big Comic Original"). November 20, 1995.***

tation, is a wonderfully vague term that can refer to males between the ages of fifteen and forty, but as the readership of manga ages it is being increasingly abused. Of the scores of what are often referred to as *seinen* magazines, some of the biggest sellers are titled, appropriately, *Big*—the name of a family of high-quality magazines published by the giant Shōgakukan and designed to appeal to a broad range of ages. There are currently five titles: *Big Comic, Big Comic Original, Big Comic Spirits, Big Comic Superior*, and *Big Gold*.

In the manga industry, if a monthly magazine sells well, it is normally turned into a semimonthly, then a biweekly, and finally a weekly in order to capture an ever larger readership. The Shōgakukan *Big* strategy has been to differentiate magazines by targeting increasingly narrow age groups. The plan has worked very well and has helped counter a problem that manga magazine publishers face; as readers mature, so do their tastes, and either the magazines have to mature with them or new magazines have to be created. Here's the lowdown on the *Big* family.

BIG COMIC

The grand-daddy of the *Big* family, *Big Comic* serializes works by big-gun artists. Long-running stories have included the famous *Golgo 13,* by Takao Saitō, about a Zen-like professional assassin who always gets his mark; *Hotel,*

DATABOX

Big Comic

Publisher:	Shōgakukan
Date founded:	1968
Price:	¥240
Format:	B5, folded/stapled, biweekly
Avg. no. of pages:	314
Sale date:	10th and 25th of each month
Est. circulation:	1,450,000
Rubi pronunciation key:	no

Big Comic Original

Publisher:	Shōgakukan
Date founded:	1972
Price:	¥230
Format:	B5, folded/stapled, biweekly
Avg. no. of pages:	302
Sale date:	5th and 20th of each month
Est. circulation:	1,700,000
Rubi pronunciation key:	no

by Shōtaro Ishinomori, about the inner workings of hotel life; and the gag strip *Akabe-ei*, by Hiroshi Kurogane. Don't look for sex and titillation here, though. This is serious stuff, written mainly by men over fifty and read by a faithful but aging male readership mostly over thirty. Some stories, like *Golgo 13*, have been serialized for twenty-five years. Ads are scarce and are mainly for cars, marriage services, energy drinks, hair tonics, hair pieces, and so forth.

BIG COMIC ORIGINAL

The sister magazine to *Big Comic*, *Big Comic Original* targets a very similar readership. Like *Big Comic*, it serializes many long-running, popular works by older and famous artists, including Fujiko Fujio Ⓐ, Koh Kojima, and Jōji Akiyama. One of its most popular stories in 1993 was "Master Keaton," by Hokusei Katsushika and Naoki Urasawa, about a half-Japanese, half-English veteran of the Falklands War who works as both a lecturer on archaeol-

Biggu Komikku Supirittsu *("Big Comic Spirits"). November 20, 1995.*

ogy and an insurance investigator. *Original*, like *Big Comic*, has few ads. The biggest difference, in addition to the fact that it goes on sale in weeks when *Big* doesn't, is that it always has amusing airbrushed paintings of animals on the cover. *Big Comic* always has caricatures of famous people drawn with enormous heads.

BIG COMIC SPIRITS

Unlike its two older siblings, *Big Comic Spirits* is a weekly, and it is aimed at young salarymen between the ages of twenty and twenty-five. The story selection reflects this. There is a greater emphasis on sports, gags, and guy-gal interaction, and opening pages often have photographs of attractive young women in bathing suits. Huge hits such as *Oishinbō* ("The Gourmet"), which triggered a boom in comics for males about cooking, have appeared here. Unlike any American comic book, there are ads for cigarettes and whiskey. In June 1993 the newsmagazine *Aera* commented that the *seinen* genre of manga magazines was suffering from lack of direction in the wake of a general crackdown on eroticism in manga. *Spirits* was particularly hard hit and circulations declined; to boost sales, in 1995 it was priced ¥10 less than *Big* and *Original*, despite having more pages. The typical reader is said to be a twenty-eight-year-old company employee or "salaryman," a systems engineer who works at a finance company,

LEFT: **Biggu Komikku Superiōru** ***("Big Comic Superior"). November 15, 1995.*** *RIGHT:* **Biggu Gōrudo** ***("Big Gold"). November 17, 1994.***

likes to eat at ramen noodle shops, and is starting to look seriously at ads for matchmaking services. Cover designs always feature characters with heads made of vegetables or fruit.

BIG COMIC SUPERIOR

There is a tiny gap in the ages targeted by *Big*, *Original*, and *Spirits*—those between twenty-five and thirty—and *Superior* fills it. Popular works it serialized in the early nineties included *Sanctuary*, an exciting tale of Japanese gangs and politics by Shō Fumimura and Ryōichi Ikegami, and a comedy titled *Bow* by Terry Yamamoto, featuring a silly dog reminiscent of the Budweiser mascot of a few years back. (*Sanctuary* is published in English by Shōgakukan's subsidiary in San Francisco, Viz Communications.)

BIG GOLD

Big Gold is the newest addition to the *Big* family and the biggest in size, price, and sophistication. Square-backed and glued instead of folded and stapled, it showcases now-graying male and female industry legends such as Mitsuteru Yokoyama; Leiji Matsumoto and his wife, Miyako Maki; Shigeru Mizuki; and Machiko Satonaka—all creators of the golden age of manga in the early seventies. According to Sadao Ōtomo, an editor at *Big Gold*, readers range in age from the twenties to late forties, with 45 per-

DATABOX

Big Comic Spirits

Publisher:	Shōgakukan
Date founded:	1980
Price:	¥230
Format:	B5, folded/stapled, weekly
Avg. no. of pages:	350
Sale date:	every Monday
Est. circulation:	1,470,000
Rubi pronunciation key:	no

Big Comic Superior

Publisher:	Shōgakukan
Date founded:	1987
Price:	¥230
Format:	B5, folded/stapled, biweekly
Avg. no. of pages:	302
Sale date:	1st and 15th of each month
Est. circulation:	700,000
Rubi pronunciation key:	no

Big Gold

Publisher:	Shōgakukan
Date founded:	1992
Price:	¥580
Format:	B5, squareback, monthly
Avg. no. of pages:	456
Sale date:	28th of each month
Est. circulation:	210,000
Rubi pronunciation key:	no

cent company employees, 12 percent public employees, 11 percent housewives, and 6 percent students. Twenty percent are women, very high for a nominally "male" magazine. Most readers, Ōtomo says, have read manga all their lives, and intend to keep doing so.

With a readership that clearly goes beyond the normal definition of *seinen*, or "youths," *Big Gold* hints at a future that more and more manga publishers are beginning to salivate over. A drop in the birthrate has given Japan one of the most rapidly aging societies on earth. In the near future, members of this huge well-heeled, leisured, and "silver" population (as it is called) will certainly all be reading their own manga magazines. The cover illustrations for *Gold* have a lyrical and relaxed European flavor to them, and they are usually drawn by Shigeru Tamura, a renowned illustrator and manga artist (who was also one of the first people in the industry to do his work on a Macintosh).

Morning

「週刊モーニング」

MANGA IN THE MORNING, MANGA IN THE AFTERNOON

Manga magazines often have a short life because readers are fickle and competition is fierce. But one magazine that is here to stay is Kōdansha's *Morning*. First published in 1982, it has already made quite a mark on the industry.

Morning is a weekly with a circulation of around 1.3 million. Physically, it is fairly typical for its category. It is immediately identifiable as being mainly for adult males by its advertisements that, while few in number, hawk cars, cigarettes, beer, music albums, bodybuilding equipment, anti-balding remedies, and, occasionally, body hair remover (for those who want the now fashionable silky-smooth look). Also, the text in the comic balloons doesn't have any *rubi*, the little pronunciation keys supplied next to *kanji* characters in children's magazines. But unlike many other adult manga, *Morning* is a serious magazine: it carries no ads for porno videos, and it uses hardly any erotic or violent images.

Many manga in Japan have clearly defined editorial policies—such as the "friendship," "perseverance," and "victory" of all-time bestseller *Weekly Boys' Jump*. *Morning* does not. According to Yoshiyuki Kurihara, the editor-in-chief, *Morning*'s main policy is summarized by the slogan that has graced its cover since 1982: *Yomu to genki ni naru*, which literally means "You'll feel great if you

Shūkan Mōningu ***("Weekly Morning"). January 7–13, 1994.***

read it" but which Kurihara prefers to translate as "Manga Energy."

Morning thus has a greater diversity of stories and art styles than most mainstream manga magazines. Each week around seventeen or eighteen serialized and concluding stories are featured (along with shorter gag strips). Some have become quite famous. Kenshi Hirokane's enormously popular salaryman tale, *Kachō, Shima Kōsaku* ("Section Chief Shima Kōsaku"), emerged from *Morning* (a personal favorite of one-time Tokyo-based *Washington Post* correspondent T. R. Reid, it was often mentioned in the U.S.-media and was made into a live-action film in Japan). Kaiji Kawaguchi's long-running *Chinmoku no Kantai* ("Silent Service"), a tale about a renegade Japanese submarine that continues to humiliate the U.S. Navy, stirred debate among the media and politicians about defense policy with its deliberately provocative theme. Tochi Ueyama's *Kukkingu Papa* ("Cooking Papa"), a light-hearted tale of a man who loves to cook for his family, includes actual recipes in each story. It has been compiled into over forty paperback volumes and broadcast as a weekly animated series on television.

In the early nineties *Morning* also carried the obligatory sports stories, such as a boxing drama, *Aishite Iru* ("I Love You"), by manga veteran Shin Morimura; a sumo adventure, *Aa Harimanada* by Sadayasu Kei; and the baseball drama *Reggie*, by Guy Jeans and Hiramitsu Minoru—a delightful tale of a black U.S. major league player who joins up with the Japanese team called Gentlemen and struggles to adapt to Japanese baseball customs. *Reggie* predated the Hollywood movie *Mr. Baseball* and was drawn in a completely original semirealistic, semideformed style.

Other stories in *Morning* have more unusual themes. In the early nineties Akira Ose's nostalgic drama *Boku no Mura no Hanashi* ("A Story of My Village") depicted the conflicts that occurred between farmers, students, and riot police when Narita International Airport was built in the Chiba area east of Tokyo. Masashi Tanaka's *Gon* was a beautifully drawn, totally original, and implausible story with no words at all about a baby dinosaur surviving among mammals (ideal for export, it is issued in book form by the Belgian publisher Casterman). Yūji

Afutanūn *("Afternoon"). January 1996.*

DATABOX

Morning

Publisher:	Kōdansha
Date founded:	1982
Price:	¥250
Format:	B5, folded/stapled, weekly
Avg. no. of pages:	378
Sale date:	every Thursday
Est. circulation:	1,100,000
Rubi pronunciation key:	no

Afternoon

Publisher:	Kōdansha
Date founded:	1987
Price:	¥500
Format:	B5, squareback, monthly
Avg. no. of pages:	1,000
Sale date:	25th of each month
Est. circulation:	200,000
Rubi pronunciation key:	no

Aoki's award-winning *Naniwa Kin'yūdō* ("The Old Osaka Way of Finance") told the story of loansharks in the Osaka area and was drawn in a detailed, blocky style, complete with dialogue in the Osaka dialect.

In addition to the originality of many of its stories, what sets *Morning* apart from its competitors is its use of foreign artists and writers. Japanese manga borrowed heavily from U.S. comic books and animation for their format after the war, but the manga market has been like much of Japan's market for imported manufactured goods—if not closed, then extraordinarily difficult to enter. U.S. comics like *Spider-man* and *Superman*, when introduced, have usually bombed.

To their credit, rather than pandering to readers' established tastes, editors at *Morning* have deliberately sought out novel material and encouraged submissions by foreigners. In California, *Morning* has run ads in local newspapers soliciting comics writers and artists. Thus far, according to the editors,, *Morning* has featured artists from the U.S., Canada, the U.K., France, Germany, Italy, Spain, Czechoslovakia, Taiwan, China, and Korea. The greatest number of artists have come from France, Spain, and the U.S., but by far the most popular and commercially successful artists are from Taiwan and Korea. The work of Cheng-wen, from Taiwan, has been compiled into three paperback volumes; despite a larger format and a price higher than usual, they have sold over 200,000 copies. One thing discouraging established foreign artists, however, is that they are required to draw with Japanese conventions of pacing and a right-to-left (as opposed to the English left-to-right) layout. Sometimes the foreigners are writers, not artists, in which case such problems are irrelevant. Robert Whiting, the author of some of the best books on Japanese baseball and, by extension, U.S.-Japanese cultural differences (*You Gotta Have "Wa"* and *The Chrysanthemum and the Bat*), was the writer for the popular baseball series *Reggie*. "Guy Jeans," his manga pen name, is a pun on the word *gaijin*, or "foreigner."

Like nearly all Japanese manga magazines today, *Morning* has established a feedback system with its readers to tell it whether a story is popular or not. In addition to the standard response card, readers can provide comments and news with a twenty-four-hour fax hot line. Readers' comments are featured in the letters to the editor section and in sidebars on the comic pages themselves—words of encouragement to a favorite hero or heroine are common. Faithful (and lucky) readers can also win presents.

If a story the editors like doesn't fit into *Morning*, there's probably room for it in its sister publication, *Afternoon*. *Afternoon* features similar stories for a slightly younger audience and at ¥500 for 1,000 pages gives readers even more bang for the buck. It weighs over 1 kilogram (2.2 pounds).

Take Shobō and Mahjong Manga

竹書房の麻雀マンガ

FOR SERIOUS GAMERS

I'm not a mahjong player. I hate smoking cigarettes and staying up all night—which is what most mahjong players seem to do. Yet I've often felt left out when Japanese friends get together to play mahjong because the game is such an integral part of student and salaryman culture, and because it is so essential for "male bonding." Luckily, there's a way for me to experience mahjong culture without the smoke and red eyes, and that's by reading mahjong comics such as those from publisher Take Shobō.

Take Shobō began publishing in 1972 with a monthly magazine titled *Kindai Mājan* ("Modern Mahjong"). The magazine was mainly text, but a few years later clever editors transformed it into Japan's first dedicated manga mahjong magazine—*Kindai Mājan Orijinaru*, or "Modern Mahjong Original." Today, this is one of Take Shobō's three mahjong manga magazines; the other two are *Bessatsu Kindai Mājan* ("Modern Mahjong Supplement," known among fans as "Bekkin"), and *Kindai Mājan Gold* ("Modern Mahjong Gold"). All claim circulations between 180,000 and 200,000 per month.

The three magazines look identical. Bold *kanji* characters for "MODERN MAHJONG" form the titles on the covers, and crown illustrations of handsome-but-serious-looking males holding winning mahjong tiles. Inside are a series of serialized and concluding manga stories—comedy, love, or science fiction, but all with an exciting mahjong game at their core—as well as an assortment of information-intensive articles and features.

Close inspection reveals slight differences in the magazines. Publication dates are staggered to cover the month. *Bekkin* uses a slightly more modern *kanji* font for the title on the cover. And each magazine has a different slogan. *Bekkin* stresses (in English) "Attractive Mahjong," *Gold* stresses "Comics for Mahjong Enthusiast," and *Original* emphasizes "Pleasant Gambling." Michiyuki Miyaji,

LEFT:* Kindai Mājan Orijinaru (*"Modern Mahjong Original"*). *November 13, 1995.* *RIGHT:* Bessatsu Kindai Mājan (*"Modern Mahjong Supplement"*). *December 1995.

one of the editors, explains that the magazines are put together by separate editorial staffs, and each has its own emphasis, artist line-up, and readership. *Bekkin* and *Original* readers range in age from sixteen to twenty-two, but the average age for *Gold* is around twenty-five and increasing.

"Mahjong's most interesting after you've been playing it two or three years," Miyaji notes. "Our readers are actually more interested in the mahjong than the manga, so the manga stories are really a vehicle to learn about mahjong." *Bekkin,* he adds, is active in popularizing mahjong and in promoting tie-ins with other media, so it often has "guest appearances" by celebrities like the eccentric avant-garde manga artist and TV star Yoshikazu Ebisu, who demonstrated his style of play in a June 1994 comic strip. *Gold*, for its part, heavily promotes Shōichi Sakurai, one of the top mahjong experts in Japan who is also a famous former *ura*, or "underground," mahjong professional.

Most gambling in Japan—with the exception of such state-sanctioned ventures as the lottery and horse, bicycle, and boat racing—is illegal, but millions of people, including off-duty police, bet on mahjong games. Nonetheless, flagrant abuse of the law is frowned upon, so true "professionals" work underground. Sakurai, who reportedly earned millions of dollars during his long

Kindai Mājan Gōrudo *("Modern Mahjong Gold"). December 1995.*

©1995 TAKE SHOBŌ

career, is a "retired professional," which thus enables him to operate publicly. In *Gold* he has been elevated to hero status and is featured not only in photo articles illustrating mahjong technique, but in manga stories based on his life. Video films produced by Take Shobō glamorizing Sakurai's life are heavily advertised in all three of its mahjong manga magazines.

Like real-life mahjong players, the vast majority of mahjong manga magazine readers are males, a fact evidenced by the ads rather than the stories, which are fairly straightforward and sex-free. After the small ads for mahjong parlors, the most common ads are for telephone sex outfits merchandising masturbatory fantasies; back covers often hawk depilatories for hairy men anxious to achieve the fashionable "smooth, and body-hairless look."

Women readers are nonetheless increasing in number. Miyaji attributes this partly to the popularity of a gag mahjong comic strip called *Super Zugan,* by Masayuki Katayama, which was shown as an animated series on late-night television, where it won many female fans. One of the most popular artists in *Gold* in 1994/95, Miyaji notes, is a woman—Rieko Saibara—whose short essay-manga gag strips became one of Take Shobō's best-selling works when compiled into paperback. Both *Original* and *Bekkin* are aggressively trying to increase female readers

DATABOX

Kindai Mahjong Original

Publisher:	Take Shobō
Date founded:	1977
Price:	¥300
Format:	B5, folded/stapled, monthly
Avg. no. of pages:	240
Sale date:	13th of every month
Est. circulation:	180,000–200,000
Rubi pronunciation key:	no

Kindai Mahjong Bessatsu

Publisher:	Take Shobō
Date founded:	1979
Price:	¥300
Format:	B5, folded/stapled, monthly
Avg. no. of pages:	240
Sale date:	1st of every month
Est. circulation:	180,000–200,000
Rubi pronunciation key:	no

Kindai Mahjong Gold

Publisher:	Take Shobō
Date founded:	1988
Price:	¥300
Format:	B5, folded/stapled, monthly
Avg. no. of pages:	240
Sale date:	23rd of every month
Est. circulation:	180,000–200,000
Rubi pronunciation key:	no

by holding women's mahjong tournaments and mahjong dating forums.

Publishing mahjong manga magazines can be a tough business—a *real* gamble—because the popularity of the magazines depends on the popularity of the game itself. Take Shobō, luckily, is an aggressive company, and it has diversified beyond mahjong into a wide variety of publications, including what was in 1993–94 a highly lucrative market for *hēa nūdo* ("hair nudes")—deluxe photo collections of nude young women that sold like hotcakes after the Japanese government lifted its ban on any works that showed or depicted pubic hair.

In the mid-eighties there were over ten mahjong manga magazines, but recession and a subsequent industry shake-out took a heavy toll; by the end of 1995 Miyaji reported that Take Shobō had the field all to itself. "During the late-eighties period of Japan's go-go 'bubble' economy," Miyaji says, "mahjong had a depressing image, and the number of mahjong parlors dropped dramatically. The industry has made a comeback recently, however, with more fashionable mahjong parlors equipped with waiters, free drinks, and hot face towels." He attributes Take Shobō's survival at least in part to the enormous popularity of a beautifully illustrated series titled *Naki no Ryū* ("Weeping Dragon"), by Jun'ichi Nōjō. Nōjō later moved on to drawing *shōgi*, or Japanese chess, manga in Shōgakukan's *Big Spirits*, a much more mainstream manga magazine.

Mahjong manga magazines rely heavily on technical information, but they also contain some very sophisticated artwork. In addition to being a good way to improve one's mahjong skills, they are an entertaining introduction into a very different world.

Pachinko Manga Magazines

パチンコ漫画雑誌

AN ARTISTIC CHALLENGE

In the early 1990s, the already overflowing magazine racks in Japan had a new addition—manga magazines devoted to pachinko.

What is pachinko? To the uninitiated, it is best described as a vertical variant of American pinball, with the added thrill of illicit gambling. Legally, customers at pachinko parlors can only trade the silver balls the machines disgorge for prizes like toothbrushes, lighters, and chocolate, but nearly everyone goes around the cor-

Manga Pachinkā *("Manga Pachinker"). November 1995.*

© 1995 BYAKUYA SHOBŌ

ner to a designated "exchange" spot—usually a tiny hole in a wall—and converts their prizes to cash. Pachinko parlors, with their garish designs, rattle of silver balls, and blaring march music, are a fixture of every town in Japan. The stressed-out urbanites who fill them are not just gambling, but engaged in a very modern sort of glassy-eyed, brainwash meditation. The game is arguably Japan's most popular and proletarian form of entertainment; in 1994 aficionados reportedly spent around ¥30 trillion (nearly $300 billion) on it annually—a figure that is more than the gross national product of Switzerland and dwarfs that of nearly every industry in Japan, including that of manga.

Individual manga stories about pachinko are nothing new. As early as 1971, Jirō Gyū and Jō Biggu created the now-classic *Kugishi Sabuyan* ("Sabu the Pin Artist"), about a young "pin-adjuster" in a pachinko parlor who constantly had to pit himself against *pachi-puro* ("pachinko professionals") trying to thwart the machines. But manga magazines devoted *entirely* to pachinko appeared around 1991. The man generally credited for this is Akira Suei, a director and editor-in-chief of the maverick publishing firm Byakuya Shobō and a minor legend in the publishing world.

Byakuya Shobō is notorious for its erotic manga and photo magazines. Before Japan's censorship laws on nudity were relaxed, Suei was hauled into the police station for the alleged excesses of at least one photo magazine he presided over. The late eighties found him publishing much safer pachinko magazines (filled with how-to articles and text-based information about the game). These sold quite well, and Suei thought that a *manga* magazine exclusively devoted to pachinko might work too, particularly since pachinko was enjoying one of its periodic booms. At the time, however, Suei says that "most people in the industry believed such magazines would never work because it was too difficult to create stories about pachinko in manga format."

Pachinko machines, despite their gaudy design, flashing lights, and flickering bumpers and "tulip" slots, are inorganic and static boxes. Unlike mahjong (which is played with four people and thus has a built-in theatrical element), pachinko is a game between one person and a machine. To create drama, Suei realized, one needed to create plots about the world surrounding the machine.

Pachinkā Wārudo *("Pachinker World"). December 2, 1995.*

DATABOX

Manga Pachinker

Publisher:	Byakuya Shobō
Date founded:	1991
Price:	¥280
Format:	B5, folded/stapled, monthly
Avg. no. of pages:	222
Sale date:	27th of each month
Est. circulation:	160,000
Rubi pronunciation key:	no

Pachinker World

Publisher:	Byakuya Shobō
Date founded:	1992
Price:	¥280
Format:	B5, folded/stapled, biweekly
Avg. no. of pages:	220
Sale date:	1st, 3rd Thursday of each month
Est. circulation:	180,000
Rubi pronunciation key:	no

And what a rich world it is. Like mahjong manga, today's typical pachinko manga feature mysteries, comedies, and sex stories, along with technical information and strategy tips. All the stories however, have a pachinko machine and a game at their core.

Suei was himself not an expert in pachinko. In preparation for his involvement with pachinko magazines, he took what amounted to a crash course in the game. As a November 1994 article on Byakuya Shobō in the media magazine *Tsukuru* notes, meticulously kept company records show that over a period of four months Suei spent 172 hours and 30 minutes playing pachinko. He spent ¥576,700 (around $6,000) and won 307,650 pachinko balls for a cashed-in return of ¥174,140, or nearly $2,000.

Under Suei's direction, Byakuya Shobō's main two pachinko manga magazines—*Manga Pachinker* and *Pachinker World*—appeared in 1991 and 1992, respectively. They have nearly identical formats and for a few years were both biweeklies with staggered publication dates, thus functioning almost like a single weekly (in 1995, due perhaps to Japan's recession, *Pachinker* switched to a monthly schedule). The first few color pages have photos of various machine designs with detailed descriptions of their merits, expert analyses of the controlling ROM (read-only memory) computer chips, and graphs of payout probabilities. Then there is the usual mix of serialized and concluding manga stories, as well as articles by pachinko experts and—since the readership is largely young males—ads for telephone sex, circumcision (increasingly popular now), and good luck charms.

In the old days, players fed balls individually into the machines and spring-fired them by deftly snapping a lever (hence the onomatopoeic "pa-chin-ko"). Now that the machines are all high-tech and the balls are auto-fired by turning a dial, it might seem even more difficult to depict such a passive game visually. On the contrary, Suei, explains, modernization has helped popularize high-tech tales. One series in *Pachinker World* in 1994 was *Digital Boy*, by Yoshihiro Ōkuma and Kōhei Ishihara, about a young technoid hacker who tries to beat computerized pachinko machines by breaking their codes.

Still, creating pachinko manga is not always easy. "Sometimes," Suei admits, "the artists don't know much about pachinko, and they have to be taught so they don't make mistakes. Sometimes they find it boring to draw the machines, but it's important for the readers, many of whom have a fetish about machine designs and hate it when artists use photocopies."

Byakuya Shobō's success with pachinko manga magazines has generated many imitators in the "me-too" manga industry. At one point it had eight competitors, but by the end of 1994 only six survived. As Suei points out, unlike the imitators who contract out the production of their pachinko magazines, Byakuya Shobō has the know-how to produce them in-house, and it has strong tie-ins to its non-manga, "how-to" style pachinko magazines. Furthermore, the company has successfully exploited a new sales route in Japan—the 40,000 "7-11"-style convenience stores that, unlike bookstores, are open twenty-four hours a day.

Mainstream publishers have shied away from pachinko manga magazines. Suei believes this may be because the pachinko industry's links to organized crime—the yakuza—have given it an unsavory reputation. Like Japan's huge sex industry, the illegal aspect of pachinko, the gambling, thrives in an extralegal environment that the authorities have tacitly condoned and that is rife with tax evasion and corruption. In the mid-1990s the police tried to regulate cash flow by encouraging computerized pachinko operations and the use of prepaid cards. But as the newsmagazine *Aera* noted in a series of articles in 1994, the huge pachinko industry quickly started coopting the police; the companies that control the pachinko prizes and the prize-for-cash system are increasingly populated by retired police higher-ups.

Which is all good fodder for pachinko manga stories. The November 27, 1994 issue of *Pachinker* had a story about an off-duty policewoman and police chief who visit a pachinko parlor for a few games on their day off. The regular parlor patrons and owners—resentful of increased police control of their industry—challenge the pair to a game of pachinko "strip poker" and win, sending the authorities home humiliated and buck naked.

Combat Comic

「コンバットコミック」

JAPAN'S MILITARY MANGA MAGAZINE

Japan may be the comic book capital of the world, but one genre of material that has been conspicuously lacking is jingoistic war comics. Devastating defeat in World War II, heavy censorship of militaristic values in the arts by the Allies during the Occupation, and a U.S.-imposed constitution that "renounces war" created a national allergy to most things glorifying the military. The company with the largest presence in the small military comics market today is Nippon Shuppansha. Since 1985 it has been issuing Japan's sole war comic magazine—*Combat Comic*—and compiling its serialized stories into paperback volumes.

Nippon Shuppansha has a history dating back over fifty years. Prior to World War II, under the name Kōasha Nippon, it issued popular non-manga magazines such as the monthly *Senzen Bunko* ("Front Line Library"); supervised by the Imperial Navy, in 1942 this publication reportedly had an impressive circulation of nearly 2 million. After the war the Allied Occupation forces stopped Kōasha Nippon from publishing for a year because of its role in promoting militarism. In 1946, the firm was revived with the new name Nipponsha and published Japanese literature classics and entertainment magazines. In 1966, Nipponsha went bankrupt, but in the same year it was restructured as Nippon Shuppansha. Around 1972, it began publishing manga.

Today Nippon Shuppansha publishes pulp novels, manga (in paperback and book form), books, and calendars. Around 60 percent of its manga and books fall into the erotic category. Military-related books and comics comprise between 10 and 20 percent of the company's total output. In an affiliation with Marvel Comics of the United States, the company also publishes the comic book *Psychonauts*, based on an American script.

The flagship of Nippon Shuppansha's military manga line is *Combat* magazine. Square-backed, with a "quality" feel in paper and binding, it sells for the relatively high price of ¥620 and has a claimed circulation of nearly 100,000. According to the editor, Tetsuya Kurosawa, the readers are almost all male and tend to be *mania*, or hard-core fans of guns, "survival games," and "mecha" (weaponry and hardware). Their average age is around twenty, but some are in their forties and fifties. Many are members of Japan's Self-Defense Forces.

Like many other manga magazines, *Combat* contains a mix of around ten serialized and concluding manga stories, plus a few short strips, editorial pages, and text-only articles. Special manga features are often timed to coincide with historical events. The July 1994 issue featured fiftieth-anniversary D-Day stories, as well as stories

Konbatto Komikku *("Combat Comic"). January 1996.*

about the battle for Leyte in the Philippines. An ad for the latter proclaimed, "The giant guns of the Imperial Navy's battleships, *Musashi* and *Yamato,* roar!" indicating the strong romantic appeal these ill-fated ships still have in the public mind. Similarly, issues in the summer of 1995 featured stories about final battles leading up to Japan's August 14 surrender.

Popular stories serialized in *Combat* magazine are compiled into a line of manga paperbacks, amusingly named "BOMB comics," that retail for around ¥880. According to Kurosawa, as of spring 1996, fifty-two different BOMB titles had been issued.

The stories in the magazine and in the paperbacks fall into three or four main categories: stories about the Pacific War (battles in the Pacific in World War II), Germany in World War II, "simulation" stories, and "parallel" SF stories set in the present or near future with a link to the past.

Past bestsellers have included a book on the Persian Gulf War (200,000 copies), a book on World War III, and a book on Vietnam (100,000 copies). The Vietnam book came out in 1987 and received a big boost from the release that same year of the Oliver Stone movie *Platoon*. Movies, especially American movies like *Platoon* and *Top Gun*, have a big influence on sales, as do political events. Japan's limited and brief involvement in Cambodia with the United Nations Peace Keeping Organization, or PKO, helped sell a manga book on the PKO in the mid-nineties.

Gyakuten!! Taiheiyō Sensō ("The Pacific War: Reversal!") is an example of a "simulation" book that has done very well; by 1996 it had sold over 60,000 copies. It analyzes specific battles in the war and uses a "What if . . ." scenario to postulate how different decisions might have affected the outcome. Since I live in San Francisco, I was particularly struck by the cover illustration, which shows the battleship *Yamato* sailing under the Golden Gate Bridge. Contrary to what I was expecting, however, I found the treatment to be a fairly well-reasoned speculation about what might have happened if the U.S. had lost a series of Pacific Fleet battles and General Patton had run amok and attacked the approaching Soviet Army in Europe. In the simulation, U.S. and Soviet forces are embroiled in a fight, the Allied coalition falls apart, the Soviets attempt to enlist the aid of Japan, and the U.S. finally agrees to a cessation of hostilities with Japan. In a treaty signed with the U.S. in San Francisco, the Japanese empire abandons many of its territories in exchange for peace.

As Kurosawa notes, since the simulation genre requires a great deal of information in order to create a sense of reality, the stories are filled with history and lengthy text passages as well as occasional photographs. "In general," he says, "our books have about three times more words than most manga."

In Japan and abroad there has been considerable criticism of the simulation genre—not only in manga, but video games, board games, and novels—since they often depict Japan as the victor in World War II. But it is easy to understand why such material would be immensely popular. One of the main constraints on the World War II war-comic genre in Japan has always been the fact that Japan lost the war. This makes for painful reading, as

DATABOX

Combat Comic	
Publisher:	Nippon Shuppansha
Date founded:	1984
Price:	¥620
Format:	B5, squareback, monthly
Avg. no. of pages:	225
Sale date:	29th of each month
Est. circulation:	100,000
Rubi pronunciation key:	no

one's favorite characters often wind up dead; it is certainly a reason that many war comics until recently have been tragic in tone, if not antiwar. In manga, most war comics still exist outside a political context and hardly seem to indicate a revival of militarism. Interestingly, at Nippon Shuppansha, nearly half of the stories star not Japanese, but foreign armies.

In reading the manga stories in *Combat*, it is hard to avoid the conclusion that a great deal of the current fascination with weaponry and war among young readers stems precisely from the fact that several generations have grown up in unprecedented peace, insulated from warfare and global conflict. One of the world's strictest systems of gun control has left them ignorant of weaponry and armed conflict, and this may conversely have contributed to an intense, naive curiosity about such matters.

Nippon Shuppansha is very sensitive to the way its comics are perceived by the public. While interviewing the editors, I was careful not to be judgmental, and they were clearly relieved by this. Nonetheless, the president of the company (whom I did not meet directly), sent a personal message to me, stressing that his firm was not pro-war and that his comics were strictly for entertainment, designed to provide a "realistic" look at what war is really like. At Nippon Shuppansha, Kurosawa also pointed out, the editorial policy is not to portray either side in a conflict as "good" or "bad."

June

「JUNE」

INVERTED-LOVE

Nothing better illustrates Japan's ability to stand "Western" conventional wisdom on its head than the bimonthly *June*, a magazine for female readers exclusively featuring stories of love between males. *June* (pronounced "ju-neh") was first published in 1978 by the Sun publishing group, which has specialized in entertaining, highly erotic magazines for the masses. In its 1995 incarnation *June* was a 300-page bimonthly in the standard square-backed B5 format, with a mix of manga stories and essays on gay-male-love themes. It had a circulation between 80,000 and 100,000.

Toshihiko Sagawa, currently an editor at Sun, claims to have developed the magazine's concept. A longtime manga fan, in the 1970s he was fascinated by girls' comics artists such as Moto Hagio, Keiko Takemiya, and Yumiko Ōshima (referred to as the "1949 Gang" for their year of birth). These women often drew stories with boy heroes instead of girls and used homoerotic themes. At the time, Sagawa notes, the emerging, mostly female-oriented *dōjinshi* amateur fanzine market was gravitating toward depictions of what are called *bishōnen*, or "beautiful boys." Gender-bender rock stars like David Bowie and Queen were also popular among young women.

"So I proposed a magazine for girls and young women devoted to this theme, and it was accepted," Sagawa says. "It was designed to have a cultish, guerrilla-style aura about it, to be something the more established, major publishers wouldn't be able to imitate."

The artists employed were almost all young women and—because the company couldn't afford to pay high page rates—mostly newcomers to the industry. In effect, *June* became a type of "readers" magazine, created by and for the readers.

This formula proved so successful that four years later Sun moved beyond manga and issued *Shōsetsu June* ("June Novels"). Now a 270-page bimonthly, in 1995 it was being issued alternately with *June* in the slightly smaller A5 size. In defiance of a general trend in Japan for people to prefer manga over novels, *June Novels* is almost entirely text-based tales of male-only romances. Whereas the manga *June* bills itself as "Now, Beyond a Dangerous Love . . . ," the literary magazine proclaims, "Now, Awakening to Dangerous Text . . ." Its circulation, moreover, exceeds that of the manga magazine. According to Sagawa, almost all the writers are females raised on manga. When writing text-only stories, "they are merely creating manga with words."

Following common practice when an idea sells well, in 1996 Sun further subdivided its "June" line up, adding a large-format magazine titled *June*, heavily illustrated with photos of young boys; a gay novel and manga combo magazine titled *Roman June* ("Romantic June") with *real* gay stories for older women; and the venerable *Shōsetsu June*. The original manga June was retitled (what else?) *Comic June*.

In addition to the four *June* magazines, the Sun publishing group issues paperback manga books, audio cas-

June. *September 1995.*

settes and CDs, and original animation videos with *June* themes. Reflecting its cultish nature, in 1995 the manga magazine retailed for ¥750, more than double the normal price of a major manga magazine. For the truly devoted, Sun sells—by mail-order only—a deluxe, twelve-volume hardback compilation of every issue of *June*. Each volume sells for ¥3,500 plus shipping charges, so to collect the entire set (nearly 8,400 pages) would cost almost ¥48,000 yen, or over $480.

There are now so many *June* imitators in Japan that the word itself has become a synonym for the whole genre of relatively serious male-love stories for female fans. According to Sagawa, his firm's projects have been aided by a number of new developments in Japanese society. Among them, he notes, are the explosion in popularity of girls' and women's manga in general, the new visibility of gay culture, the growth of the now-huge, mostly female amateur manga market, and the popularity among Japanese women of foreign films with a gay theme, such as the 1984 British movie *Another Country*. But "June" stories, as they are known, also represent an extension in manga of a genre of Japanese art and literature known as *tanbi mono* or "esthetic works"—works that exalt beauty above morality and reality. The late Yukio Mishima's novels, for example, often had a dark, homoerotic, fetish quality to them, a worship of beauty that produced aberrant or antisocial behavior.

Why are female readers so attracted to love stories about gay males?

"The stories are about males," Sagawa says, "but the characters are really an imagined ideal that combine assumed or desired attributes of both males and females. Thus the heroes can be beautiful and gentle, like females, but without the jealousy and other negative qualities that women sometimes associate with themselves. The women readers are also attracted to the friendship and bonding that they assume takes place between males; the idea that men would die for each other on the battlefield, for example, is seen as a type of 'love,' when for men it's probably seen as comradery. On the surface these characters are gay males, but in reality they are a manifestation

DATABOX

June (1995)

Publisher:	(Magajin Magajin) San [Sun] Shuppan
Date founded:	1978
Price:	¥750
Format:	B5, squareback, monthly
Avg. no. of pages:	326
Sale date:	25th of every other month
Est. circulation:	80,000 – 100,000
Rubi pronunciation key:	no

of females; they're like young women wearing cartoon-character costumes.

"Also, girls and young women in Japan still have constraints on them socially. They feel the characters are freer if they are male, both socially and sexually.

"Finally, society expects men and women to fall in love, but there are still taboos associated with homosexual love. Therefore, to many of our readers, gay love seems more 'real.' Gay characters have to overcome many social obstacles, thus engendering sympathy and occasional tragedy, and again making their love seem very 'real.' This makes it easier to create stories. For a while suicide endings were very popular, but now readers want characters to have happy endings."

The magazines' readers, Sagawa notes, are females ranging from high school students to housewives in their forties. There are very few gay readers, he claims, because the perspective is different. To preserve this female point of view, most of the editors are women, as are the artists and writers. "The only reason I'm able to do this work," he says, "is because I've read so many girls' comics over the years."

Comic Amour

「COMIC AMOUR」

FEMALE SEX FANTASIES UNLEASHED

"Ladies' comics"—or *redikomi* as they are affectionately called in truncated Japanese—first appeared in the 1980s. These magazines targeted adult women—college students, office workers, and housewives—and by 1993, there were reportedly fifty-seven of them, with a combined circulation of over 120 million. Some magazines today focus on nonsexual areas such as marriage and child-raising or mystery stories, but most include so much erotic material that *redikomi* has almost become a synonym for racy reading material for women. A shakeout in the industry in 1994 put many *redikomi* out of business, but *Comic Amour*—arguably the top erotic comic magazine for women in Japan today—continues to thrive by providing high-quality, high-risk adult entertainment.

Amour was first issued in 1990 by the Sun publishing group, which has long specialized in erotic publications. Edited by Masafumi Mizuno and a staff of three men and three women, it is currently a square-backed monthly with 400+ pages that sells for ¥390 (less than ¥1 per page!). According to Mizuno, *Amour* now has a jaw-dropping circulation of 430,000 copies per month.

"We're developing the magazine as we go," Mizuno says. "Men have their erotic manga magazines, but we're different. We're pursuing a female viewpoint. Both males and females like eroticism, but for the female reader it can't be too direct. In a man's manga, for example, in sixteen pages the story might start, the sex occurs, and that's it. But in erotic manga magazines for females it's necessary to depict some psychological interaction, to show the relationship between characters, and perhaps have a psychological struggle. For this, we also have to have female writers and artists, or it doesn't work."

For those who have entertained notions of Japanese women being particularly chaste or, conversely, sexually repressed, *Amour* is a great place to be disabused of such

Comic Amour.
June 1994.

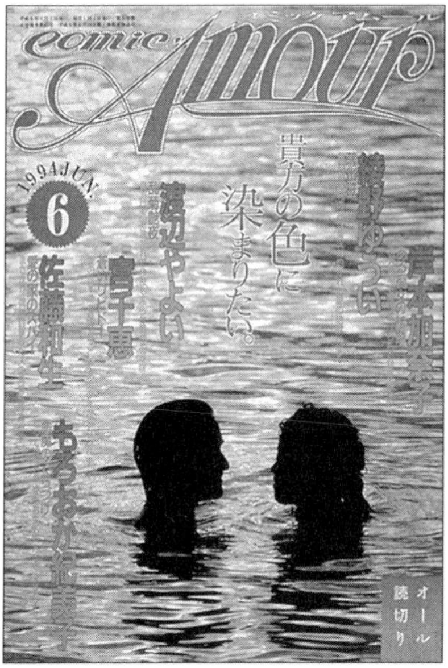

illusions. For if manga are a visualization of people's fantasies, then the women of Japan today have some of the richest and disturbing sex fantasies on the planet. The stories in *Amour* (which are almost all concluding and not serialized, as is normally the case in magazines) span the spectrum. The stories one would expect—the first love, the seduction of the coworker, the affair with a husband's friend—are all there. But so, too, are stories that would make many American and European feminists wince—a woman seducing a son's very young friend, a woman becoming a molester of men on a subway, and women characters who apparently enjoy enduring gang rapes, sodomy, and every other form of sexual torture and humiliation imaginable.

Yayoi Watanabe, one of *Amour*'s most popular artist/writers, authored one clever piece in June 1994 titled *Rangiku En'ya* (roughly, "Scattered Chrysanthemums, Sensual Nights") about a young woman determined to keep her virginity until marriage. The woman is kidnapped by a classmate who forcibly exposes her to a full range of carnal acts but miraculously leaves her hymen intact. Sure enough, when the woman finally does marry her fiancé, she has been so conditioned to unorthodox sex that the orthodox is boring. She quickly dumps her hubby for the classmate. The moral, presumably, is that it is foolish to prize one's virginity. Appropriately, the piece is subtitled "A Depiction of the Darkness Dormant in a Woman's Flesh."

Women's erotic manga may have more "psychological" depictions than those for men, but it would be wrong to assume that the visual depictions of sex are particularly discreet. In fact, although everything in *Amour* is drawn from a woman's perspective (and drawn quite well), the artists provide remarkably graphic depictions of sex, typically tiptoeing around the edges of Japan's now almost nonexistent obscenity laws. Genitals are depicted clearly, if slightly blurred (usually but not always minus pubic hair), and they are depicted often. Words regarded as obscene in Japanese are used heavily, with one or two characters replaced by little circles (just as newspapers in the United States coyly replace the middle letters of English obscenities with asterisks or dashes). And on nearly every page there is much exaggerated panting, gasping, groping, sweating, and massive oozing of bodily fluids.

In fact, except for the emphasis on the "woman's perspective" and on foreplay and "relationships," *Amour* and many other *redikomi* are almost identical to erotic manga magazines for men. One typical *Amour* issue in 1994 had a color photo spread about "women in heat" having car sex. Then, in addition to the manga stories, there were serialized erotic fiction stories, graphically illustrated articles on how to have better sex, reports from readers about adulterous affairs (the *furin* so fashionable in Japan since the early eighties), and—most surprising, perhaps—reports about the side of the huge sex industry in Japan that caters to women. Sex massage parlors for women, for example, were analyzed and rated with a star system indicating the degree of eroticism, the price, and the level of "risk." Advertisements, which do seem somewhat more numerous in *Amour* than in men's erotic comics, include those for weight-loss programs, bust-enlarger contraptions, depilatory devices, and adult videos. Reader feedback is important in all manga maga-

DATABOX

Comic Amour

Publisher:	(Magajin Magajin) San [Sun] Shuppan
Date founded:	1990
Price:	¥390
Format:	B5, squareback, monthly
Avg. no. of pages:	402
Sale date:	30th of every month
Est. circulation:	430,000
Rubi pronunciation key:	no

zines, and in *Amour* opinions are solicited not only about the magazine, but about preferred oral sex techniques, etc.

Comic Amour was so successful that in 1994 Sun began issuing *Young Amour* for readers in their late teens. Drawn in a slightly more "youthful" style by younger women artists, it has a nearly identical format to its sister publication. As one might expect, many of the stories are about ways to lose one's virginity. The magazine started with an initial print run of 250,000 per month.

Japanese females may have a long way to go before they achieve equality with males in the workplace, but in the erotic manga they read—for better or worse—they are rapidly approaching parity, with *Amour* leading the way.

Yan Mama Comic

「ヤンママコミック」

FOR YOUNG MOTHERS WITH ATTITUDE

I was surprised when I first learned of the unique problems of young mothers in Japan, particularly during their "park debut." This modern ritual takes place when new mothers bring their babies to the local park for the first time to meet other mothers in the neighborhood. It apparently can be quite stressful. The mothers have to worry about what to wear or say, for if they are a little dif-

Yan Mama Komikku (*"Yan-mama Comic"). December 1995.*

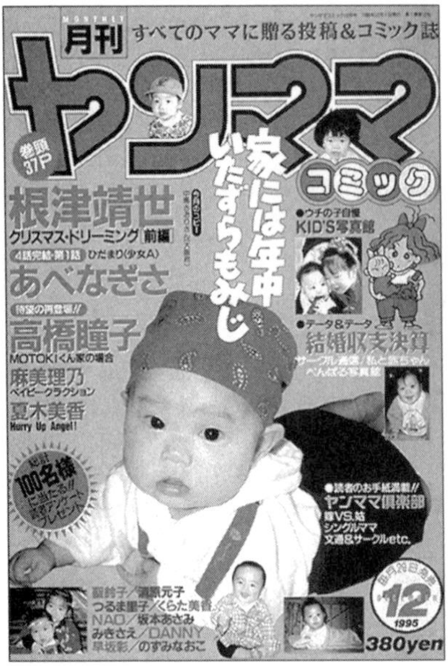

ferent from the middle-class, rapidly aging norm they may have trouble winning acceptance. And if they are so-called *yan mama,* very young mothers of a particularly modern sort—one-time social rebels with reddish dyed hair and flamboyant clothing, for example—they may even be ostracized. This rigidity among the playground moms has led to the formation of hundreds of *yan mama* "circles" or support groups in Japan.

Sure enough, there is even a monthly manga magazine for these women: *Yan Mama Comic*, published by Kasakura Shuppan. When I visited its editorial office in late 1994 I was pleasantly surprised to find that the magazine's editor-in-chief, Keiko Tamura, was herself a woman of twenty-seven, this in an industry where head editors are usually much older and almost always male.

Tamura (who is said to have coined the term *yan mama*) said that when she gave birth to her own child three years ago she spent a great deal of time reading books on child-rearing but found them too difficult. "Ladies'," or adult women's manga, for that matter, tended to concentrate too much on sex. If only, she thought, there were manga for people like herself. The result, in October 1993, was *Yan Mama Comic*, drawn for new mothers, by mothers. "Unlike most manga magazines," Ms. Tamura says, "we depict very real experiences, the sort of everyday things that all mothers go through, and we show mothers that their problems are not unique. Our readers say they feel we're writing about them personally."

Intrigued by the title, I asked Tamura about *yan mama* and learned the term has two nuances—"young mother" and "*yankii* mother," both of whom the magazine targets. One often hears the word *yankii* in Japan today, but in my ignorance I had always assumed it came from the English word "Yankee" and simply implied outgoing and brash young females. Tamura quickly and curtly explained to me that the term actually has little to do with America and is far more complex, having originated in the Osaka area, where *yankii* females are often affiliated with the *bōsōzoku*—Japan's gangs of live-fast-die-young car- and motorcycle-crazed delinquent youths. *Yankii* women affect an "attitude"; they may dye their hair reddish, assume an uncultured *unko suwari* ("shit squat"; see the color cover on page 80 for an infant version of this pose), smoke in public, and, if gang members (sometimes referred to as *redisu* or "ladies"), wear outfits that are a mix-and-match homage/parody of kamikaze pilot and day-laborer garb, embroidered with bold slogans.

Before starting *Yan Mama Comic*, Tamura edited a magazine for the guys and gals in the *bōsōzoku* scene titled *Champ Road*, filled with photos of cool cars and gang uniforms and articles on subjects like the danger of sniffing too much paint thinner. More and more of the young women in this scene were giving birth and sharing problems not being addressed anywhere else, so many of them became the core readership of *Yan Mama*.

A year after start-up, Tamura was proudly presiding over a monthly manga magazine with a claimed circulation over 120,000. By then the readership had broadened to include many ordinary mothers in addition to the core *yankii* or former *bōsōzoku* gang members.

The degree of reader involvement in *Yan Mama* is remarkable, reflecting not only a clever editorial policy but the extreme social isolation of many young Japanese

DATABOX

Yan Mama Comic

Publisher:	Kasakura Shuppan
Date founded:	1993
Price:	¥380
Format:	B5, squareback, monthly
Avg. no. of pages:	312
Sale date:	ca. 20th of every month
Est. circulation:	130,000
Rubi pronunciation key:	no

mothers. Some manga stories are based on letters from readers. *Kōen no Shikitari* ("Rules of Behavior in the Park"), a 1994 short work by the artist NAO, for example, describes how one *yan mama*, for her park debut, tried dyeing her reddish hair back to its original black and faking a more respectable attitude in order to gain acceptance. She in the end found comradery with another semi-ostracized mother—a *maru-kō* (written with the character for "high" in a circle and meaning a woman who gives birth at a high-risk age). Other stories in *Yan Mama* are more mundane and focus on pivotal experiences in child-rearing such as a child's first steps or first cold.

Elsewhere in the magazine are photos of babies mailed in from proud young mothers throughout Japan. Also in the mix are illustrated articles describing reader's tiny homes, analyses of readers' limited household budgets, reports from *yan mama* circles throughout Japan, and appeals from lonely readers for similarly situated pen pals. The biggest concerns readers have, Tamura says, are children, husbands, and how to get along with mothers-in-law, especially if living under the same roof, as is common in Japan. The magazine's last two pages are a questionnaire for readers to send in with information about children, problems, relations with neighbors, and so on.

Most readers appear to range in age from sixteen to the mid-twenties. Tamura claims that only 9.2 percent of them are unwed mothers. This hardly means the rest are conformists, however. The vast majority, Tamura proudly notes, are not on the standard middle-class social track in Japan and are definitely not obsessed—as so many Japanese mothers are—with getting their children onto the exam treadmill and into elite schools.

And what of Tamura's plans for the future? At the end of 1995, with more and more young fathers reading her publication, she was dreaming of bringing out a *Yan Papa* manga magazine.

Garo

「ガロ」

A DIFFERENT TYPE OF MANGA MAGAZINE

Japan's manga industry is without question the world's most enormous and diverse, yet it remains plagued by the same disease that affects commercial entertainment everywhere: a tendency to shallowness and imitation. There are manga magazines that today specialize in mahjong, business, sports, and sex, and magazines that target every age group of each gender. But only one magazine—*Garo*—has consistently been dedicated to the fostering of creativity.

Garo was created in the summer of 1964 by Katsuichi Nagai. A will-o'-the-wisp yet tough-as-nails man, whose sunken cheeks in later life showed the effect of decades of bouts with tuberculosis and hard living (and whose imminent demise was often prematurely prophesied), Nagai created *Garo* with the financial help of the now legendary artist Sampei Shirato. The idea was that it would serve as a monthly forum for Shirato and other artists to experiment. Shirato's classic tale of ninjas and class struggle in feudal Japan, *Kamui*, was thus one of the first stories the magazine serialized, and its enormous popularity in those days among intellectuals and radicalized students helped boost the magazine's sales. The title of the magazine, *Garo*, in fact comes not from the same-sounding Japanese word for "art gallery" but from one of Shirato's ninja characters.

Unlike the editors of almost all other, more com-

Thirtieth anniversary issue of* Garo*, September 1994. Katsuichi Nagai proudly posed with the beautiful Natsuo Ishidō, star of the 1994 movie* Ōtobai Shōjo *("Motorcycle Girl"), based on a manga story first published in* Garo *in 1973.

mercial manga magazines, from the start Nagai meant to encourage the development of unique art styles and storytelling and to push the envelope of comic creativity. As he stated in his 1982 autobiography, his rules for selecting material for serialization were simple: (1) that they be interesting and (2) that content be emphasized over form. In other words, Nagai viewed the magazine as sort of a training ground where people with unpolished technique but good ideas could find a forum for expression. The technique, he knew, would come later with practice.

Perhaps because of Nagai's radical approach, *Garo* was one of the first manga magazines in Japan to appeal to older readers, to university students and factory workers. And early on it quickly attracted a different breed of artist; not someone who wanted to create Disneyesque tales for children or action-adventure strips for adults, but true creators who were intent on personal and intellectual exploration.

Over the years, there have been several identifiable trends in *Garo*, starting with the enlightened ninja stories of Shirato and then moving into an abstract, surrealistic phase, an "illustrator" phase, and an erotic/grotesque phase. While never regarded as a "major" manga magazine in Japan, *Garo* has always been a trendsetter and a powerful creative force in both the manga industry and the world of commercial illustration. Many artists who debuted or cut their teeth on the magazine later went on to considerable fame. In recent years, in the manga world they have included women such as the modern manga-ukiyo-e artist Hinako Sugiura, the radically autobiographical manga artist Shungicu Uchida, and men like the black humor satirist Yoshikazu Ebisu. In the illustration/graphic design world *Garo* graduates include Seiichi Hayashi and Shigeru Tamura, whose lyrical illustrations grace many Japanese posters and magazine covers, and Teruhiko Yumura (aka King Terry), who spawned a revolutionary "bad-good" art movement.

The most remarkable aspect of all this is that most of the time Nagai did not pay the artists who drew for his magazine a nickel (or even a yen). He couldn't afford to. In a land where several manga magazines sell millions of copies per week, *Garo* often sells only 7,000 per month, and for years it was run at a loss. In the 1980s, in fact, circulation actually declined by around 150 copies per year. Nonetheless, aspiring artists—even established artists—still submitted their works, and the 200+ page magazine has survived over thirty years, making it ancient by industry standards. How could this be?

DATABOX

Garo

Publisher:	Seirindō
Date founded:	1964
Price:	¥550
Format:	B5, squareback, monthly
Avg. no. of pages:	266
Sale date:	1st of every month
Est. circulation:	20,000
Rubi pronunciation key:	no

IN ENGLISH

Two anthologies of *Garo* works have been published in the United States:

Sake Jock. Seattle: Fantagraphics, 1995.

Comics Underground Japan. Edited by Kevin Quigley. New York: Blast books, 1996.

Invariably, the reason the artists give for their participation is the magazine's reputation for artistic freedom. In mainstream manga magazines, editors pressure artists to conform to a certain style or to create whatever type of story is fashionable. In *Garo*, Nagai did not. He only published artists that he himself liked, and once he decided to publish them he gave them virtually free rein to experiment. The result was a broad range of styles and technical ability. Nagai also gave equal opportunity to women, making *Garo* one of the few true "unisex" manga magazines. In 1989 he claimed that nearly 70 percent of new submissions were from women artists.

If a particular work proved popular enough in *Garo*, it was compiled in book form and published by Seirindō, Nagai's tiny publishing outfit. From this point the artist would finally begin to be paid for his work in the form of royalties on book sales, which over time could be quite substantial. In the early nineties, books by *Garo* artists could be seen in bookstores and manga specialty shops in the section "Pāsonaru Komikkusu," or "Personal Comics," the place for works that concentrate on the artist's private, internal vision. Sales of Seirindō books have, in fact, subsidized *Garo*.

Seirindō never had much overhead. Headquartered for decades in an old, dilapidated building in the Kanda book area of Tokyo, and surrounded by towering, fancy buildings belonging to more "successful" manga publishers, it long consisted of just Nagai and five other employees, who worked hard to keep their vision intact and their expenses down. Publishers in Japan physically go to collect finished pages from manga artists, rather than have them mailed or hand-carried in, as is the usual practice in other countries. As Nagai and his staff proudly pointed out in an interview I did with them in 1989, however, when *they* had to go pick up the artwork their artists had completed, unlike the big corporate publishers, they always took inexpensive local trains instead of taxis.

By 1994, thirty years after *Garo*'s founding, an ailing Nagai—whose imminent demise was again being rumored—finally began receiving the recognition he deserved in the Japanese press. Retrospectives on his magazine appeared in mainstream magazines. The Kawasaki city museum had a special exhibit of work by former *Garo* artists. The contribution of *Garo* to Japan's manga and intellectual culture was also apparent, not only in the increasingly high profile of former *Garo* artists in mainstream manga art and the appearance of *Garo*-style competitors, but in the film world as well, where several *Garo*-inspired films had been made.

On January 5, 1996, the rumors finally came true. At age 74, Nagai succumbed to illness, and an important era in manga ended.

As for Nagai's magazine, it still struggles on. In 1991, it was bought out by a personal computer and game software company, and a new president still in his twenties was installed. Ads for computer games based on *Garo* stories began appearing, and there was an increase in music and rave-related articles, giving the magazine a new, hip content. Nagai was retained as the chairman until his death, however, and the new president vowed to continue the spirit of the original magazine. Even today the title page displays an English-language logo that still captures the soul of the publication—"Monthly Eccentric Comix Magazine."

4 ARTISTS AND THEIR WORK

マンガ家&マンガ作品

JUST AS THERE ARE HUNDREDS OF MANGA MAGAZINES, SO TOO are there thousands of manga artists. Not all become full-time professionals, and of those that do even fewer become commercial or artistic successes. Ultimately the most important quality required is originality, and a unique personal vision.

Hinako Sugiura

杉浦日向子

THE ROOTS OF JAPANESE COMICS

Most manga artists never think of themselves as inheritors of a centuries-long Japanese tradition of cartooning. Before their professional debut, in fact, most spend time copying and tracing over their favorite modern manga artists (which is why so many drawing styles look the same). The artist who has most consciously drawn on native traditions, both for story inspiration and art style, is Hinako Sugiura. In her manga as well as in real life, she has been an apostle of the aesthetics of the Edo period, the years from 1600 to 1867 when Japan was isolated from the outside world.

In Japan's early feudal period, most art was created in a superficially religious context, even when it was primarily for entertainment. In addition to painted scrolls, humorous, cartoonlike art included monochrome *Zenga* (Zen pictures), originally executed as a meditative aid, and *Ōtsu-e*, or "Ōtsu pictures," color print-drawings that

A **kibyōshi**-*style modern manga:* **Hanageshiki Kitsune Kōdan** *("Tales of Foxes at Flower-Viewing Time") in the collection* **Ehimosesu. The title comes from the last five characters in Japan's traditional syllabary and can be read as "to not be intoxicated."**

were originally designed near Kyoto as Buddhist amulets for travelers. During the Edo period (when there was an unprecedented 250 years of peace), the feudal system began to change, a money economy emerged among the urban merchant class, and inexpensive art as pure entertainment came into full bloom, aided by mass production based on woodblock printing technology. In the 1800s the great artist Hokusai Katsushika produced *Hokusai Manga,* a fifteen-volume collection of drawings and sketches (from which the modern word for Japanese comics derives). Erotic prints, violent and fantastic warrior prints, and Kabuki actor bromides flourished.

Museums around the world today are filled with

serious Japanese art, but so much of the material from the Edo period is humorous, entertaining, and fantastic that one occasionally wonders if overly image conscious museum directors haven't formed a worldwide conspiracy to ignore it. Townspeople in the Edo period were crazy about humorous woodblock illustrations and trashy illustrated storybooks. Many of these, although they lacked sequential picture panels or word "balloons," bore a striking resemblance to modern comics. They usually had twenty or more pages, with or without text, and were bound with thread or opened accordion-style. In the Osaka area, *toba-e* books featuring pictures of long spindly limbed characters in amusing antics were all the rage. In the early 19th century, *kibyōshi*, "yellow-cover" booklets, were produced by the thousands. Like modern comics, *kibyōshi* evolved from illustrated tales for children and gradually encompassed more and more sophisticated adult material. Most pages consisted of a drawing combined with the text in a block above it to form an illustrated, running story. Like comics today, *kibyōshi* were frequently published as a series.

Hinako Sugiura studied visual communication and design in university and dreamed of one day becoming an art director for commercials. But she became increasingly fascinated by feudal Japan and dropped out of college to study with Shisei Inagaki, the author of over a hundred books and perhaps the top consultant for theatrical and television films set in the Edo period. In 1980 Sugiura made her debut in the experimental manga magazine *Garo* with a short story titled *Tsūgen Muro no Ume* (roughly, "Trends and Artificial Beauty"). It was set in the Edo period and although somewhat roughly executed had a novel retro-yet-new style. The story established Sugiura as a chronicler of life in old Tokyo, especially in the colorful and wildly popular red-light district of Yoshiwara. In her subsequent work as well, Sugiura made the Edo period seem very much alive.

Sugiura is one of the few manga artists who occasionally draws in the *ukiyo-e* style practiced by woodblock masters over a hundred years ago. Sometimes she dips so deep into tradition that the pages truly look like the *kibyōshi* of old, which she acknowledges to be a powerful influence. Her short story, *Hanageshiki Kitsune Kōdan* ("Tales of Foxes at Flower-Viewing Time"), published in the early 1980s, is an example. It is a simple tale about a samurai warrior in springtime who wades into a rice paddy, hoping the leeches in the field will cure his foot fungus; the local people all gather to watch, thinking he has been possessed by a fox-deity. Sugiura not only draws the story with careful attention to period clothing and tradition, but executes it in *kibyōshi* format. She abandons the drawing pens, sequential panels, word balloons, and typeset text of modern *manga* for a brush and a traditional narrative layout. Text is hand-lettered in calligraphic style. Sugiura's main concession to modern times is to adapt the language—few Japanese would be able to read Edo-period Japanese without a dictionary.

A thoroughly modern person who once listed her hobbies as assembling plastic model kits and playing with computers, Sugiura comes from a family of kimono makers in Tokyo, and she grew up with a rich sense of tradition. She has often been called a "modern *ukiyo-e* artist," but she is really a bridge between two eras separated by the chasm created by Japan's rapid modernization. As she wrote in the afterword to *Gassō* ("Co-burial"), one of her paperback collections:

Ukiyo-e *style manga:* Asaginu *("Morning Silk"). A prostitute chides a man for falling in love with her. In* Garo *magazine, November 1981.*

IN ENGLISH

> Part of an episode titled *Unagi no Kai no Hanashi* ("Story of an Apparition of an Eel") from Hinako Sugiura's *Hyaku Monogatari* ("One Hundred Tales") appeared in issue 40 of *Mangajin*.

> To most people, the "Edo era" seems like another dimension, something from the world of science fiction. It's hard to imagine that our forefathers once wore topknots and strolled around streets that look like . . . [a movie set], but the Edo period and "today" exist in the same continuous flow of time; we now live on the same land that our top-knotted ancestors once lived upon.

In the late eighties and early nineties Sugiura spent more and more time writing and speaking about the Edo period, frequently on television as a talk-show celebrity, dressed in a kimono. She won the Japan Cartoonists' Association Award of Excellence in 1984 and the Bunshun Manga Award in 1988. Unfortunately for manga lovers, in 1993 she decided she was ill-suited to the life of a manga artist. At the age of thirty-five, claiming to be dissatisfied with her artwork and unwilling to keep up with the brutal pace of commercial manga publishing, she announced her retirement. She intended, she said, to become a scholar of the customs of the Edo period.

King Terry

湯村輝彦

THE BAD-GOOD ARTIST

Japanese manga are a wellspring of ideas for illustrators, graphic designers, and not surprisingly, for more than a few fine artists, many of whom once dabbled in manga themselves. The one artist/illustrator whose work exists in a continually symbiotic relationship with manga is Teruhiko Yumura, aka King Terry, Terry Johnson, and Flamina Terrino Gonzalez.

King Terry is a man who can make the rare boast of having used his own esthetic to redesign the cosmos. Born in 1942 and educated at Tama University of Arts, he burst into prominence in Japan in the late seventies and early eighties, drawing a series of covers for *Garo* and creating short pieces with crazed-penguin themes in collaboration with the famous copywriter Shigesato Itoi. Terry's influence vastly exceeded his actual output as a cartoonist, for he appeared in Japan when formalism and realism were under attack, not only in comics, but society at large (deliberately amateurish comedy and music shows, for example, were wildly popular on television). Terry became the guru of a revolutionary art movement known in Japan as *heta-uma,* or "bad-good," which invigorated the comics world and subverted that of commercial illustration.

Of his early experiments with Shigesato Itoi, creating works such as *Penguin Shuffle* and *Jōnetsu Penguin Gohan* ("Passionate Penguin Dinner"), he said in a 1989 interview, "I wanted to draw the pictures *I* wanted in the space provided, rather than tell a story. I started drawing whatever I wanted in each panel, and because I can't draw the same face twice, the character faces all changed." The result was manga with a weird mix of primitivism, energy, and dadaist storylines—comics where the art, the text, and the entire concept fused together in an elegant bad-good style, where in one episode an existential penguin floating on an iceberg dreams of dinner and suddenly romps through the Wild West, a boudoir, the Amazon jungle, and flying saucers, finally returning to contemplate the ocean with the lines, "Oh, Ocean/Not Sky/Only Ocean/ You are a parking lot for tears." Then, with a "Yum" he sits down to dinner on his iceberg.

At first glance Terry's cartoons and illustrations appear to be bad art, but on closer inspection, they are also good. Hence they are *heta-uma*, or bad-good. Terry believes that everyone starts as a "bad" artist and tries to become good. But simply becoming "good" is not enough. Artists who try too hard to become "good" begin to emphasize technique over soul, and then the life goes out of their drawings; their spirit fails to keep up with their technique. Terry's philosophy in art, therefore, has

King Terry shows how to draw "bad-good." From* Heta-uma Ryakuga Zuan Jiten *("A Bad-Good Sketch and Design Dictionary").

TALES OF LOVE THAT COULD BE YOURS!
With a Boy's ARMS AROUND ME!

been to avoid becoming too good, and to preserve a graffiti-like soul. He believes that there are essentially four types of art:

> (1) *Heta-uma* [Bad-good]—a high level of achievement, requiring great practice. The goal to be attained.
>
> (2) *Uma-uma* [Good-good]—the truly amazing "professionals," those who can astound everyone with their works. The crème de la crème.
>
> (3) *Heta-heta* [Bad-bad]—the truly bad amateur, who has neither technique nor sensibility. The average person.
>
> (4) *Uma-heta* [good-bad]—the professional whose technique is good but whose work lacks life. No soul.

In case anyone fails to understand the concept, in 1986 the publisher Seibundō Shinkōsha released *Heta-uma Ryakuga Zuan Jiten* ("A Bad-Good Sketch and Design

IN ENGLISH

> King Terry's work is featured in *Raw* magazine, issue 7, 1985.

Dictionary"), a 285-page manual in which Terry teaches aspiring "bad-good" artists how to draw nearly everything—vehicles, animals, faces, fight scenes, and sex scenes—in his unique style. In 1995 the book was out of print but so in demand by fans that Terry was working on a new 600-page expanded edition titled (in translation) "The *Decisive* Bad-Good Sketch and Design Dictionary."

Terry spawned a host of imitators in Japan, both in the comics and illustration world. One distinguishing feature of Terry's *heta-uma* art, however, is its "American" mood. Many of Terry's non-penguin, human characters in his comics are Westerners who speak fractured English. Terry has even been accused of being "more American than Americans." Where did Terry's weird All-American sensibility come from? He grew up in a period when Japanese infatuation with America was at its peak. But instead of high-brow culture, Terry was especially attracted to the trashy layouts and graphic designs of sixties and seventies pulp magazines and comic books. In the early 1990s he visited the mainland U.S. several times. But when I interviewed him in 1989 he hadn't been to America for sixteen years. Commenting on his first trip, he said, "I had a strong, romantic image of the U.S. before actually going there, but seeing the real thing sort of destroys the dream. People often think I've lived a long time in the U.S., but if you live there the influence is diluted. When I do go, I want to notice interesting things."

In Japan, Terry can enjoy his own version of America. A soul music aficionado, he claims to have nearly 40,000 LPs and CDs. And his company, Flamingo Studios, has undertaken graphic design work that subtly transforms mundane American packaging and advertising concepts into works of art with Terry's own brand of humor. "I like the beauty of English," he says, "Especially the graphic design element."

Perhaps because of the "American" element of

Terry's work, he has received some attention in the United States. In 1985, Terry created "The Shogun Tofu" for the New York avant-garde comic magazine *Raw*. An all-English masterpiece, it had typical Terry titles such as "Filled with Krazzzzzzzy Confusions" and "New Shock, New Violence, and *Great* Satisfaction." Samurai dialog ran along the lines of "Ancient time samurai was very great. So he killed every time, everybody . . . (THWAKKK) (This page is over but this cartoon keeps alive!! See next page!)." In 1990, Terry was written up in *Elle* magazine. In Japan, in 1995, Terry was creating the covers to the very hip annual manga magazine *Comic CUE*.

Z-Chan (Shingo Iguchi)

『Zちゃん』(井口真吾)

Z-CHAN: COMICS AS ALTERNATIVE REALITY

In 1989 I discovered a Japanese manga unlike any other I had seen. Titled *Z-Chan* ("Zed-chan," or "Little Z"), and created by Shingo Iguchi, it appeared sporadically in *Garo*. I was intrigued.

Most young cartoonists in Japan develop their technique by imitating established artists or working as their assistants, so it is usually possible to tell the "lineage" of an artist just by his art style. But not so with Iguchi. Unlike the wild abandon that characterizes many Japanese manga, he has made the world of *Z-Chan* rigid and controlled; lines are sparse, white space abounds, and there is almost no complex detailing or shading. The result is a streamlined, almost inorganic look, and a fantasy setting devoid of any Japanese context. Surreal English words are often used for graphic effect. Sometimes, however, orderly images suddenly disintegrate into geometric patterns and rough sketches.

When I first read *Z-Chan*, I couldn't detect any plot at all. But the more I read, the more I realized its characters existed in a self-contained universe, one that operated under its own unique set of rules and logic. The hero of *Z-Chan* is a little boy of the same name who wears a dunce cap and a black mask. His sidekick is Richard Sex, a blue mouse who lives in another dimension on the other side of a wall but who appears regularly through a mouse hole. They live in a little house on top of a hill, in Z-zone and the garden of nothingness, in Lotus Heaven, beyond hope and despair. They both like to take Z powder, which makes them first forget everything, and then remember everything. One of the blue mouse's jobs is to water tulips. Often the two engage in absurd, riddle-like dialogue:

> Z-Chan: *"I can't tell the difference between myself and a cup."*
>
> Richard Sex: *"What? Did you say something?"*

I was fascinated, and I resolved to meet the artist.

We met at a coffee shop in Tokyo. Iguchi was tall and thin, with heavy frame glasses, a frowzled mop of hair, and a slightly anemic complexion. Except for the color of his hair, he bore a striking resemblance to Andy Warhol.

He was born, he said, in Hiroshima in 1957 and came to Tokyo in 1982. While working as a part-time dishwasher he became involved in Tokyo Funky Stuff, a group of young artists that included Teruhiko Yumura, aka King Terry, and who were then staging events and happenings in the area. Iguchi had previously dabbled in both drawing and writing and his affiliation with the other artists made him feel as though he, too, should do something "interesting." He began drawing manga and fused both of his interests. When he submitted a work to *Garo*, it was accepted.

The hero of *Z-Chan* was originally a female character that Iguchi had created earlier, but he turned it into a boy by adding the dunce cap and the mask. "I can only draw one face," he says with a self-deprecating smile. After creating Z-Chan, he had to think of what the boy should represent. Since "Z" was the last letter of the alphabet, he decided it could also be equated with the last year in the millennium, 2000, and that Z-Chan should be a child who lives to the year 2000 as part of a total "Z-plan factory" that would grant all wishes by then. As Iguchi drew more and more, he began holding exhibits

Z-Chan's friend calls to report a big problem. "Relax, Rose," Z-Chan says, "Easy does it. . . ." From Z-Chan, serialized in Garo *magazine in February/ March 1990.*

related to *Z-Chan* here and there, and he found himself forced to develop a more complete context for his character. A comic strip that had started almost as an accident gradually became a universe. Preserving this "accidental" approach to developing the universe became part of Iguchi's methodology.

Iguchi is a man in the process of constructing his own reality. The more I questioned him, the more animated he became. Every element in *Z-Chan* has Iguchi-meaning, and every element fits into a larger Iguchi-context. Soon the words began flowing from him in a torrent. Z-Chan, he told me, is simultaneously a child of total despair and total happiness. He is a zero-child, with no past memory, who knows no history and thinks only inside his dunce cap. As for "Z," he comes from a long line of ancestors, going back all the way to "A." For my benefit, Iguchi then launched into an awesomely detailed explanation of each ancestor's complicated personal history. I began to imagine that it would take him several days to reach "Z," but out of consideration for me he jumped a few ancestors, and to my surprise said that they actually only went to "N." "N," in total despair, had fallen over, thus becoming "Z" (in case you have trouble following this, try turning the capital letter "N" on its side).

As Iguchi's alternate reality developed, it became more than complex; it became a total commitment, one that Iguchi plans to stick to until at least the year 2000. "My entire life," he lamented in 1989, "has become the world of Z-Chan." At the end of 1995, nearly ten years after starting his series, Iguchi was still going strong. *Z-Chan* was still appearing in *Garo*, and Iguchi had even managed to publish it in a beautifully bound hardcover edition. Not content with manga alone, he had also launched a Z-Chan project to distribute tulip bulbs by mail around the world. He had written Z-Chan stories and Z-Chan music and put on Z-Chan art exhibits and public performances, including a Z-Chan parade of seventy-five friends wearing dunce caps in downtown Tokyo. As for the near future, while not yet possessing a computer, Iguchi spoke passionately of getting a Z-Chan site up and running on the Internet. As he said once with a sigh, "It's getting harder and harder to explain what I'm doing to the outside world. It's the sort of thing I'd feel a little uneasy having my parents know too much about. I'm afraid they'd worry about me."

Yoshikazu Ebisu

蛭子能収

THE PRINCE OF ULTRA-NONSENSE MANGA

Anyone who watched Japanese television in the late eighties and early nineties has seen Yoshikazu Ebisu. He is an omnipresent personality on talk shows and commercials, where he projects an aura of reassuring mediocrity; a Japanese "everyman" with clothing slightly rumpled, hair out of place, and a disarmingly crooked grin.

In reality, Ebisu is one of Japan's more eccentric and intelligent manga artists, a "prince of ultra-nonsense manga" who delights in dissecting the neuroses in human nature and in modern Japanese society. But don't look for his work in the highly commercialized *manga* magazines for children. He has a cult following, and his humor is definitely outside the mainstream.

Ebisu's unique skills as a *manga* satirist are a product of his unusual background and personality. Many *manga* artists in Japan debut in their late teens, become "stars" in their early twenties, and fade from public view before reaching thirty. Ebisu began to reach notoriety in his forties—and he has not taken the normal commercial route. He had an early interest in drawing, graphic design, and scenario writing, but after high school held a variety of jobs, including working as a sign painter for six years and working for a year and a half with a Tokyo *chirigami-kōkan* (paper recycling) firm. In 1973 he did what many maverick aspiring manga artists of his generation did and submitted a piece to *Garo*. When it was accepted, he says, "It was the happiest time of my life. They told me they couldn't pay me, but I didn't care."

Convinced that he could turn professional, Ebisu quickly quit his job, only to come up against the hard crunch of reality and the need to support a family. He went back to work and for years was employed as a Duskin salesman (Japan's version of the Fuller Brush Man). Eventually, however, he found sidework drawing for erotic manga magazines and for *Garo*, and several of his stories sold well when compiled into paperback. The freewheeling policies of these publications let him experiment visually and hone his own style. Unlike most artists, who first work for long years as apprentices to famous mentors and thus have highly derivative art styles, Ebisu emerged into the world as a one-of-a-kind.

Ebisu draws in a stark, almost primitive style with no shading. His characters, alter egos with average names like "Tanaka," are average citizens whose averageness cloaks a paranoid psyche. When disturbed, beads of sweat form on their brows. Their faces cloud over during fits of brooding. And they live in an utterly normal world—the world of modern Japanese cities, drab office buildings, business-

In front of the boss, a coworker demands to know Tanaka's true opinion, which the poor man doesn't have. Ebisu writes at the bottom of the page: "Tanaka seems to be in serious trouble here, but he's all right. Not having any opinion at all is really one of the best ways to win everyone's general approval." From **Ebisu Yoshikazu no Sarariiman Kyōshitsu** *("Yoshikazu Ebisu's Salaryman Classroom") in the collection* **Watashi wa Nanimo Kangaenai** *("I Ain't Got No Think").*

suited men, mahjong parlors, bill collectors, trains, and nightclubs. But the normalcy here can crumble at any moment. To create a sense of ominous absurdity, Ebisu often has flying saucers, "bullet" trains, and horses suddenly materialize out of nowhere. "I like to tell ordinary stories that self-destruct for shock effect," he says.

Many of Ebisu's ideas come from his own life experience and his struggle to survive. And many of his best works revolve around "salarymen," the faceless white-collar denizens of Japan's corporate landscape. His series like *Sarariiman Kiki Ippatsu* ("The Salaryman Had a Narrow Escape") and *Sarariiman Kyōshitsu* ("Salaryman Classroom") are classics. Black-humor survival guides to working in the neurotic hierarchy of Japanese company organizations, these works tear at the heart of Japanese social structure, depicting average employees tying themselves in intellectual knots trying to conform to their

IN ENGLISH

> *Jigoku no Tenshi* and *Wakaranakutte mo Daijōbu* appeared in *Comics Underground Japan* as "Hell's Angel" and "It's All Right If You Don't Understand," respectively. Edited by Kevin Quigley. New York: Blast Books, 1996.

bosses' whims, engaging in backstabbing conspiracies, and lapsing into fits of paranoia and delusion.

Ebisu's stories are also a direct reflection of his idiosyncratic personality. A gambler, he is a risk taker, in comics and in life. His three favorite hobbies are mahjong, pachinko, and professional boat racing—favorite pastimes of the Japanese working class. He draws and writes about gambling for gambling magazines (including mahjong and pachinko manga magazines) and clearly gets ideas for both characters and absurd situations from the gambling scene. Losing money may even be good for him. "When I have no money," he says, "I begin wondering why others have it, and wondering how to get some. It helps stimulate my imagination."

Ebisu also prides himself on a lack of what many Japanese cherish above all else—*jōshiki*, or the common sense knowledge of the complex codes of social behavior that rule Japan. Actually, he knows the rules backward and forward, but he is intellectually capable of freeing himself from them. "I have no *jōshiki*," he says, "so when I draw it often seems like great satire to other people."

Kazuichi Hanawa

花輪和一

ONE-OF-A-KIND ORIGINAL

On a trip through the northern island of Hokkaido in 1992, I stopped briefly in the city of Sapporo and finally met Kazuichi Hanawa in a local coffee shop. I had interviewed him on the phone a few years earlier, and found him both shy and open, sharing his views on art as well as his personal problems. In a society that places a high premium on conformity, I suspected that Hanawa was so inherently unorthodox that he couldn't conform, even if he tried. A small gentle man, he wore a cloth cap over a nearly shaved head and walked awkwardly. Only later, when I looked at a photograph I had taken of him, did I notice that he seemed to be holding his hands in a *mudra*, a symbolic gesture often used in tantric Buddhism.

A self-taught artist completely outside the manga mainstream, Hanawa over the years has enjoyed a steadily growing cult following. Born in 1942, he says he first wanted to be an illustrator, but after encountering the work of Yoshiharu Tsuge—one of the first serious surrealist manga artists to appear in the sixties—he realized that comics did not always have to be cute and lovable and that he, too, could draw them. His first work, *Kan no Mushi* ("Irascible") appeared in *Garo* in 1971 and was a short story of an incorrigibly bad boy whose mother takes him to a sadistic acupuncturist for a "cure." With detailed backgrounds somewhat reminiscent of Tsuge and a cast of characters drawn in both realistic and deformed styles, it had an eerie, surreal quality to it. But that was just the beginning.

Soon after, Hanawa began drawing stories in an entirely unique style best described as Japanese retro-kitsch-horror. *Akai Yoru* ("Red Night"), one of his first forays in this area, established the tone. It is a lurid story of a deranged samurai thrill-killer who forgets his original vow of revenge and is tricked into committing suicide by his disappointed wife. Such a plot alone isn't particularly exceptional in the world of manga; what is striking is the art style. While still adhering to the basic comics format of illustrated sequential panels, *Akai Yoru* evokes the atmosphere of trashy illustrated tales from the early Meiji period. Pages are heavily detailed and dark. Faces have an elongated *ukiyo-e* look. The lettering is almost all in the distinctive phonetic script *katakana*, using a retro typeface that makes the story appear exotic and decadent, as well as awkward to read. Throughout is the lurid esthetic of violence used by woodblock masters like Yoshitoshi Tsukioka—blood spatters, splatters, and gory disembowelments.

Hanawa thus established himself as an artist who

Frontispiece illustration for Kazuichi Hanawa's Akai Yoru ("Red Night"). The line of text at the top says in very old-fashioned Japanese, "A manga in bad taste."

drew on his own terms. But this didn't win him any lucrative contracts with mainstream children's magazines. Subsequent stories in the same vein, like *Kikan* ("The Return"), *Tatakau Onna* ("Fighting Woman"), and *Niku Yashiki* ("Flesh House"), probably branded him in the eyes of many readers as an *ero-guro* ("eroticism and grotesquerie") artist with a fetish for violence, sadomasochism, and nightmarish perversion. Such a characterization was not completely warranted, for many of Hanawa's stories were intended as a parody of traditional Japanese values and militarism. But by the mid-1970s this no-holds-barred approach to manga had apparently reached its limit, for Hanawa virtually disappeared from view.

When Hanawa returned in the early 1980s, he had abandoned his bloody grotesqueries in favor of an entirely different approach and style. In mainstream manga magazines for adults, such as *Action*, *Super Action,* and later *Afternoon*, he began drawing stories set in Japan's distant past. Many of these works are collected and sold today as paperback and hardcover books, and they reflect another side of Hanawa, his fascination with history, Buddhism, local customs, botany, and supernatural beings. Early on, Hanawa developed the technique of blending his own fecund imagination with historical fact and legend to concoct something entirely new. "I read a lot of books," he says, "and develop my own image of a period and its clothes, houses, and crops. Often I'm inspired by old narrative scrolls. I like the Heian period of history the best, but the Heian period I create exists only in my manga."

Nue: Shinkonjaku-monogatari ("Chimera: New Tales of the Past and Present") is an example of Hanawa's method. A collection of fanciful tales of chimeras and human oddities in the late Heian period (late 11th and 12th centuries), many of the stories in it are inspired by Japan's famous illustrated narrative scrolls. One, *Shigisan*, begins with actual reproductions from the famous 12th-century scroll of the same name (which depicts a levitating rice bowl and flying storehouse), but then Hanawa begins to move the characters in it according to his own imagination, creating an original version of how the monk Myōren gained his magical powers of levitation.

Since the early eighties, Hanawa has continued to "create" his own Japanese history. Often his stories deal with elements of madness and depravity in ancient times, and often, as in the 1987 collection *Ukikusakagami* ("Re-

IN ENGLISH

Kazuichi Hanawa's *Jiniku* ("Mercy Flesh") was included in *Comics Underground Japan.* Edited by Kevin Quigley. New York: Blast Books, 1996.

A Heian-era character designed by Kazuichi Hanawa.

flections of Transience"), set in the 15th century, his stories unfold through the eyes of an independent-minded little girl.

Like several other well-known avant-garde manga artists before him, Hanawa occasionally suffers from severe slumps and, by his own admission, bouts of depression. Yet his anxieties probably boost his overall creativity by pushing him in new directions. Nearly all Japanese manga artists today live in the megalopolis of Tokyo—the cultural epicenter of modern Japan—but to Hanawa, Tokyo is an oppressive environment. He eventually abandoned it for faraway Hokkaido and closer contact with nature. To achieve personal peace, he chanted Buddhist sutras daily and read the works of Vernon Howard, an American author of such books as *The Esoteric Encyclopedia of Eternal Knowledge* and *Secrets of Mental Magic*. These efforts seem to have worked, for over the years Hanawa's manga became far more peaceful and were accepted into the mainstream; his popular *Tensui* ("Weird Water Spirit") was even serialized in the mid-nineties in the very respectable monthly *Afternoon*. But no matter how popular Hanawa's stories became, there was always something slightly quirky and mildly disturbing about them. I knew Hanawa loved old steam locomotives, but apparently he had other hobbies, too. In December 1994 Hanawa was arrested for possession of model guns that had been converted to the real thing, and under Japan's strict gun-control laws he was sentenced to three years in prison. At the end of 1995, Hanawa languished in jail incommunicado; his sentence was being appealed, but his serialized story in *Afternoon* was canceled, despite protests from fans.

Murasaki Yamada

やまだ紫

PERSONAL VISIONS

There is a strong women's culture in Japan and an especially strong women's culture in manga. In 1995 there were forty-five titles of *manga* magazines specifically for girls (called *shōjo* manga) and fifty-two for adult women (called "Ladies'" manga), published in biweekly, monthly, and quarterly formats. Almost all the stories were authored and drawn by women.

To the average male, stories for girls often seem to feature nothing but pretty, leggy, saucer-eyed heroines in saccharine plots, endlessly falling desperately in love or staring wistfully into space; sometimes it seems that manga for adult women are only a more mature variant of the same, with the addition of sex. A hallmark of both manga for girls and manga for women, however, is that, compared to manga for men, they are more stylized and introspective, with a greater emphasis on emotion and human psychology.

Murasaki Yamada may be a female manga artist, but her work does not fit the conventional mold at all. In fact, her work often transcends manga and takes on the quality of poetry and feminist literature. Although Yamada has never achieved mass popularity, she has had a big influence on other women manga artists such as Hinako Sugiura and Yōko Kondō, both of whom have worked as her assistants in the past.

A very direct cat says: "Hug me . . ." From Murasaki Yamada's* Shōwaru Neko *("The Malicious Cat").

Yamada made her debut in 1969 at the age of twenty in *COM*, an experimental publication founded by manga god Osamu Tezuka. Later she often drew for *Garo*. From the beginning, her readers were mostly adults. Also, unlike most other self-taught women manga artists, Yamada had had some formal art training. These two factors probably explain how she was able to avoid many of the more stifling conventions adhered to by so many female manga artists. Yamada's stories have no heroines with saucer eyes, no walking fashion shows of fluffy dresses and detailed kimonos, no blissful romances, no teary tragedies, and no sex and violence. Yamada's drawings are realistic, but minimalist, streamlined, and smooth, with few backgrounds, lots of white spaces, and fine lines. Often she will draw characters with no facial features at all. What Yamada does share with many other women artists is the ability to impart a special introspective, lyrical quality to her work and to explore the workings of the heart. In her slow-paced and measured style, she depicts everyday things closely linked to her own daily life.

The words in Yamada's manga are as important as

the pictures. In both choice of words and story pacing (she alternates between giving her alter-ego heroines dialogue and displaying their introspective thoughts) there is a refined sense of poetry. Yamada herself is a poet and throughout her career has written many essays. Many of her manga, in fact, are collaborations with other women poets, such as the beautiful 1995 hardback *Yume no Maigo-tachi* (literally "Lost Children Dreaming," but subtitled in French as *Les Enfants Reveurs*) with Yōko Isaka. Critics have often said that Yamada's comics are the graphic equivalent of the confessional Japanese "I" novel. Some men find her feminist outlook unsettling.

In the past, Yamada has mainly drawn two types of stories; those with humans, and those with animals. *Shin Kilali*, a semi-autobiographical collection named after an onomatopoeic word in a poem by Yūko Kōno, is one of the best examples of the stories about people. It is a series of episodes in the everyday life of a Japanese mother of two who finds that her marriage of ten years is gradually falling apart. Each chapter is drawn in a subdued, understated fashion; the climax approaches as the wife gradually develops an independent perspective on her marriage and her future and, over her husband's protests, decides to look for a job. Yamada shows her protagonist's resentment over being taken for granted and treated as less than equal, and in the process provides an intimate glimpse of a Japanese woman's gentle revolt against a male-dominated society. In *Blue Sky*, serialized in the serious women's non-manga magazine *Fujin Kōron* from 1990, Yamada explores life after the divorce, her heroine struggling to survive economically, ignoring the criticism and constraints of the tightly meshed society around her when she begins living with a man a decade younger than she is.

An example of Yamada's animal stories is *Shōwaru Neko* ("The Malicious Cat"). This is a collection of story-poems about relationships, realistically drawn and written from the perspective of cats, who function as surrogates for human characters. "My stories with a 'home' theme," Yamada told me when I interviewed her in 1989 (she was wearing bib overalls), "can be an extension of my real life, but because of that they tend to be

After talking things over with her much younger boyfriend, the protagonist/alter-ego of Murasaki Yamada's* Blue Sky *announces to her children that he will be living with them. In the drying laundry in the background Yamada shows a clever use of "screen tones."

more polite and reserved. In my animal stories, I can say whatever I think through the animal characters. They can say things for me that I normally wouldn't dare say."

In 1995, Yamada added another genre to her repertoire when she began a manga version of the Japanese classic *Otogizōshi*, a popular series of twenty-three stories from the Muromachi period (1392–1573). This was, she noted, a completely different direction for her, but she still intended to give the work a very feminist perspective.

Yamada believes that women artists are getting better and better in Japan, and that this is partly a reflection of a larger social phenomenon. The men in Japanese society are still reserved and have trouble communicating their thoughts and ideas, whereas the women are becoming more outgoing and forthright. Women, socially and creatively, are getting stronger and stronger.

Suehiro Maruo

丸尾末広

SEX AND VIOLENCE

Yes, it's true. Ordinary Japanese manga often contain an enormous amount of sex and violence, and some of the so-called erotic or *ero-manga* for adults include stories that in other countries would land the artists in jail. But *ero-manga* themselves produce more than mere titillation. They are a fertile breeding ground for some of the most talented artists in Japan today.

Suehiro Maruo is a typical example. A self-taught artist, high school dropout, and former shoplifter who began drawing comics at the age of eighteen, Maruo says he submitted his first work to the popular weekly manga magazine *Shōnen Jump* and was promptly rejected. But that may have been just as well. Commercialized, mass-market magazines often impose a dreary conformity on art styles and suck the originality out of promising artists. At twenty-four, after a hiatus of several years, Maruo again began drawing, this time for *ero-manga*. It was, he says, mainly a way to use his talents to earn money, but it was also part of a quest for artistic freedom. *Ero-manga* require endless sex scenes, but beyond that editors could care less what their artists do. "It's impossible to draw stories that are just fantasy-dreams in the mainstream magazines," Maruo said when I first met him in 1989. "They always want them to be easy to understand, and the art style to be 'happy,' and 'upbeat.' Since I draw in a dark style, my work was unacceptable."

Today, Maruo has a cult following that extends far beyond the readers of pornography or even normal manga readers. His work is increasingly sold in deluxe, hardback book form, and limited editions of his lithographed prints sell for high prices. But that does not mean he has joined the mainstream camp. His manga are among the most disturbing published in Japan today.

Maruo draws nightmares. In the tradition of the *muzan-e* ("atrocity print") woodblock masters of the 19th century, he draws short stories of axe murders, abortion,

A frontispiece illustration from Suehiro Maruo's Itoshi no Shōwa *("My Beloved Shōwa Era"), serialized in* Garo, *July 1988. Three very stern boys in Japanese school uniforms announce that they are the Meiji (1868–1911), Taishō (1911–25), and Shōwa (1925–1989) eras of Japan, respectively; each holds an artifact emblematic of the period—a sword, flute, and baseball bat.*

rape, incest, sadomasochism, and other unspeakable perversions in as much graphic detail as the obscenity codes allow. In a land where people lead extraordinarily well-behaved lives under extraordinary pressure, Maruo visualizes the most twisted elements of the subconscious mind. One of his favorite images is that of an old woman licking a young boy's naked eyeballs. "Maruo is to pornography what the nuke is to the cherry bomb," said John-Ivan Palmer in an interview-article titled "Blood of the Paper Psycho: Suehiro Maruo and the Sado-Erotic Manga" in the magazine *Your Flesh* (no. 26, 1992).

But Maruo is also one of the great retro artists working in the manga field today. Esthetically his heart is in the 1930s. "Ever since I was a child," he says, "I've liked the design sense of the period—the costumes, the architecture. I often wish I'd been born in either Germany or Japan back then." Many of his tales, such as *Nemuri Otoko* ("Sleep Man") and *Shi, Yo, Banzai* ("*Banzai*, O Death"), are lavishly detailed with buildings and objects of the prewar fascist era creating a sinister, decadent mood.

In reading Maruo's stories, one can't help thinking that right-wing novelist Yukio Mishima would have loved their esthetic, and also have been disappointed when he realized many are a satire on militarism and warlike attitudes. *Nihonjin no Wakusei* ("Planet of the Jap") is Maruo's fantasy of what would have happened to the United States if Japan had won World War II; atomic bombs are dropped on San Francisco and Los Angeles, the samurai ethic runs amok, and General Douglas MacArthur is beheaded with a sword (his executioners graciously allow him to keep his sunglasses on). *Itoshi no Shōwa* ("My Beloved Shōwa," later retitled "Farewell Shōwa") uses three schoolboy brothers representing Japan's Meiji, Taishō, and Shōwa periods (covering the era of modernization to the present day) who anxiously await the birth of a long-overdue new sibling; in the end they take off their masks and reveal themselves as monsters. The story is a searing criticism of modern Japan and its modern era.

Maruo may love the past but he could only be a child of modern Japan and its goulash of conflicting ideas and cultures. Writer Inuhiko Yomota has called his visual esthetic a "museum of 20th-century kitsch art," citing elements taken from Nazi Germany, Japan's Taishō and early Shōwa periods, modern television, and manga. Maruo himself says his artistic influences range from the 19th-century woodblock artist Yoshitoshi Tsukioka, who also dealt in violent, bloody imagery, to Andy Warhol, whom he adores for his "cool, inorganic look," to Kazuichi Hanawa. Back in 1989, he told me he was a big fan of the weird films of American director David Lynch and of punk rock groups like the Sex Pistols. Sometimes

MacArthur loses his head to the Japanese Imperial Army. From Suehiro Maruo's **Planet of the Jap**, *in the collection* **Paranoia Star**.

in his stories he lists the names of appropriate albums to listen to while reading.

Whatever Maruo's influences are, his execution is superb. Whether he is depicting blood-spattered scenes or simple emotion on a character's face, his elegant control of line and his innovative page designs are unrivaled. And his artistic sense is attracting more and more attention. His artwork adorns the cover of *Naked City*, a CD by American free-form jazz musician John Zorn. He has been paired with Kazuichi Hanawa in a deluxe art book

IN ENGLISH

"Michael Jackson Bad" in *The New Comics Anthology.* Edited by Bob Callahan. New York: Collier Books, 1991.

Mr. Arashi's Amazing Freak Show. New York: Blast Books, 1992.

"Planet of the Jap" was included in the anthology *Comics Underground Japan*. Edited by Kevin Quigley. New York: Blast Books, 1996.

Suehiro Maruo also illustrated Leonard Koren's *How to Take a Japanese Bath*, and *How to Rake Leaves.* Berkeley: Stone Bridge Press, 1992 and 1993, respectively.

titled *Bloody Ukiyo-e*, half of which is devoted to reproductions of the "atrocity prints" of 19th-century woodblock artists Yoshitoshi Tsukioka and Yoshiiku Ochiai, and half of which contains modern versions by Maruo and Hanawa (the introduction contains accolades to Maruo from famous Japanese cartoonists, novelists, and musicians). In the fall of 1992, after great difficulty finding a printer willing to handle the material, Blast Books of New York published a translation of Maruo's book *Shōjo Tsubaki* ("Camellia Girl," retitled as *Mr. Arashi's Amazing Freak Show*), keeping the original right-to-left Japanese format. Maruo's work is also showing up in non-print media. In 1995, in what seems a bit of a media mismatch, "Camellia Girl" was made into a sixty-minute animated film directed by Hiroshi Harada. Maruo wrote the lyrics to the closing song. At the end of the year a collection of Maruo's work on CD-ROM had also been announced.

The ultimate testimony to Maruo's strength as an artist is the fact that often his most powerful and lyrical works are his simplest ones—the stories with the least sex and violence. Perhaps recognizing this, at the end of 1995 he said he was preparing a new work for serialization in the very mainstream manga magazine *Young Champion*. It would, he said, be "short, humorous, and quite 'cute.'"

Silent Service (Kaiji Kawaguchi)

『沈黙の艦隊』（かわぐちかいじ）

SUBMARINE METAPHORS

The U.S. and a shadow Japanese government develop Japan's first nuclear-powered submarine to help protect Japan's sea lanes, keeping the project top secret to avoid offending the Japanese public's antinuclear sensibilities. The 60,000-horsepower sub is an American design, but it incorporates superior Japanese technology and is commanded by an elite Japanese crew led by the charismatic Commander Shirō Kaieda. Everything goes according to plan until the sub embarks on a test run with the U.S. Seventh Fleet. Commander Kaieda and his crew suddenly mutiny and take off with U.S. ships in hot pursuit. And that's just the beginning. Kaieda is no ordinary mutineer. He commands the world's most powerful nuclear sub, and he has an agenda. . . .

* * * * *

Thus begins Kaiji Kawaguchi's bestselling series *Chinmoku no Kantai*, or "Silent Service," which began serialization in the weekly *Morning* in 1989. Over seven years and 7,000 pages later, it was still running.

Silent Service is a rip-roaring, good-old-fashioned undersea adventure tale. But along the way, it manages to address many of the important political issues that lurk in the background of Japanese politics—the future of the Security Treaty with the United States, the real meaning of Japan's American-authored constitution, the future of its military, and even the future of the nation state.

* * * * *

When Kaieda resurfaces, he has christened his sub the Yamato. *He declares, moreover, that* Yamato *is no mere submarine, but an independent, autonomous nation. The U.S., unable to stand idly by, resolves to destroy* Yamato, *and so does the Soviet Union. The affair turns into a scandal in Japan, but after the initial uproar the Japanese government* *has difficulty deciding whether it should cooperate completely with the United States or somehow try to save* Yamato* *from destruction.*

Yamato *becomes a sort of high-tech "Moby Dick." Through a series of brilliant maneuvers and submarine acrobatics, it causes the virtual destruction of the U.S. Third Fleet and a Soviet fleet, humiliating both superpowers [this is a manga, so anything's possible of course]. In the process,* Yamato *forces the U.S. and the Soviet Union to cooperate, and it drives a wedge between the United States and Japan. When Commander Kaieda announces that Yamato (the independent nation) wants to enter into a treaty with Japan, Japan vacillates, and the U.S. threatens to reoccupy Japan, even nuke a few cities.*

Kaieda reveals himself to be no ordinary nuclear terrorist. His actions, no matter how destructive they may be to others, are always taken in the context of "legitimate self-defense" (or at least it seems so to Japan). His real goal, it is gradually revealed, is world nuclear disarmament and the creation of a transnational military force to enforce world peace. His arguments resonate with the remarkably resolute prime minister of Japan, who boldly agrees to enter into a treaty with Yamato, *if* Yamato *will only return to Japanese control. In exchange, and in order to reassure the rest of the world of his peaceful intentions, the prime minister offers to place the entire Japanese Self-Defense Forces under the command of the United Nations. Yamato heads for the U.N. in New York, sailing under the Arctic ice cap and fighting off attacks by U.S. subs along the way. After it arrives off the coast of New York it destroys or disables nearly all the ships the U.S. sends out in an attempt to sink it. Yamato causes chaos not only in Washington, D.C. and capitals around the world, but in Japan. In Tokyo, old political parties disintegrate and new ones are formed, each with a different idea of how to resolve the situation. The*

* "Yamato" is the name of both ancient Japan and one of the most famous but doomed battleships of World War II. The battleship is particularly popular in Japanese fantasy. In Leiji Matsumoto's manga/animation smash-hit, *Space Battleship Yamato* (known as *Star Blazers* in the U.S.), the sunken WWII ship was salvaged and turned into a high-tech spaceship.

During a tense moment on the Yamato, crewmembers forward crucial information to Commander Kaieda. Framed against the fixtures of his submarine periscope, in a typically beatific pose, he remains cool, calm, and collected. From Kaiji Kawaguchi's Chinmoku no Kantai ("Silent Service").

wild card in dealing with Yamato is always the question of how many nuclear warheads it has, and whether Kaieda is willing to use them to attain his goals.

* * * * *

As soon as it appeared in 1989, *Silent Service* became a sensation. It was discussed by politicians in the Japanese Diet, it won the 1990 Kōdansha Manga Award, and it was featured in all the major media in Japan, and even in national newspapers in the United States. On October 26, 1990, Kōdansha ran large ads for it on the editorial pages of the *Asahi* and *Nihon Keizai* national newspapers, claiming "Heisei Era Japan Finally Awakened from Its Slumber by a Comic." Eventually, in 1995, Kōdansha published a collection of articles by political, economic, and technology experts analyzing the story—articles that had originally been serialized in a Self-Defense Agency public relations magazine called *Securitarian*. At the beginning of 1996 the story had been animated for television, and the twenty-nine paperback volumes in the series had sold over 22 million copies.

Why was *Silent Service* so popular? It was a good story, but it also stimulated discussion about political issues rarely mentioned—and it appealed to a latent nationalism. Fans of *Silent Service* span the political spectrum, but some of its biggest admirers have been members of the Self-Defense Forces. In the July 7, 1990 issue of *Comic Box*, critic Yoshio Suzuki claimed it had become the bible of young rightists who regard Kawaguchi as a new "Yukio Mishima" (a reference to the brilliant, outspoken novelist whose fascination with militarism led to his ritual suicide in 1971)."This is a dangerous manga," Suzuki wrote. "It is a coup d'état in the manga world, and a manga that invites a coup d'état." It was an exaggeration, of course, but so is the whole manga.

Silent Service also surfaced in the public consciousness of Japan when people were still somewhat giddy from the economic and technological successes of the 1980s. There was a sense that Japan's superior technology and enlightened views of mankind would lead the world into a new, better era , and that the United States, in particular, was old and in the way. *Silent Service*, in a fashion, thus articulated many of the rarely vocalized national aspirations of the general public. But with the bursting of the economic bubble at the beginning of the 1990s and the sudden realization that Japan—once thought to be charging ahead of the U.S. in nearly all areas of technology—was perhaps ten years behind in the computer network revolution, this confidence became somewhat deflated. What once seemed "historically inevitable," as Commander Kaieda once put it in the *Yamato* story, is now far less certain.

As time passed, *Silent Service* lost much of its impact and its novelty. The story dragged on too long, and exciting action scenes increasingly gave way to pontificating by politicians and even Kaieda at the U.N. and other forums. Although the plot was linked to real-world events, it was also overtaken by reality. The world changed so fast that even Kawaguchi couldn't keep up—who would have guessed in 1989 that the Soviet Union would collapse, that the United States and Russia would become de facto allies, and that U.S. global hegemony would only increase? Furthermore, many of Kawaguchi's unstated goals (reform of Japanese politics, for example) have at least been partially accomplished. As for the U.N. being

IN ENGLISH

> Part of *Shiken Kōkai* ("Test Voyage"), or episode 5 of *Silent Service,* appeared in issue 13 of *Mangajin*.

given more global responsibility, Japan's controversial involvement in peace-keeping operations in Cambodia and the failure of U.N. forces to keep the peace in Bosnia, Somalia, and various other troublespots around the world have no doubt dimmed the appeal of this idea.

Silent Service was, however, for years listed among the most popular manga when such surveys were done. At Komiketto and other amateur manga fan conventions, parodies of *Silent Service* became a standard target of parody publications. Young fans took the characters and situations in Kawaguchi's story and drew and developed them in ways he never intended—from the comedic to the pornographic.

While *Silent Service* may have had many fans for its fascinating political subtexts, true military hardware buffs were apparently not among them. According to Tetsuya Kurosawa, the editor of *Combat* magazine, his readers didn't like *Silent Service* because it was too unrealistic in its portrayals of what submarines can actually do.

Akira Narita

成田アキラ

A (FORMER) TELEPHONE CLUB ARTIST

I first became friends with Akira Narita when he came to San Francisco in 1980. After a whirlwind drive around the U.S., he showed up in a car with a strange gray color. He had slept the previous night in his car near Mt. Saint Helens volcano, and when it erupted his once-white vehicle had been covered in ash. He was quite a character then. He is a celebrity today.

Narita made his professional debut as a manga artist in Japan in 1971 at the age of twenty-six, drawing an SF fantasy series with a slightly psychedelic touch for a men's weekly. The story was fairly popular for a couple years, but then readers' tastes changed, and for several years he was forced to support his family drawing cartoon illustrations for magazines. The trip to America, which turned into a year-long stay, was a way to recharge his batteries and come up with something new.

When Narita returned to Japan he began drawing educational manga in book form for young people, on subjects like Einstein's theory of relativity, the brain, and mathematics. It seemed a good genre to work in, since Narita had three children of his own, and a degree in electrical engineering, and as a youth had often assisted his uncle, Tsunezō Murotani (a famous children's manga artist). But sales never took off.

Aside from comics, one of Narita's big interests in life had always been women, and sex. No ordinary cheat-on-your-wife type, Narita enjoyed a rather radical family situation, with everyone—his wife, parents, and children—aware of his exploits and, if not overtly encouraging them, at least not objecting. To Narita, regular, frequent, and varied sex was part of a normal mental and physical fitness program. Eventually, however, it turned into a quest for something else.

In the mid-eighties, the sex industry in Japan hit upon the innovative and very Japanese idea of what are called *terekura* or "telephone clubs"—rooms with banks of phones, the numbers of which are advertised in women's magazines. Men pay up to ¥3,000 an hour to wait by these phones for calls from anonymous women, and when the calls come in they engage in conversation. If the man is a particularly clever conversationalist and the woman likes him, she may agree to meet him at an mutually arranged spot. Whether sex, romance, or mere conversation ensues is up to the pair. When Narita began frequenting these outfits he not only had an extraordinarily high rate of success in persuading women to meet him, but to sleep with him.

Around 1986, Narita began drawing a series of humorous stories based on his experiences with *terekura*, and when serialized they became instant hits. With a humanistic and confessional approach to sex (often the

"When I strap this thing on, it makes me feel like a man. . . . How many men have I turned into women with it? Hey, nobody ever said 'no,' except for those with bleeding hemorrhoids. . . . Deep down all men are part fags. . . ." On one of his frequent "telephone club" dates, Akira Narita discovers that one married mother has some aggressive tendencies. After a moment's shock, in the spirit of adventure he decides to go along. From Oku no Iromichi (*"Road to the Deep Eros"*), by Akira Narita.

men fail to perform), his stories were fun reading for both men and women. He had finally found the perfect medium for his talents and interests. He credits eccentric American artist Robert Crumb, whom he read in the U.S., as an influence.

By 1992, Narita's manga stories were appearing in mainstream but second-tier magazines such as *Manga Sunday* and *Shūkan Taishū* and in the evening newspaper *Naigai Times*. Periodically he also did non-manga reportages on the sex lives of Japanese. Narita had become an "authority" on *terekura* and on sex in general. Both he and his wife appeared frequently on late-night TV talk shows, discussing sex and sexuality. By 1995 his work was appearing in top mainstream magazines and over twenty paperback volumes of his adventures had been published in manga format. He had even written (with the help of a tape recorder) two novels based on his adventures. At one point he claims to have grossed over half a million dollars a year just from royalties and page rates.

Eventually, Narita became so famous that he no longer had to go to the *terekura*. He made arrangements with the clubs and had the calls routed directly to his studio, where he worked with three assistants. One magazine even published a special hot-line number directly to him for women. "I get forty to fifty calls a day on my studio speakerphone," he told me, "but I obviously can't answer all of them, so I only pick up the interesting ones." Always prepared, next to his desk he kept a black leather bag filled with whips and vibrating dildos, just in case.

Why did so many women call? "Loneliness is the biggest reason," he says, "but many women are simply curious about this sort of thing. Probably half of the women are married and sexually dissatisfied. The telephone club system works because Japanese people still have few opportunities where they can easily meet members of the opposite sex. In the United States people can strike up conversations with each other in a bar or on a bus, but here that's difficult. The funny thing is, Japanese people aren't very good at socializing, but on the phone where they can't see each other's faces the inhibitions disappear and they talk a mile a minute. It's a very Japanese type of interaction. The fact that Japan is a fairly safe country also helps."

Narita himself nonetheless has to be able to live with a certain level of risk. Between the time he started his *terekura* series and 1995, he estimates he interacted with over 400 women. With AIDS an increasing danger, he has been tested and is HIV negative, but he stresses that he always tries to be very careful and uses condoms.

Narita also has to be fairly tough. He once drove

IN ENGLISH

> "When Socrates Drinks, Everybody Drinks!"—a short work with no sex at all by Akira Narita (with Fred Schodt and Leonard Rifas) appeared in *Food Comix*, issue 1, 1980 (published by Educomics).

from Tokyo north to Sendai, Morioka, Matsumoto, Suwa and back —a good 1,000 miles or so—in two days, participating in trysts with four women who had called him. He returned at four in the morning and started drawing the next day. "Unless you really like women," he says, "you can't keep doing this sort of work."

Eventually the "work" became a true family affair. In 1994, Narita's younger brother, Kōji, an established artist in his own right but a shyer personality, issued a manga paperback titled *Narita Kyōdai no "Etchi"-Tsū-Oh!* ("The Narita Brothers' Nasty [H]$_2$0!"; the "$H_2$0" was a pun on the chemical equation for water and *etchi*, a Japanese

One of the brothers' parties gets out of hand and winds up in the bath. Akira far left. Kōji, in the foreground, laments his ruined guitar. From* Narita Kyōdai no Etchi-Tsū-Oh! *("The Narita Brother's Nasty [H]$_2$O!")

word for "naughty" or "nasty"). The work humorously described what it was like to have inherited an oversexed brother. Narita, for his part, has also created a series about his wife's adventures.

In 1994 Narita began an entirely different series. In the popular and respectable weekly *Morning*, he began serializing *Chōai no Hito*, or "Transcendent-Love Man." Perfect for the age of safe sex, it was about a man trying to learn why people love others, about romance and desire without necessarily having sex. As he wrote his readers (male and female) in the last episode on May 25, sex had become something of a spiritual quest for him:

> My main interest in life is still sex between men and women. But as the years pass . . . my views of sex have changed. . . . Ultimately, men and women should be able to enjoy carnal ecstasy with their clothes on, without having any physical contact at all. But in order to do that they must be connected by a powerful feeling of love. I began drawing *Chōai no Hito* in order to depict such a relationship.

Shungicu Uchida

内田春菊

THE LIGHT AND DARK SIDE

I have never met Shungicu Uchida, but I feel I know her. In her manga, she quickly draws the readers into her world. In her life, she has made a career out of being open, if not flamboyant, and she would probably feel flattered if compared to American female rock stars like Cyndi Lauper or Madonna. In the past, in fact, she sang in a latin band, and one of her first collections of manga stories opened with the Lauper hit lyric "Girls just want to have fun." A new type of Japanese woman, she is capable of playing with peoples' notions of women's and men's social roles, all the while remaining very much in control.

Uchida made her debut as a professional manga artist in 1984. Instead of working as an assistant for an

A chapter frontispiece from Shungicu Uchida's* Nami no Ma Ni Ma Ni *(English title on paperback: "An Old-fashioned Love Elegy"), about a fictional young maid who is constantly abused. First serialized in* Garo *in 1988.

established woman artist or drawing exclusively for girls' or women's comics—both of which would have locked her into a more conventional "women's" art style —she honed her skills outside the mainstream, drawing for the avant-garde manga magazine *Garo*, men's erotic magazines, women's magazines, men's newsweeklies, music magazines, and even mahjong magazines.

Like many other women artists, Uchida draws female characters with big eyes. But when she draws carefully (often working from Polaroids of models posing), her women have an unusual realism. Rather than being tall and skinny (as so many characters drawn by women are), they are often short, buxom, and a little plump, with an erotic quality that can make people unfamiliar with her work think the artist is a man. Sometimes Uchida uses different art styles in the course of a single story, shifting from a realistic look to a deformed "cartoony" look for comic relief. She rarely draws any backgrounds because her stories are usually about male and female relationships and feature close-in frames of heads, faces, and bodies, both clothed and naked. Most of her stories are, needless to say, for adults.

Uchida also draws in a variety of genres that include long, serious tales with a heavy dose of psycho-realism as well as short gag strips, comic-horror, and thriller pieces. *Tarafu-chan to Oryōri* ("Cooking with Tarafu-chan") shows off her wonderful sense of humor; it is a tongue-in-cheek short piece done in 1986 about how to use a microwave oven to cook ramen and make wire sparklers, among other things. In the 1986 series *Hen na Kudamono* ("Strange Fruit"), Uchida has a short piece about three women who decide to visit a family restaurant and harass the staff. When the obsequious waiter comes to the table to welcome them with a deep bow and ridiculously formal language, Uchida's characters all stand up, bow back to him, and introduce themselves.

The 1988 series *Isshinjō no Tsugō* ("A Personal Affair") is one of many lighthearted tales Uchida has written about Japan's "OL," or "office ladies," their plots and affairs and their struggles to obtain respect in a male-dominated organization. Some of her female characters are innocents in a sea of schemers. Some are naive *burikko*, experienced young women who fake a naive, virginal exterior. And of course there are the usual married workers having affairs.

Several of Uchida's stories have a distinctly dark side. In longer narratives like the 1991 *Maboroshi no Futsū Shōjo* ("The Illusory Ordinary Girl") and the 1992 *Monokage ni Ashibyōshi* ("Marking Time in the Shadows"), she depicts the underbelly of Japanese society, a world not of high technology, ever higher standards of living, and smooth human relations, but of broken families, unwanted pregnancies, juvenile delinquency, and drug use. These stories have elements of the confessional Japanese "I" novels, for they are thinly disguised allusions to Uchida's own youth.

In the early nineties Uchida began to speak publicly about what is still a taboo subject in Japan—the abuse she had experienced growing up. At age fifteen she accidentally became pregnant. Her stepfather, with her mother's consent, forced Uchida to have sex with him with the ludicrous claim that this would induce an abortion. After suffering years of such treatment, Uchida dropped out of high school, left home, and never returned. She eventually wrote about her early suffering not in manga format but in a confessional novel with the provocative title *Father Fucker* in 1994. The book began with the line, "I am often told that I have the face of a whore."

Uchida washes her hair, but baby won't leave her alone. From Shungicu Uchida's* Watashitachi wa Hanshoku Shite Iru *("We Are Reproducing").

IN ENGLISH

Short selections from *Maboroshi no Futsū Shōjo* ("The Illusory Ordinary Girl") appeared in issues 37–38 of *Mangajin.*

Uchida clearly has a strong desire to take control of her own life. She is a success today not only as a self-taught comic artist, but as an illustrator, essayist, and novelist. One of her manga stories, *Minami no Koibito* ("Minami's Sweetheart"), has been made into a popular live action television drama with animation. Her *Mizu Monogatari* ("Water Story") became a 1991 live-action film in which she had a starring role.

In the early 1990s Uchida gave birth to a baby she named Alpha. Although she was living with one man she was not married to, she had another man, who was merely a friend, serve as the child's biological father. Sure enough, in 1994, she published a collection of manga that presented her birthing experience in highly personal terms. Titled *Watashitachi wa Hanshoku Shite Iru* ("We Are Reproducing"), it won a prestigious literature award. Whatever Uchida does today, whether in her private life or in her comics, she does it her way, on her own terms.

Shigeru Mizuki

水木しげる

THE SPIRIT WORLD

I first met Shigeru Mizuki briefly in the early eighties at a gathering of cartoonists in Japan. He was hard to overlook. In an industry where many artists are in their late teens or early twenties, he was in his late fifties, and the left arm of his coat hung empty. But he exuded vitality. I met Mizuki again in 1993, in San Francisco, after he had just returned from an arduous research trip in Hopi Indian territory in Arizona. He was nearly seventy then and accompanied by an entourage of much younger men. After a late dinner and drinks, they were all exhausted, but he insisted on slipping into a porn shop to look at the

A chapter frontispiece from Shigeru Mizuki's **Ge Ge Ge no Kitarō** *("Kitarō, the Spooky"), with Kitarō in the foreground and Nezumi Otoko ("Rat Man") in the background.*

girlie magazines. His companions rolled their eyes in amazement.

Mizuki was born Shigeru Mura in 1924 in the town of Sakaiminato on the isolated western seaboard of Japan. He exhibited a precocious drawing ability as a child, even garnering a mention in the local *Mainichi* newspaper. Much later, after the war, he briefly attended Musashino Art University in Tokyo, but since formal art training can destroy the originality required for good cartooning, he fortunately was not ruined by the experience. Today he often draws highly realistic, detailed backgrounds while rendering human characters in quirky, "cartoony" shapes.

Mizuki's cartooning ability was aided by the voracious curiosity he developed at an early age. An elderly local woman he called "Auntie Non-non" often took care of him as a child and helped him develop a passionate interest in the spirit world, especially in local tales of goblins and ghosts.

Mizuki's other formative experience was war. In 1943 he was drafted into the Imperial Army and sent to Rabaul on the island of New Britain in what is now part of Papua New Guinea. As one of the lower-ranking, late arrivals in a hierarchical and feudalistic command structure, he was constantly beaten by his superiors. While on sentry duty in the field one day, his detachment was completely wiped out in an attack by Australian and native forces. Mizuki made a harrowing escape alone back to Japanese lines, only to be reprimanded by his superiors for losing his rifle and (in Imperial Army style) for surviving. Later, during a raid by Allied airplanes, he was badly wounded and lost his left arm. After lingering on the verge of death and battling malaria, he was eventually nursed back to health. During this time he developed a deep affection for the natives of New Guinea, and he claims to have realized that a spirit force was guiding his life. Indeed, had he not been put out of commission, it is most likely that he would not be alive today. In a fairly famous incident, a unit to which he would have been attached was sent out on a suicidal "banzai" charge. Miraculously it survived, but since the men's "glorious death" had already been reported to HQ, the unit was sent back to the front with orders not to return alive.

After repatriation, Mizuki worked for a time drawing for the *kami-shibai*, or "paper-play," market—an inexpensive pre-TV form of street entertainment wherein raconteurs embroidered tales with a sequence of illustrated panels. He also drew stories for the manga pay-library market—a series of for-profit libraries that lent manga (and books) for a small fee to entertainment-starved readers. His debut work, published in paperback form in 1957 when he was already thirty-three years old, was titled *Rocketman*.

Commercial success and recognition eluded Mizuki until 1965, when he drew a story called *Terebi-kun* ("TV-kid") for a supplement of the boys' weekly *Shōnen Magazine*. *Terebi-kun* was about a young boy who discovered how to enter his TV set, steal the products displayed on commercials, and give them to his poorer, real-world friends. The only people who could see him do this on the screen, though, were children who watched television. It was a novel plot, and with the huge boom in TV sets in Japan after the Tokyo Olympics, a formula for success. It won the prestigious Kōdansha Manga Award the next year.

Thereafter, Mizuki began to win the hearts of Japan, especially with his ghost and goblin stories. He drew heavily on Japanese spirit traditions, but the paranormal world he depicted was completely his own, and the monsters and goblins that populated it were, rather than scary, endearing. Kitarō, his most famous creation, in the series

After playing catch with hand grenades, Mizuki's sergeant is mortally wounded. Seconds later he asks Mizuki for a spare grenade, and finishes himself off. From* Komikku Shōwashi *("A Comics History of the Shōwa Era").

IN ENGLISH

> In 1993, Osaka-area fans published five of Mizuki's stories in English in a beautifully bound limited-edition book titled *Tales of Shigeru Mizuki* and issued by Kagome-sha. The stories included *Kappa* ("The Story of the Boy Who Met the Water Imp"), *Gōkaku* ("Successful in an Examination"), *Yamata no Orochi* ("The Legend of the Orochi Dragon"), *Marui-wa-no-sekai* ("The World As a Round Circle"), and *Terebi-kun* ("TV-kid"). Unfortunately, the book was never sold publicly.

Ge Ge Ge no Kitarō ("Kitarō the Spooky") was born of a family of ghost-goblins (his father was a mummy), the last of their kind on earth. Both parents "die," but the father's eyeball survives (with little arms and legs) and becomes Kitarō's guardian. Since Kitarō himself only has one eye, the father's eye sometimes hides in Kitarō's eye socket. Kitarō lives in modern, normal human society, but along with a character called Rat Man he is poverty-stricken and an outcast. With his supernatural skills, he often helps people.

This blend of the weird and the normal proved tremendously popular. *Ge Ge Ge no Kitarō* was animated for television in 1968. A loose translation of a line from the theme song lyrics (written by Mizuki) illustrates one reason children loved it:

> Boo, boo, boo boo-boo-boo-boo . . . in the morning
> I am snoring in my bed . . . Oh, it's so much fun, it's
> so much fun, goblins don't have to go to school or
> even take exams. . . .

The other genre of manga in which Mizuki excels is war stories. Many of them have an antiwar theme and commiserate with the plight of the average soldier, thus allowing Mizuki to exorcise his own personal demons. Of these, the 1973 *Sōin Gyokusai Seyo!* ("The Banzai! Charge") is Mizuki's best. It is an account, in dramatic manga-style, of the fate of Mizuki's doomed unit in New Guinea. Its gruesome detail and Mizuki's obvious anger over the way arrogant Japanese officers squandered the lives of their men make it one of the most powerful anti-war comics ever created. (Ironically, Mizuki's older brother was tried and convicted as a Class B war criminal.)

In the early nineties, with renewed interest in Japan in psychic phenomena and the spirit world, Mizuki's popularity soared. In addition to comics, he published several essays and books on Japanese folk beliefs. In 1991 and 1992, a story by him about "Auntie Non-non" was broadcast as a prizewinning drama on the public television network NHK. And around the same time, he received the prestigious Medal of Honor with Purple Ribbon from the Emperor of Japan.

At the end of 1994, Mizuki completed a marvelous 2,000-page series titled *Komikku Shōwa-shi* ("A Comics History of the Shōwa Era"). It wove his own tumultuous history into that of one of Japan's most dramatic and controversial periods—the reign of Emperor Hirohito (1925–89)—using one of his ghost characters as an interlocutor and including meticulously researched footnotes and historical references. Had anyone else attempted to create such a work, it might have seemed forced or presumptuous. But Shigeru Mizuki made it seem a very natural thing to do.

Emperor of the Land of the Rising Sun

『日出処の天子』

RYŌKO YAMAGISHI'S REVISIONIST IMPERIAL HISTORY

"Subversive" is usually not the word that comes to mind when thinking of *shōjo*, or girls', manga, but it can be. One of the most popular girls' stories of all time depicts a revered founder of Japan as a scheming, cross-dressing homosexual with psychic powers. Ryōko Yamagishi's *Hi Izuru Tokoro no Tenshi* ("Emperor of the Land of the Rising Sun"), serialized in *Lala* magazine between 1980 and 1984, is a fictionalization of the life of Prince Shōtoku, who was regent, or de facto ruler, of Japan from A.D. 574 to 622 and whose countenance until recently graced the face of all ten-thousand-yen notes.

Prince Shōtoku helped establish Japan's first centralized government headed by an emperor, and he helped introduce Buddhism into Japan. He promulgated a "constitution" or code of administrative ethics for court officials, and he oversaw construction of the famous Hōryūji temple in Nara. An extraordinary individual, he became the subject of legend, and in many areas of Japan today he is still worshiped as a semi-deity. The title of Yamagishi's story comes from a letter the adult Prince Shōtoku reportedly sent to the ruler of China (which then regarded its neighbors as subordinates), boldly addressed as being "from the emperor of the land of the rising sun to the emperor of the land of the setting sun."

Yamagishi's story starts when Prince Shōtoku is ten years old and follows him into adulthood. It is told mainly from the perspective of Emishi Soga, the eldest son of Umako Soga, one of the wealthiest nobles in the court. Emishi, out for a walk, accidentally comes across what appears to be a young girl bathing, and the image of her beauty is burned into his mind. Only later does he realize that it is the young Prince Shōtoku. Thereafter he sometimes encounters the Prince as a girl, with flowers in her hair, and sometimes as a boy, but from the beginning it is clear that the prince has strange powers. He can levitate things, and sometimes he can make Emishi understand his thoughts.

In the tradition of the best Japanese manga, the story quickly develops a novel-like complexity, featuring dozens of characters and plots and subplots in over 2,000 pages. As the young prince matures his powers are magnified, and he starts subtly manipulating people in the court around him, increasing his own influence. This is a fascinating period of Japanese history, a time when some members of the court backed the traditional animist religion, Shinto, and others backed the new import from the continent, Buddhism. Intrigues abound as people jockey for power and mysterious murders take place. In one thrilling scene during a horrible drought, the court has a Shinto priestess conduct a ceremony to bring rain. She fails, but Prince Shōtoku succeeds, enhancing his prestige—and that of the Buddhism he champions—enormously.

Buddhist and Shinto factions in the palace jockey for influence, and the young Prince Shōtoku explains why a rainmaking ceremony, designed to bolster the Shinto faction, won't work. From Ryoko Yamagishi's* Hi Izuru Tokoro no Tenshi *("Emperor of the Land of the Rising Sun").

The period in which the story is set is ideal for girls' manga, not only because the costumes are exotic and different but because the human relationships (the true subject of girls' manga) are extraordinarily complex. Men had several wives and numerous children, and families were linked together in complex political and incestuous alliances involving marriages of close cousins (Yamagishi includes family trees in each paperback in the series to help readers). Some extraordinarily complicated love affairs—doomed love, unrequited love, or impossible-to-begin-with love—result.

Prince Shōtoku falls hopelessly in love with Emishi, who is interested but is basically heterosexual. Emishi falls hopelessly in love with a vestal virgin who works at the local Shinto shrine. Emishi's younger sister, however, falls hopelessly in love with Emishi, tricks him into sleeping with her, and bears his child. Prince Shōtoku, who hates women, marries for political purposes and takes Emishi's younger sister as one of his wives, thus making Emishi his brother-in-law.

In portraying these relationships, Yamagishi is probably being faithful to the mood of the times, if not to its actual history, for few people of rank were able to marry the people they really loved.

The format of Yamagishi's story has all the ingredients of the best girls' manga. These include beautifully drawn costumes, pages occasionally embroidered with flowers and natural elements for effect, lots of introspection (as opposed to vocalized speech), and, occasionally, pages of beautiful symbolic scenes, such as the young Prince Shōtoku wordlessly gliding through space in a form of meditation-astral travel.

Gay love, a central theme in *Emperor of the Land of the Rising Sun*, was by no means a new idea in girls' manga when Yamagishi began her series in 1980. Homoerotic relationships have been a staple of girls' comics for years, starting with stories that featured cross-dressing women, then beautiful boys in boarding schools falling in love with each other, and so forth. But in taking an icon of Japanese history like Prince Shōtoku and turning him into a cross-dressing gay character, Yamagishi was taking a radical step. In an interview in the September 1992 issue of *Crea* magazine, she said that at first her editors begged her not to turn the story into another "gay" girls' manga. By the time she finished, however, she says the same editors were telling her to stress the gay theme because, "nowadays girls' comics with a gay theme sell, and those without one don't."

For students of Japanese the language in *Emperor of the Land of the Rising Sun* may be rather difficult; it is filled with formal speech and long, complex names (Prince Shōtoku's real name is Umayadonotoyotomimi-noōji), but footnotes are included for many historical terms. Ultimately, it is recommended reading both for those interested in a unique slant on Japanese history and those who just enjoy good manga. In 1983, it won the Kōdansha Manga Award.

Criminal Defense Stories

『マンガ版刑事弁護ものがたり』

THE CASE OF THE LEGAL MANGA

One way to learn about Japan's legal system is to read manga. And a particularly good one to read is *Mangaban Keiji Bengō Monogatari* ("Criminal Defense Stories: The Manga Version"). That it's an "educational" manga isn't particularly unusual, since manga in Japan today are used to impart information on everything from the stock market to nuclear power. What makes it rather novel is that it is published by the Japanese Government; specifically, by the Printing Bureau of the Ministry of Finance.

Criminal Defense Stories is part of a series of books published in conjunction with the Bengō Jitsumu Kenkyūkai, or "Society for the Study of Legal Defense Practices," on subjects such as divorce proceedings, automobile accidents, wills and inheritances, renting houses, and leasing land. Most of the books are text-only, but some, such as those on criminal defense and land leasing, have been turned into manga versions.

After a brief introduction explaining that criminal defense is a fascinating field because it is also the study of human behavior, seven actual legal cases are presented in 244 pages. All are interesting in their own right for what they reveal about both Japanese law practice and the educational manga format.

The first case involves an incident that took place in 1970, at a camp in mountainous Nagano Prefecture in central Japan. A group of students from a Tokyo high school rugby team were engaged in strenuous training. One of the students suddenly died, and the police suspected *shigoki*, "hazing," to be the cause. The high school teacher in charge was arrested and charged with involun-

A lawyer defending five young men accused of raping a fourteen-year-old girl visits the girl's house. Introducing himself to the victim's mother with a gift, he hopes for an eventual settlement. The ultimate result is a stay of prosecution. From* Mangaban Keiji Bengō Monogatari *("Criminal Defense Stories: The Manga Version").

tary manslaughter. The parents of the dead boy sued the teacher and his school for ¥15 million. At the district court level the teacher was found innocent, but the prosecutors appealed; at the superior court level the first verdict was thrown out and the man was given two months incarceration with a year's probation. The defense appealed to the Supreme Court but the suit was rejected. The school finally ended up paying the dead boy's parents a court-advised settlement fee of ¥13.5 million. The entire process took seven years.

The final verdict was clearly a defeat for the defense, but the trials illustrated the problems of assigning responsibility in a case where the facts were in dispute. Was the student a victim of hazing or overzealous training, or was he the victim of ill health and bad luck? How much responsibility did the supervising teacher have? These are all difficult questions to explore in manga format, but the authors and artists do a good job in this and the other cases, quoting throughout from the court record, contemporary newspaper articles, and the witnesses' testimony.

Inevitably, educational manga tend to be much

wordier than those designed solely for entertainment, and the artwork suffers from a lack of hyperbole and thrilling action—there are no titillating sex scenes or gory shootouts. Nonetheless, the drawings make the information more accessible and convey the "emotive" details: panels showing the lawyers' faces, the nervousness of witnesses, and cigarettes piling up in ashtrays during lawyers' strategy meetings are worth thousands of words.

Other cases covered in the same volume range from the mundane to the lurid; they include the trial for robbery and battery of two wino/day-laborers who steal money from a drinking buddy and bash him in the head with a sake bottle; a gangster type who is charged with the rape (which he vehemently denies) of a young woman friend; and a famous case from 1953 about a radio salesman murdered in his sleep whose wife was charged with the murder.

In this last case, the woman confessed to the police but later claimed that her confession had been coerced. She was found guilty, despite considerable evidence to the contrary, and all her subsequent appeals were denied, as were her petitions for a retrial. Finally, nearly thirty years later, she was retried and cleared of all charges, but she died of cancer shortly before the verdict was issued. Her case became the focus of several books and a film in Japan, and the episode in *Criminal Defense Stories* is used to illustrate how difficult it has been until recently to obtain a retrial in Japan.

For the average person, there is a great deal to be learned from manga like *Criminal Defense Stories*. Legal terms (of which there are many) are explained at the bottom of the page. The legal process—indictments, trials, appeals, and convictions—is introduced in the context of interesting stories (and also in a supplementary text section at the back of the book). For non-Japanese, *Criminal Defense Stories* gives many insights into the peculiarities of Japan's legal system and shows how it deals with particularly Japanese issues, such as deaths through group hazing and confessions that in the past were frequently coerced. The oft-noted Japanese aversion to direct legal confrontation is apparent in nearly every case as the lawyers for the defense approach the victims or their relatives to achieve some sort of settlement, either to avoid having the case go to trial or to have the charges reduced. In one instance, the prosecutor helps the defense lawyers by calling up a particularly intransigent party and getting him to agree to a settlement.

The language used in *Criminal Defense Stories* is considerably more sophisticated than that used in more commercial manga. There are no handy pronunciation keys given for difficult kanji characters as there are in many manga for young people. Nonetheless, legal manga are certainly easier to read than more academic textbooks. Perhaps because it is a government publication, the artist (Izumi Maki) is given short shrift and only mentioned in fine print at the back.

Fancy Dance (Reiko Okano)

『ファンシィダンス』(岡野玲子)

ZEN ROMANCE

I could never become a Zen monk, but I've always been interested in Zen and in the lives Zen monks lead. An old high school friend has been a monk in a Zen temple in rural Fukui Prefecture for nearly twenty years. I've visited him a couple of times, and I often find myself thinking about his life.

With that in mind I like to read Reiko Okano's light comedy *Fancy Dance*, which has a great introduction to modern temple life. This might seem surprising, not just because *Fancy Dance* is a manga but because it is a girls' manga. Girls' manga are known more for love stories than realism, and tales of Zen monks are hardly ordinary fare. But *Fancy Dance*—which was serialized in Shōgakukan's *Petite Flower* comic from 1984 to 1990—is no ordinary manga. Superficially, it fulfills the criteria for a girls' comic: it has romance and many fashionably dressed characters with dreamy big eyes (who often look very Caucasian). Yet it delves into philosophy and metaphysics.

The hero is a young man named Yōhei. He's a college student who fronts a rock band called the Flamingos. He's tall, handsome—an ultra hip Tokyo "city-boy"—and he hangs out with an equally hip crowd of young men and women. Yōhei likes Masoho, who is beautiful and fashionable, and she likes him, but both have an ornery streak and their relationship never quite seems to gel. Yōhei also has a "problem." He is the eldest son of the abbot of a rural Zen temple, and according to tradition he must eventually take over his father's job.

Herein lies much of the tension in the story. Yōhei resists his fate, for in modern-day Japan it has definitely not been fashionable to become a Zen priest (at least not until *Fancy Dance*). As artist Okano explained in an interview, among young people in Japan the life of a Buddhist priest conjures up dark, even funereal images. Before she began creating *Fancy Dance*, she would have regarded someone like Yōhei as being in a "tragic" situation. Even her editors were skeptical about the theme she chose for her story.

But Yōhei and his friends are the opposite of dark and dreary. They are the epitome of Tokyo youth in the roaring "bubble economy" of the late 1980s, when Japan's future seemed most glorious. They are *akarui* ("bright") and *karui* ("light"), with hardly a care in the world. And in the first three volumes of the story, which is set in the cafes and discos of Tokyo, Okano does a marvelous job of recreating the hip, upbeat banter of this crowd. When Yōhei and friends encounter Bjorn, a serious Swedish youth interested in traditional Japanese "culture," they take him to the Akihabara electronics area to tease him.

Fancy Dance really takes off after volume 4, when Yōhei and his younger brother Ikuo (a beautiful teenager with gay leanings) begin training as acolytes at a Zen temple in the mountains. Their lives change drastically. They enter a hierarchical world with more parallels to Marine boot camp than Tokyo discos. Heads shaved, they must abide by a strict schedule of meditating and working and endure the hazing of their seniors.

What starts out as a one-year training period, how-

Yōhei and his younger brother experience a little posture straightening (and a "wake-up call") while learning to meditate as Zen acolytes. From Reiko Okano's Fancy Dance*.*

ever, becomes a three-year sojourn, as Yōhei grows to appreciate Zen life. Eventually he sees beauty in discipline, appreciates Zen esthetics, and views the monks' dress as "fashionable" (remember, this is a girls' comic).

Okano does a superb job of showing life in a typical Sōtō sect Zen temple. Worship areas, monks' living quarters, and robes are all rendered in loving detail. Rituals and organizations are introduced, and difficult Buddhist terms are explained with footnotes. To draw her story Okano spent a week at one temple and visited another regularly, staying at a local hotel and getting up at four in the morning to watch the monks perform their rituals. She befriended many young acolytes. Some of the information she gleaned is introduced in special

IN ENGLISH

Part of episode 17 of *Fancy Dance—Kan Myō Shametsu no Kyō, Ten wo Hiite Kakyō ni Iru* ("Falling from a Higher State of Consciousness and Taking One Another Along to the Fiery Pit")—appeared in issue 41 of *Mangajin.*

bonus pages titled "Secret Report on Temple Life: Acolyte Fashions."

Yōhei's temple life is not all serious. Acolytes vie with each other for better assignments, sneak in snacks of Kentucky Fried Chicken, get silly-drunk on illicit nights in town, and pay the price when caught. And they dream of their girlfriends back home. Despite his three-year sojourn, Yōhei maintains his affections for Masoho, and she for him, even though she increasingly resents his absence. As Yōhei says, however, monastic life is like a Nintendo game—once you start, you have to take it as far as it goes.

Eventually Yōhei leaves his mountain temple and returns to Tokyo. He holds a variety of odd jobs, including taxi driver, janitor, and hospital morgue attendant, as he tries to figure out what he has learned as a monk and attempts to restart his relationship with Masoho. One day, while working as a professional pachinko player, he sees a mandala of the universe in the intricate design of the pinball-like machine.

Yōhei regains Masoho's affections and realizes what he wants to do in life. After a trip to Hawaii, he proposes to her, and she accepts. When the story ends, Yōhei has finally resolved his conflicts. With Masoho by his side, he will take over his family's temple and become one of the hippest Zen monks in Japan.

Fancy Dance is published in nine paperback volumes totaling nearly 1,800 pages. Although English editions have never appeared, Chinese editions have been scheduled for publication in Hong Kong and Taiwan. In the Japanese edition, since the story is designed for teenagers, difficult kanji have *furigana* or *rubi* pronunciation keys, making it easy to pronounce Buddhist terms with unusual readings.

In 1988 an audio LP/CD of *Fancy Dance* music was released. Produced by Makoto Tezuka, who later became Okano's husband and who is the son of Osamu Tezuka, it is part of a huge and lucrative genre of "image CDs" containing music inspired by manga stories; Okano even wrote some of the lyrics. In 1989 *Fancy Dance* was also made into a charming live-action film (and later video) of the same name, starring, among others, Masahiro Motogi, Kenji Otsuki, and Naoto Takenaka.

Tomoi (Wakuni Akisato)

『TOMOI』(秋里和国)

***TOMOI:* A PIONEERING MANGA ABOUT GAYS AND AIDS**

I live in the Haight-Ashbury district of San Francisco, world-famous epicenter of the 1960s "hippie" revolution. Only a twenty-minute walk from my apartment over a steep hill is the Castro district, which became famous in the late seventies and early eighties for its role in the gay rights revolution. Back then I often walked over the hill to watch movies in the Castro, and one day I started seeing strange notices tacked to telephone poles. The notices were warnings about a mysterious form of pneumonia killing many local young men, and they asked for help in identifying the cause.

Thus did I first become aware of what we now call acquired immune deficiency syndrome, or AIDS. Since then AIDS has killed many people I know and has spread to every nation and every sector of the world's population. In the mid-eighties, however, many people in Japan seemed to be in a severe state of denial brought on by the "we'll never get it 'cause we're different" syndrome. Thus it was all the more remarkable that during this period a very sympathetic portrait of both AIDS and gays came out of Japan. The moving series *Tomoi* was created by a young woman manga artist named Wakuni Akisato, and it appeared in *Petite Flower*, a bimonthly for women between the ages of eighteen and twenty-three. That such a story would appear first in manga for women, rather than men, is not as odd as it may seem, given the long tradition in girls' manga of soap-operatic stories romanticizing gay love, especially in overseas settings.

The protagonist of Akisato's tale is a young Japanese man named Hisatsugu Tomoi. Instead of taking over his father's business, Tomoi becomes a doctor and does his residency at a hospital in New York City. Tomoi is tall, dark, and handsome (like an "Arabian prince"), and while growing up he had always felt a little "different." When he arrives in New York in 1982, he realizes his true "gayness" for the first time. He falls in love with an attractive German doctor named Richard Stein and is introduced to the hedonistic pre-AIDS New York gay scene of discotheques and bars. It's a heady experience, but Tomoi matures quickly. Stein is a promiscuous playboy who quickly drags Tomoi into his complex and tangled world of jealous lovers, only to eventually dump him. More and more gay patients start showing up at the hospital with a strange lethargy and a new syndrome called AIDS, and one of Stein's former lovers dies of it. Stein becomes afraid and goes back to Germany.

Heartbroken, Tomoi returns to Japan for a while and finds himself even more of a misfit. His parents want him to have an arranged marriage, but his identity is by now firmly gay. He tries to seduce an old friend, Yukihiro, and fails miserably. Then, when he returns to New York, he falls in love with Marvin Williams, a handsome and sensitive young ophthalmologist at the same hospital (who wears, it turns out, the same cologne as Tomoi—Chanel Pour Monsieur). Marvin becomes the love of Tomoi's life, but it is a complicated relationship. Marvin is locked in a loveless marriage that his wife won't let him out of. And he, too, starts finding himself easily fatigued, and there are strange blotches on his skin. As a doctor, Tomoi realizes what is happening, but it makes him love Marvin even more; in a touching ceremony the two men exchange wedding vows and rings. But one day Marvin's enraged wife comes to the hospital with a gun. She tries to kill Tomoi. Marvin jumps in the line of fire, taking the fatal bullet.

Unable to forget Marvin and deep in depression,

In a symbolic marriage ceremony, Tomoi promises to love Marvin in sickness and in health. From Wakuni Akisato's **Tomoi.**

Tomoi volunteers to work as a physician in Afghanistan for the resistance forces fighting the Soviet invaders (this is the early eighties, remember). Needless to say, Tomoi meets a tragic end in Afghanistan, but not from AIDS.

Presenting only a synopsis of the plot of *Tomoi* makes it sound depressing, melodramatic, and even downright corny. But the artist, Akisato, does a superb job of telling her story. She tenderly illustrates it throughout and includes many gags and much humorous banter. Sometimes the story even reads like a lighthearted comedy. Yet Akisato's depiction of relationships among gays seems (to me at least) both uncontrived and sensitive. Most impressive is the way she is able to deftly weave information on the symptoms and causes of AIDS into her story, even at such an early stage of the epidemic.

The *Tomoi* series is widely available in Japan as two volumes, titled *Nemureru Mori no Binan* ("Sleeping Beauty Boy") and *Tomoi,* as part of the Shōgakukan *PF* series of manga paperbacks. The language is easy to understand, and all the kanji have pronunciation keys.

Naniwa Financiers (Yūji Aoki)

『ナニワ金融道』(青木雄二)

NANIWA KIN'YŪDŌ AND STREET-LEVEL ECONOMICS

In the spring of 1993, the magazine *Marco Polo* polled critics, literati, and its own readers on what they thought were the fifty best men's manga. The all-around winner was Yūji Aoki's *Naniwa Kin'yūdō*, serialized every week in the comic *Morning* starting in 1990. It was a manga so unusual in art style and theme that it was hard to ignore.

Naniwa is an archaic term for the city of Osaka, and *kin'yūdō* means, literally, "the Way of Finance." Instead of the usual sex-sports-gambling-action-adventure, *Naniwa Kinyūdō* is about *machikin,* or "street financiers," in Osaka. The protagonist is a young man named Tatsuyuki Haibara who lands a job at a tiny lending firm called Imperial Finance when his first employer goes bankrupt. After a rocky start he discovers he likes the work, and he resolves to become the best lender in all of Osaka. A veteran co-worker, Kuwata, befriends him and initiates him into the rough-and-tumble world of lending to the masses.

The word "financier" has a sophisticated ring to it, conjuring up images of nattily dressed bankers making loans to big corporations. But *machikin* are an entirely different breed. Their customers are individuals and owners of small firms who need money in a hurry and for one reason or another (a lack of collateral, perhaps) cannot qualify for a loan from a regular bank. *Machikin* give unsecured, unguaranteed loans after simple credit checks. In the public mind, they are closely associated with the notorious *sarakin*—lenders who often prey on salaried-workers—but *machikin* issue loans against bills of exchange and deal with a much broader clientele. Both have an unsavory reputation as heartless loan sharks and usurers; they charge exorbitant rates of interest (25 to 100 percent per annum in the past, now usually around 30 percent), and they are often mentioned in the news in conjunction with suicides and other assorted personal disasters that happen when consumers get over their heads in debt.

Naniwa is an interesting manga not just because it depicts a business with a terrible image, but because the hero, Haibara, for all his flaws, is someone we come to empathize with, and even like. In the beginning, he sympathizes too much with borrowers who fall on hard times and have trouble repaying their debts, and he agonizes over their plight. As time passes, however, he learns to read human character, and in a business where recovering loans is of paramount importance he learns that it's occasionally necessary to get tough, even ruthless.

A fine balance must be maintained in the lending business. The lender has to lend as much money as possible at a high interest rate, but he also needs to ensure that the borrower can repay the loan; if the burden is too great, the borrower will default and skip town. Haibara is therefore constantly getting involved in people's personal lives, trying to help them get side jobs, encouraging them to straighten out their finances, and maneuvering to make sure they don't default. The greater the risk in the loan, the more extreme the measures taken to prevent default. Co-guarantors have to be located, contracts have to be drawn up so property can be used as collateral, and bills of exchange have to be collected and cashed in. When one customer borrows too much and loses control of his debt repayment, Haibara is ordered to encourage the customer's girlfriend—a co-guarantor of the loan—to work as a prostitute to cover the debt. He is tormented by what he has done.

Yūji Aoki, the creator of *Naniwa*, was born in 1945 and was thus forty-five years old when he began his series in 1990. Since he was virtually unknown until then, Aoki qualifies as one of the all-time late-bloomers

IN ENGLISH

> Parts of episodes 1–3 of *Naniwa Kin'yūdō* appeared in issues 34–40 of *Mangajin.*

in the manga world, where many artists turn professional in their teens. Yet he brings to his work a wealth of world experience and a sophistication in storytelling reminiscent of masters like Sampei Shirato or Osamu Tezuka. One of his main inspirations was not a manga, but Dostoyevski's *Crime and Punishment*, which he claims to have read more than five times before starting his story.

In a world where imitation is rampant, Aoki maintains a highly individualized art style. Rather than leave lots of blank space on pages or just draw "talking heads," he fills in everything to create a hyper-detailed look. When his story takes place in offices, bars, or restaurants, instead of tracing photographs for backgrounds (as many artists shamelessly do today), he painstakingly draws everything freehand in a quirky, blocky style. Ashtrays and files on desks are drawn in great detail, as are street signs with amusing puns. The faces of Aoki's characters, while "cartoony," capture distinct personality types that inhabit the streets of the Osaka area. None of Aoki's characters are good looking, but all are true "characters," in the vernacular sense of the word.

Language is an important part of *Naniwa*, which is, in fact, a rather "wordy" manga. Aoki goes to great lengths to explain complex financial terms, both in the context of the story and in footnotes. And he writes not in standard Japanese, but in the colorful dialect of the Osaka streets. If one doesn't understand Japan's Kansai dialect, this manga is a good place to learn; Aoki, a native of the area, is uncompromising. Footnotes are included for expressions Tokyoites would be unlikely to comprehend.

At the end of 1995 *Naniwa Kin'yūdō* consisted of fourteen paperback volumes that in total had sold over 7 million copies. It had been dramatized for television, and it had won the 1992 Kōdansha Manga Award. Far more than any textbook, it is an ideal introduction to the

The title page from chapter 34 of Yūji Aoki's **Naniwa Kin'yūdō** *("The Old Osaka Way of Finance"): "If you don't have the cash, get it at a massage parlor." Novice financier Haibara looks on nervously while his superior gets tough.*

underbelly of Japan's vaunted economy. It teaches not only about co-guarantors, promissory notes, defaults, and mortgages, but about the former "bubble economy," the role of the yakuza, land speculators, politicians, and *jiageya* (property consolidators who entice or force land owners to move when in the way of building projects). Its gritty realism provides an entertaining education, so much so that former prime minister Hata reportedly said he had learned a lot from it when he was minister of finance. Seizing upon this informational aspect of the manga, in 1994 publisher Kōdansha issued a non-manga book on economics, edited and illustrated by Aoki, titled *Naniwa Kin'yūdō: Kane to Hijō no Hōritsu Kōza* ("Naniwa Kin'yūdō: A Legal Seminar on Money and Mercilessness"). It promptly became a bestseller.

Yoshiharu Tsuge

つげ義春

THE ECCENTRIC MASTER

If it can happen to William Burroughs, I'm sure it will soon happen to Yoshiharu Tsuge, too. I'm talking about becoming a big enough cult figure to be the subject of Japanese TV quiz shows. Burroughs, the notorious American novelist, former junkie, surrealist, and existentialist, is something of an acquired taste even in his homeland, but in the early nineties the Japanese quiz show *Cult Q* had local fans competing to show their knowledge of trivia such as the street address of his birthplace.

Yoshiharu Tsuge is arguably Japan's premier eccentric manga artist, and like Burroughs he has quite a cult following among intellectuals. Neither a commercial nor even a prolific artist, he has probably had more written about him than he has himself created. He is invariably introduced in the media with the words *ishoku*, meaning "unique" (written with the characters for "different" and "color"), and *kisai*, meaning "singular genius" (written with the characters for "demon" and "talent"). A quarter of a century after he created his most influential works he is being discovered by a new generation: in the last few years several collections of his manga have been reissued, and at least two feature films—*Munō no Hito* ("A Man without Ability") and *Gensenkan Shujin* ("The Master of the Gensen Inn")—have been made based on his short stories.

Born in 1937, Tsuge came of age in the devastation of World War II. His education ended in grammar school, and by the time he began working in a variety of menial jobs he was intensely introspective, plagued with an obsessive self-consciousness that caused him to blush uncontrollably. At fourteen he stowed away on a ship bound for the United States, but before it left Japanese waters he was caught and handed over to the Japanese Coast Guard. Around age sixteen he began drawing manga professionally, partly so he wouldn't have to interact with other people.

Tsuge began drawing not for major Tokyo manga magazines but for the *kashibonya*, or "book-library," market. At one point there were nearly 30,000 of these pay-libraries that rented out books and manga to readers looking for an inexpensive way to pass the time. By and large, the artists and the readers were both working class, and the pay-library stories tended to be realistic, action-oriented, and adult in theme, often featuring crime and mystery tales. If the stories were bleak, so was real life. Tsuge faced a constant struggle with poverty and depression. When a girlfriend left him in his early twenties, he attempted suicide. When he was broke and in debt, he sold his blood.

In the mid-sixties, Tsuge began drawing in a more experimental style in the avant-garde manga magazine *Garo*, using semi-realistic backgrounds populated with "cartoony" characters and weaving psychological themes into his stories. His art style was reminiscent of Sampei Shirato and Shigeru Mizuki (two famous former *kashibonya* artists who also drew for *Garo*), but his trademark was intense introspection and a tendency to surrealism. In 1967, Tsuge's now classic *Nejishiki* fired the imagination of alienated college youth in Japan and permanently established him as a "cult" artist. *Nejishiki*, or "Screw-style," was only twenty-three pages long, but it took the reader on a wild psychological ride. It reportedly was the product of a dream Tsuge had when taking a nap on the roof of his apartment building. The first page showed a disturbed-looking youth wading out of the ocean with the dark shadow of an airplane (a B-29?) flying above him. He is holding his left arm and an exposed artery which has been severed by a giant jelly fish. In a surreal quest for medical help, he begins walking through a local town and is picked up by a locomotive driven backward by a child. Finally, he finds a gynecologist who fixes him with a wrench after first "playing doctor" with him. On the last page of the story the hero is zipping across a lake in a speed boat, a valve attached to his repaired arm. The narration says, "And so it happened that my left arm became numb whenever I turned my valve off."

In *Nejishiki* and other stories such as *Numa*

Nejishiki ***("Screw-Style"), by Yoshiharu Tsuge.***

("Swamp"), *Chīko* ("Chirpy"), and *Gensenkan Shujin* ("The Master of the Gensen Inn"), Tsuge exposed his soul in a way readers had rarely seen in comics. Critics who normally never read comics called his stories "art."

Tsuge's career has been interrupted by several long bouts of depression, and during such times he draws little. In addition to his manga, however, he has illustrated essays based on trips around Japan and published records of his dreams. He likes to travel alone on a shoestring, vis-

IN ENGLISH

> Tsuge's bittersweet nostalgic story *Akai Hana* was published in English under the title "Red Flowers" in issue 7 of *Raw* magazine in 1985.

iting hot springs and recording the rundown street scenes that form the backdrop to his stories. His Japan does not consist of high-tech flash or fashion; it is an impoverished place of the past, populated by ordinary, if slightly haunted-looking, characters.

As Tsuge mentioned in an interview in *Garo* in 1993, "I'm not preaching religion or trying to change the world. It's very hard for me to adjust to the world, and I'm just trying to figure out how to exist so that I can be different without feeling insecure about it."

Banana Fish (Akimi Yoshida)

『Banana Fish』（吉田秋生）

***BANANA FISH:* ROMANTIC NEW-YORK BAD DREAMS**

The Mekong Delta of South Vietnam, 1973, a year and ten months before the fall of Saigon. A group of U.S. GIs are sitting around shooting the breeze, singing "Oh, My Darling Clementine" and reading *MAD* magazine, when suddenly one of their buddies approaches with his M-16 and begins wildly firing—at them. He has a crazed look on his face, and stops only when someone finally shoots him in the legs. The shocked soldiers try to find out what happened to their comrade and realize he is out of his mind—all he can mumble are the words *Banana Fish. . . .*

New York, March 4, 1985. Police detectives are trying to solve a strange series of suicides. Late at night, a man is shot in a dark alleyway by teenage streetgang members. Not unusual, perhaps, except that the boys had been put up to the job by a Corsican Mafia boss named Papa Dino. When their real leader—Ash Lynx—comes across the scene, he is horrified. Before expiring, the mortally wounded man hands Ash an empty necklace vial and mutters, "Find 'Banana Fish' . . ."

Ash, as it turns out, is the kid brother of the GI who went berserk in Vietnam and is now a human vegetable. Realizing the connection, Ash thus begins a complicated quest to find out what really happened to his brother and what the strange words "Banana Fish" mean.

Akimi Yoshida's action-packed mystery-thriller, *Banana Fish*, began serialization in May 1985 and quickly captured a broad range of readers in Japan. Its conclusion—ten years, 3,400 pages, and nineteen paperback volumes later—garnered mentions in major newspapers. For fans, it had become an addiction and an emotional roller-coaster ride, with every episode bringing new twists and turns in the complicated plot.

Like slowly peeling an onion layer by layer, Yoshida reveals more and more about her characters and their motivations. Ash, the hero, is no ordinary street punk, but an extraordinarily charismatic and handsome teenager with an IQ over two hundred. He also has an extremely complicated past. Abused as a child, he was coerced into prostitution by his father and eventually became the main squeeze of the homosexual Mafia boss, Papa Dino, who groomed him to take over his evil empire. With his own gang, Ash had finally managed to break free of Papa Dino's grip.

When Ash realizes the extent of Dino's evil and his possible involvement with a strange "Banana Fish" conspiracy, he declares virtual war on his former mentor-tormentor. Dino, despite his desire to crush Ash, also harbors desires of a more carnal sort and employs a full suite of nefarious tricks to again make Ash one of his obsequious minions, including kidnapping and murdering his friends.

"Banana Fish," we gradually learn, is the name of a drug accidentally discovered by three scientist brothers in 1970. A powerful relative of LSD, it is potentially the perfect mind-control weapon, but in early incarnations it mainly renders its victims insane or suicidal; in Vietnam it had been secretly tested on American troops, one of whom was Ash's own brother. When Corsican Mafia boss

***Ash, standing on the roof of a roaring truck with gun in hand, bears down upon Mafia boss Papa Dino, his tormentor. He is determined to shoot him. Dino (with shock of realization): "Ash!" "You bastard!" Sound effects:* **VROOOM.** *From Akimi Yoshida's* **Banana Fish.**

Papa Dino gets hold of the top-secret drug, he realizes its enormous potential and, working with corrupt forces in both the government and the military, tries to perfect it—to create a drug that will turn people into virtual robots who will obey any command. . . .

Set in New York, Yoshida's story is populated with a diverse mix of characters. In his confrontation with the Mafia, Ash's own racially mixed gang must form alliances with Chinese and African-American gangs and then confront them when their interests diverge. Ash himself must continually ward off attacks and attempts at abduction staged by a beautiful, young, cross-dressing, and intensely jealous Chinese gang leader. Luckily, Ash wins respect easily, and he is aided in his quest by some honest New York police, several journalists, and a Japanese cameraman named Ibe and his young protégé-pal visiting from Japan, Eiji.

Naive, sensitive, and unwittingly caught up in the drama that unfolds around him, Eiji serves as an intermediary for Japanese readers. As Eiji learns more and more about life in the streets and about violence in America, he gains respect and sympathy for Ash and eventually falls deeply in love with him. Ash, for his part, develops a deep love for Eiji and realizes he is the only person in the world he can truly trust.

Because of his unique upbringing and specialized training, Ash can operate skillfully in almost any environment. He uses guns and computers with equal ease, and he always gets "respect." But he is no angel. Like his name, Ash Lynx, he is a wild mountain cat, and he kills with little remorse. When he has to, he sells his body. Above all, he lives to survive.

Banana Fish is a hard-boiled action thriller filled with killings and blood. In addition to constant assassinations, there are gun battles in the sewers and subways of New York and even in the Museum of Natural History. The city is portrayed as a modern Wild West, and at times one wonders if there is any authority at all. There are also sex scenes, most of which are homosexual in nature and tactfully depicted. The world of *Banana Fish* is totally male, and Ash, although he happens to be highly attractive to women, isn't attracted to them in the least.

What makes *Banana Fish* so unusual a manga is that it was originally designed for young girls and serialized in the special monthly supplement issue of *Shōjo Comics*, a 524-page magazine that targets junior and senior high school girls. But the story's fans included both genders; while it was serialized, *Banana Fish* was one of the few girls' manga a red-blooded Japanese male adult could admit to reading without blushing. Yoshida, while adhering to the conventions of girls' comics in her emphasis on gay male love, made this possible by adopting a completely masculine art style, eschewing flowers and bug eyes in favor of tight bold strokes, action scenes, and speed lines. Her composition perhaps most closely resembles that of Katsuhiro Ōtomo—the artist who created a revolution in clean-line realism in male manga in the early eighties and who was one of the first to draw Japanese people with more Asian-like features.

Banana Fish's popularity coincided in the late eighties with a fascination with New York City. When everything seemed to be going right in Japan, before the "bubble" burst in the economy, New York was often portrayed as a symbol of everything that was wrong with America, from drugs to guns to racial tension to poverty—sort of a modern Sodom and Gomorrah. But at the same time, it seemed symbolic of America's raw energy and exciting individual freedoms. Not surprisingly, in this period many intrepid young artists and intellectuals began making regular treks to New York to experience its scary but seductive world.

Milk Morizono

森園みるく

"H" MANGA

Many ladies' manga—the dainty-sounding genre of manga created by women for women—became highly eroticized in the late eighties and early nineties. One of the artists in the vanguard of this trend was Milk Morizono, whose sexually charged S&M-flavored stories created something of a sensation. When I first arranged to meet Morizono at a coffee shop in Tokyo in 1994, I half-expected a flamboyant S&M queen with whips and chains to show up. She arrived looking like any other Tokyo sophisticate, however, attractively attired in a fashionable outfit and wearing dark glasses. Her open manner and good humor quickly put me at ease.

Morizono began drawing manga as a child, as is common in Japan today, but for a woman her professional debut came quite late by industry standards. In 1981, at age twenty-three, she won Shōgakukan's award for new artists. Nearly all publishers have awards to foster new talent, but Shōgakukan's is particularly prestigious (and rewarding; then ¥500,000, it is now around ¥1,000,000).

For the next six years or so Morizono drew *shōjo*, or "girls,'" comics, and for a while she dabbled in gag strips for the young men's genre. When ladies' manga became more popular, however, she found it easier to identify with their more mature readers and began drawing exclusively for them—just as the erotic content in many of the ladies' magazines was increasing. Morizono's pen name, "Milk," was the result of an attempt with an editor to come up with something catchy and feminine; other candidates at the time, she says today, were fruit names such as Melon and Mikan ("Mandarin").

By 1995 Morizono had published over thirty-five paperbacks, most with fashionably designed covers and snappy English names like *Cocktail Stories*, *Desire*, *Bondage Fantasy*, *LUST*, *Let's Go to Bed*, and *Slave to Love*. The inside flap copy for one of her bestsellers, *Slave to Love*, speculates that she will be listed in a ladies' "Who's Who" of the 21st century and raves on:

> Last genius artist of the 20th century, possessing a combination of Dali's wild extravagance and Gaugin's positivity. Born on the same day as Jesus Christ, she skillfully depicted the extremes of love in *fin de siècle* Tokyo.

Slave to Love is a collection of short stories written between 1986 and 1988 about male-female encounters; included are one-night stands, pool table sex, a little bondage, and an amusing tale of lost virginity. By 1995 standards it is tame stuff, with no genitalia or pubic hair. And unlike erotic manga for males, the stories have a fairly long lead-in before the actual sex begins, and everything is depicted quite fashionably. As with much good erotica, the stories are normal enough so that the reader can presumably imagine how such an encounter or experience might-maybe-possibly-could happen to her.

Morizono uses the standard Japanese term *etchi* when she talks about erotic material. Usually written with the capital letter "H" to stand for the Japanese word *hentai* ("abnormal," "perverted"), *etchi* can mean anything from seriously "perverted" and "twisted" to "erotic" or

In Milk Morizono's short story "Amore" ("Eros"), a channeler tells a beautiful Tokyo pop singer that in a former life she was the Greek goddess Psyche. Shortly after, she is betrayed by her boyfriend and attempts to kill herself. Losing consciousness, she is transported to the world of Greek gods, where she relives the famous Eros-Psyche myth, complete with seductions by Eros, great trials of faith, and rapes by fearsome beings. Here, the pop singer, as Psyche, realizes she is being ravished by Eros; a spy-dove sent by Aphrodite takes wing to report. **From Kamigami no Tasogare** *("Dusk of the Gods").*

"naughty-nasty" in a playful, positive sense (which is how Morizono uses it).

"'H' manga magazines are very popular now among women readers," Morizono said in 1994, "and most women artists draw for them. They're a female version of the erotic or 'Lolita complex" magazines for men. Essentially, Ladies' manga today are divided into two types: those with lots of 'H' material, and those with none. I draw mainly for the monthly magazine *Feel*, which is unusual in that it has both."

Why are erotic manga so popular among women in Japan? Morizono speculates it is because long-repressed Japanese women have pent-up frustrations but now have the freedom to express themselves directly. Many of the readers of erotic ladies' comics, she notes, are bored wives cheating on their husbands. "Sometimes they buy the magazines just for the 'telephone club' ads."

Morizono is also known for her foreign and gay stories and characters. Although these elements are common among young girls' manga in Japan, she claims she is the exception in the ladies' genre, where many writers and readers focus on more easily identifiable characters and situations.

"I have a Japanese friend in New York who happens to be gay and have a black boyfriend," she says. "I used to visit New York and go to discos with them, and the characters in my stories started to become the people I met." At various periods Morizono has been a regular customer at gay bars and bondage clubs in Tokyo. She even made a special trip to Germany once to photograph bondage scenes in Berlin. Such experiences clearly help the realism of her stories and enhance her reputation in Japan as a sexy power-woman.

Morizono is also unusual in the manga industry in that she rarely writes her own material. She usually works with a pool of four or five young and unestablished writers, choosing them according to the subject matter and sharing around 30 percent of her royalties (more experienced artists may get 50 percent). Like most successful artists, for mass production and tax purposes she has her own company, called Milky World, with five men and two women assistants.

Morizono may have been on the radical fringe of Ladies' manga at the beginning of the 1990s, but by the end of 1995 things had changed. During our first interview she had expressed her fears for the future of *Feel*—the magazine in which most of her material ran—and these had finally proven true. Like several other middle-of-the-road ladies' manga magazines with both erotic and serious material, *Feel* had gone out of business as readers' tastes polarized. "I'm thinking of switching to drawing for young men's magazines," she said, "because ladies' manga don't sell well anymore. They focus too much on 'bed scenes,' and not enough on storytelling."

Today, Morizono is clearly less interested in shock

Here, "Psyche" is assaulted by terrifying creatures: "Open your mouth!!" "Eek . . ." "Ahh . . ." "No!" When "Psyche" regains consciousness in this world, and her boyfriend declares his true love for her after all, she kills herself by jumping out the hospital window to be with Eros. From the short story "Amore" in Kamigami no Tasogare *("Dusk of the Gods").*

and more in substance. Among her other works are *Kamigami no Tasogare* ("Dusk of the Gods" or "Götterdämmerung"), erotic love stories based on Greek myths, and a two-volume story about AIDS titled *Soshite Tsutaete, Hibi no Owari ni* ("Tell People, to the End of Our Days"). In *Feel Young* in 1995, she serialized a story about Marilyn Monroe based on a book by Natsuo Kino, with a subplot about Robert Kennedy and the CIA.

One of her long-expressed goals is to draw more story-oriented "H" manga, and even create erotic manga versions of novels by famous Japanese writers like Yukio Mishima, Edogawa Rampo, and Junichirō Tanizaki.

By the end of 1995, Morizono was achieving some

recognition overseas. One of her manga stories, *High Life*, was being published in Italian. But she wasn't limiting herself to manga. She had issued a CD featuring herself singing with two S&M queens, and she was also scheduled to work as the writer on an upcoming erotic live-action film.

The Way of Manga (Fujiko Fujio Ⓐ)

『まんが道』（藤子不二雄Ⓐ）

THE WAY OF MANGA

I was not the first person surprised to discover that Fujiko Fujio was two people, and not one. Until the late eighties, "Fujiko Fujio" was known as the creator of such mainstays of Japanese children's culture as Obake no Q-tarō ("Q-tarō, the Ghost"), Ninja Hattori-kun ("Young Hattori, the Ninja"), and Doraemon, the robot cat—manga characters that roared through the Japanese national consciousness in the sixties, seventies, and eighties, spawning television shows, movies, popular songs, and toys. The entity "Fujiko Fujio," however, was really the pen name of two artists—Hiroshi Fujimoto and Motoo Abiko—who had an extraordinarily close relationship.

Manga artists often collaborate with writers and use assistants who help fill in backgrounds and details. Abiko and Fujimoto were unique in that, on the surface at least, they seemed to share nearly everything, from scripting to drawing to income. Both men had a genius for seeing the world through the eyes of children and for creating naive, magical stories about the everyday world. Of all the works that were first issued under the name Fujiko Fujio, I found a fictionalized autobiography titled *Manga Michi*, or "The Way of Manga," to be the most interesting. It's also one of the best histories of postwar Japanese manga.

The Way of Manga stars two young boys—pals—named Michio Maga and Shigeru Saino (a semi-fictionalized Motoo Abiko and Hiroshi Fujimoto). The story starts in 1951, when, as junior high school students in Takaoka City, they go to visit their idol, Osamu Tezuka (known as the "God of Manga"), in Osaka. Inspired by Tezuka, the boys had been drawing comics together since the fifth grade, putting two desks side by side at Saino's house and creating a little artist's "studio."

The story then follows both the manga career of the two lads and the development of the long, narrative story-manga genre pioneered by Tezuka. As students, the boys send stories to children's magazines like *Manga Shōnen*, winning prizes and getting their works printed. After graduation from high school, and briefly holding down day jobs (one day in Saino's case), they resolve to become professionals. When Osamu Tezuka moves to Tokyo and energizes the manga industry there, they (and other talented young artists from all over Japan) follow him. Unlike others, Maga and Saino live and work together and use a single pen name—Shigemichi Ashizuka—à la Fujiko Fujio.

The life of a young artist isn't easy. The boys first live in a two-tatami-mat room with barely enough space for two people to lie down to sleep, let alone work together. Earning enough to pay the rent is a constant struggle. Gradually, however, they learn how to work faster, and they get better jobs. They move into a four-and-a-half-mat room in a rundown apartment building named Tokiwasō (the building, now legendary, is where Osamu Tezuka and other young artists once also worked and has been the subject of books and television documentaries).

Alas, Maga and Saino soon fall into the trap that awaits many young cartoonists. They accept too much work, panic, and fail to meet their deadlines. In doing so they lose the good standing that they had worked so hard to achieve in the booming manga industry. In despair, they nearly give up on their new careers, but after being encouraged by Tezuka and others they struggle hard, and work their way back.

The Way of Manga runs over 4,000 pages. If it were just a success story it would quickly become boring. What makes it fascinating is its autobiographical detail and historical accuracy. Many of the legends of the manga industry—Osamu Tezuka, Shōtaro Ishinomori, Fujio Akatsuka, and others—appear in it as young men. It

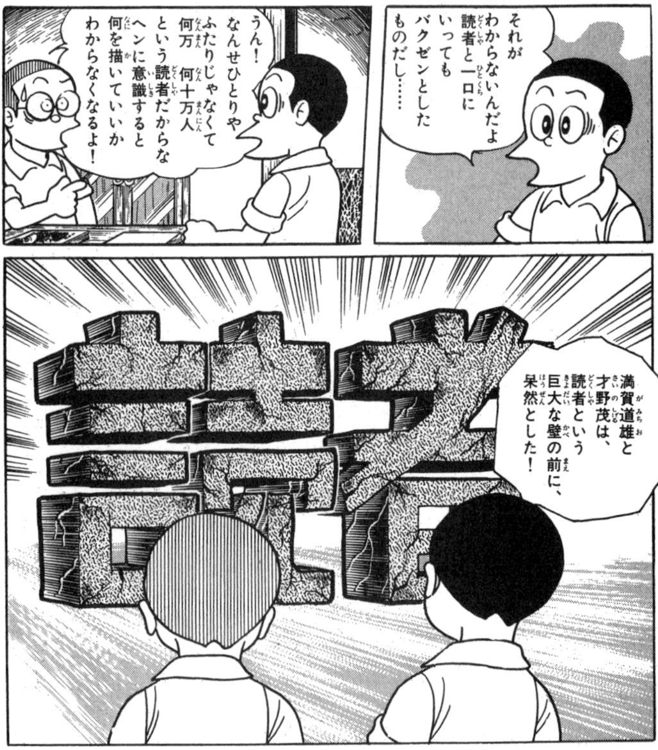

Michio Maga and Shigeru Saino realize how important it is to consider the audience when creating comics, and the kanji for "READERS" flash in front of them. From Fujiko Fujio Ⓐ's Manga Michi ("The Way of Manga").

also provides a great deal of information about the manga industry: how plots are developed, how artists interact with the publishers and their editors, how editors use the *kanzume* ("canning") system to isolate artists in a room and force them to meet deadlines, and how important (and difficult) it is for artists to stay healthy. When pages of works by the fictional characters "Shigeru Saino" or "Michio Maga" are introduced in the course of the story, drawings from the period by the real duo—Abiko and Fujimoto—are reproduced. *The Way of Manga* is of special interest for the way it references many popular films of the 1950s. Manga artists were heavily influenced by American movies, and Abiko and Fujimoto were no exception. Lavish illustrations and descriptions show how cinematic techniques and themes were adapted and became an integral part of the manga style.

When I first met "Fujiko Fujio" in the early eighties,

IN ENGLISH

> Selections from Fujiko Fujio Ⓐ's *Warau Sērusuman* ("The Laughing Salesman") appeared in *Mangajin. Tomodachiya* ("Matchmaker") ran in issues 33–34. *Yume no Karaoke Hōru* ("The Karaoke Hall of Dreams") appeared in issues 36–37. An interview with the artist is included in issues 36–37.

the two men were middle-aged and married, but they really did act as though they had spent nearly every day of their lives together (and indeed they practically had). Still, they were clearly very different personalities. Fujimoto was shy and reserved but very sweet. Abiko, whom I eventually got to know quite well, came from a long line of Buddhist priests and was a strict vegetarian, but he was also an avid golfer and an experienced drinker. For a man famous for his innocent children's stories, his sense of humor was cutting edge, almost existential.

Sometimes even the best friendships are hard to maintain. In the mid-eighties, "Fujiko Fujio"—or Abiko and Fujimoto—split up and began working on their own, thus ending one of Japan's most unusual artistic collaborations. Today both continue to draw manga, and both are extremely successful. Abiko draws stories mostly for adults, often with a "black humor" edge to them. In the early nineties a story in this vein that he had actually created in 1969, *Warau Sērusuman* ("The Laughing Salesman"), became an extremely popular animated show on television. Fujimoto, despite health problems, has also continued drawing for both children and adults. Much like the property of a couple going through a divorce, however, the large body of works the two men originally issued under one name had to be split and wherever possible reissued under separate copyrights and individual names. Their combined name was too great an asset to sacrifice completely, however, for the pen names they use today are Fujiko F. Fujio and Fujiko Fujio Ⓐ.

The Way of Comics is published as a multi-volume collector's edition by Chūo Kōronsha. It is written in easy-to-understand Japanese with pronunciation keys for all the kanji. Since the work was essentially Abiko's, the last volume was issued under his—Fujiko Fujio Ⓐ's—name, as were subsequent reprints of the earlier volumes. The story has also been made into an NHK television drama. In 1996, Abiko, or Fujiko Fujio Ⓐ, began serializing a sequel, subtitled "Youth," in a special supplement issue of *Big Comic Original.*

Doraemon (Fujiko F. Fujio)

『ドラえもん』(藤子・F・不二雄)

***DORAEMON:* THE ROBOT CAT**

He has infrared eyes, radar-capable whiskers, a kangaroo-like Fourth Dimension pouch, a huge mouth, a bell around his neck, and a nuclear reactor in his chest. He reportedly weighs 285 pounds, but he's only a tad over four feet tall, and cuddly cute as can be. It's Fujiko F. Fujio's Doraemon, the robot cat that climbed out of the desk drawer of young Nobita Nobi one day and became his pal, and the pal of nearly every child in Japan and Asia.

Fujiko F. Fujio, whose real name is Hiroshi Fujimoto, is one of the most consistently successful children's manga artist's in Japan today. In a field in which many artists burn-out or out-grow, he has survived and thrived. Longtime former partner Motoo Abiko—Fujiko Fujio Ⓐ, a top children's artist in his own right—calls him one of the few "true naturals." Many in the industry refer to him as a "genius." In the manga world, *Doraemon*—which first appeared at the beginning of 1970 in Shōgakukan's manga-style educational magazines for young children—has been the equivalent of a home run with the bases loaded, repeated again and again. There are over forty-five *Doraemon* paperback volumes in the main series and seemingly endless spin-off editions. Every year, Fujimoto creates a new *Doraemon* manga story that is faithfully made into an animated feature film in time for the spring holidays; watching it has become a national ritual for children and parents. By 1996 over seventeen *Doraemon* feature films had been released, each one usually among the

DATABOX

THE DORAEMON *SUCCESS STORY*

BOOKS	VOLS.	EST. COPIES SOLD
Tento Mushi series manga paperbacks	44	100,000,000
Doraemon super manga ed. (*Daichōhen*)	16	1,700,000
Doraemon film animation books	16	3,200,000
Doraemon illustrated books, etc.		4,000,000
Total:		**108,900,000**

VIDEOS	VOLS.	EST. COPIES SOLD
Theatrical features	16	2,000,000
Educational videos	22	200,000
TV animation series	22	280,000
Total:		**2,480,000**

THEATRICAL FEATURE FILMS (1980–95, 17 FILMS)	
No. of theatergoers	60,720,000
Distribution income* from rentals to theaters	¥29,772,000,000 (US$297,720,000)

GENERAL MERCHANDISE ROYALTIES**	
1979–94	¥15,300,000,000 (US$153,000,000)

* Yen-dollar conversions at ¥100 per dollar.
** Includes toys, apparel, stationery, video games, advertising, etc. Does not include royalties from publications, movies (including video tapes or laserdisks, or music; an estimated 100–150 different types of Doraemon items are sold per year).
Source: Akira Fujita, Shōgakukan Productions, January 1996.

year's top-grossing domestic films. On television, the robot cat still captures top ratings. He even stars in at least two touring musicals.

"*Doraemon* was the result of an accumulation of experience and lots of trial and error," Fujimoto says, "during which I finally found the pattern or style of manga to which I was most suited." It began with *Obake no Q-tarō* ("Q-tarō, the Ghost"), the story of a friendly cute ghost who lived in an ordinary family. Created in 1964 with Motoo Abiko (they still share copyrights to this one), *Oba-Q*, as it was known, also took Japan by storm after it was animated, resulting in a flood of merchandise. Its formula for success involved taking a familiar, ordinary environment and then introducing into it a single unusual element to create a variety of unexpected results. *Doraemon* was an extension of this formula, but instead of being about a ghost in ordinary life it was a gentle science-fiction comedy starring a high-tech robot-cat from the future who lived with an otherwise unexceptional family.

Success wasn't immediate. "My forte," the soft-spoken and shy Fujimoto says, "is what I call 'ordinary-life gag manga,' and when I started creating *Doraemon* the genre was waning in popularity because there was a boom in *gekiga* ["dramatic pictures," or more "realistic" manga]. But I did my best and kept drawing."

Nearly ten years later, after the manga *Doraemon* had been animated for television and paperback books were out, the situation changed and the series exploded in popularity. When the animated theatrical features started in 1980, *Doraemon* became a national institution.

Another reason for *Doraemon*'s success, Fujimoto suggests, is that it falls into what he calls the "wish fulfillment" genre of manga. "Both adults and children have wishes, and although the wishes manifest themselves in different ways they have much in common. We may wish for something to happen, to become stronger, smarter, or for an easier life. In a very abstract sense, many of the wishes may be fulfilled in this genre of manga."

From his Fourth Dimension pocket, Doraemon pulls out gadgets that delight children—some of the most popular being propellers worn on the head that make flying possible, an "any-where door" that when opened becomes the door to wherever one wants to go, and a time machine. In 1993 there was a boomlet in tongue-in-cheek books for adults that "explained" the "secrets" of the most popular manga. In *Doraemon no Himitsu* ("Doraemon's Secrets"), the authors (the Setagaya Doraemon Research Club) noted

Doraemon shows Nobita how to make a paper flying saucer—and it really works! From **Doraemon SF no Sekai** ***("Doraemon's Sci-Fi World").***

of the "any-where door" that "it is one of the most fervently wished-for gadgets by salarymen who have to suffer through rush-hour hell on trains."

For a modern children's manga, *Doraemon* is remarkably gentle, eschewing violence, eroticism, scatology, and sensationalism in favor of a low-key, optimistic, and reassuring approach. This certainly helps explain Doraemon's popularity among small children, and also among their parents. And it also may explain why it has been so popular overseas in different cultures. *Doraemon* was one of the first Japanese manga to achieve wide success abroad, either in animated and printed (often pirated) form, and although it has never been given exposure in North America it has been shown widely throughout Latin America, the Middle East, Europe, and especially Asia, where it has achieved overwhelming popularity.

Fujimoto has had a string of successful children's manga in addition to *Doraemon*. Other than his popular formula, he speculates his own basic personality helps. "You can't draw children's comics from the perspective of

IN ENGLISH

In 1981 an English version of a large-sized *Doraemon* book containing five episodes was published by Shōgakukan, but never sold publicly.

adults and try to create what you think the children will like," he says. "You have to create something you really enjoy, that they also happen to enjoy. You have to be at their eye-level, in other words, with their perspective. I guess I have a bit of the child in me that refuses to grow up, because I'm extraordinarily lucky in that what I like to draw, they like, too."

It's not easy to draw the same way all the time, however, so sometimes Fujimoto creates science fiction works for adults. "*Doraemon* is positive, yang energy," he says, "but sometimes I want to draw stories that are more adult, dark, and hopelessly depressing. Alternating helps me keep my balance."

Fujimoto is nationally famous, and by all rights fabulously wealthy. But that doesn't necessarily mean he's had an easy life. He has undergone major surgery for ulcers, and in the early nineties he was forced to cut down drastically on his work. When I last talked with Fujimoto in 1994, I ribbed him about how none of his three daughters had expressed any interest in following in his footsteps, as would have been expected were he a traditional Japanese artist or craftsman. Fujimoto smiled wryly and said, "The manga artist as a profession is glamorized, but it's unstable work. When your work doesn't sell, you have no money. When it sells, you have no time to use your money. And when you have lots of income, most of it is taken away in taxes. It's not the sort of job most artists would recommend to their children."

Still, Fujimoto wouldn't have it any other way for himself. If he were to be reborn as a salaryman in Japan's lifetime employment system, he jokes, he would surely be a *madogiwazoku*, one of the "sit-by-the-window tribe"—the incompetents consigned to useless busywork. "Being a manga artist has been great for me," he says. "It's the only talent I have."

King of Editors (Seiki Tsuchida)

『編集王』(土田世紀)

KING OF EDITORS: LIFE BEHIND THE PANELS

Editors usually work behind the scenes and rarely get credit; they may even be hated by those they help. Given this, Seiki Tsuchida's *Henshū-Ō* ("King of Editors") is particularly entertaining. A fictionalized introduction to the life of manga editors, it portrays them in a highly sympathetic light. It first began serialization in *Big Comic Spirits*, a weekly magazine for young men, in 1993.

The construct Tsuchida uses is simple and clever. Opening scenes show a rural lad named Kanpachi Momoi—weeping with his school chums over dramatic scenes in a manga boxing story. Momoi resolves to become a boxer, and then we see him years later as a struggling prizefighter getting knocked out yet again in the ring. When a detached retina finally ends his career, an old pal at a major manga publisher gets him a job at the office of the weekly *Young Shout*.

The story then follows Momoi as he struggles, despite his limited education and rough-and-tumble manner, to learn how to be an editor. He is an underdog hero, but he has *junjō*, a pure, unsullied state of earnestness and sincerity. By nature he prefers to settle matters with his fists than his brains, and this is the source of much drama and melodrama in the story.

In Japan, one of the main jobs of an editor is to go to the home or studio of the artist and physically collect the completed comics pages. If the pages are not ready, the editor must sometimes resort to *kanzume* ("canning"), corralling the artist and confining him in a hotel room until he finishes them. Threatening and cajoling are part of the editor's repertoire as well.

One of Momoi's first jobs is to accompany an editor to collect the manga pages of a famous but now merely-resting-on-his-laurels artist. An enormous fan of manga, Momoi learns in the process how cynical some artists can be, and how bureaucratic the practice of producing manga has become—how many salaried editors no longer work to create good stories but have become mere errand boys. Despite the fact that the artist in question is famous, highly paid, and the object of groveling demonstrations of respect, his stories are far less interesting than those of lesser-known artists. Momoi's naive and earnest *junjō* qualities lead him to tell his superiors, and even the artist's manager, that parts of the story should be redrawn. The manager, impressed by Momoi's sincerity and obvious love of comics, ultimately redraws and rewrites part of the work himself.

In another chapter in *King of Editors*, Momoi helps out a twenty-two-year-old young man who has become a manga star but lost confidence in himself. Pressured by his editors into drawing more "breast shots" and other erotic scenes in his manga to improve sales, he has become so disgusted with the story's direction that he can no longer bear to continue. The magazine, however, depends on him, for it is already reaping huge profits from animation and merchandising based on his story. Momoi helps the young artist exit his dilemma, but first he has to help him meet a deadline; with friends he does the work normally done by the artist's assistants—adding balloons around the words, inking backgrounds, and drawing panel frames.

In the same chapter, the over-reliance of manga magazines on ratings and statistics is also highlighted. Following a practice established by the weekly *Jump*, nearly all manga magazines today rely on questionnaires filled out by their readers. The result can be a pandering to readers' tastes—a "flavor of the month" approach that exacerbates trends like eroticism and violence and can result in quick termination of artists whose popularity sags.

Manga editors also have to coddle egotistical artists, supply them with ideas, and sometimes serve as ghostwriters. Even after they have the artwork in hand, they have to edit text portions and take them to the printer, lay them out, and paste the words into the balloons on the pages. It requires long hours and the ability to get along with difficult personalities. In yet another chapter of *King of Editors*, Momoi accompanies a young female editor on

Kanpachi Momoi watches as an artist's manager improves on the work of his boss, and the two men develop a rapport. From Seiki Tsuchida's Henshu-Ō *("King of Editors").*

her rounds, collecting work from the artists for whom she is responsible. As one of the few female editors in the entire industry, she has to work twice as hard as others, and even then is not always accepted. One artist complains his work has deteriorated ever since she was assigned to him, because she is not a male and therefore can't possibly understand his problems.

Like many good manga, *King of Editors* uses melodrama, comedy, and gags to spice up its somewhat informational approach. The protagonist readily punches out people who offend him. He adopts some stray puppies that always follow him around. He can only go to the bathroom when he is buck naked. Despite the visual gags and occasional deformation, the artwork is quite realistic, with several of the fictional editors' faces seemingly modeled after those of real people—perhaps industry insiders. And although the story is serialized in a magazine published by Shōgakukan, the headquarters of the fictional *Young Shout* is modeled after that of Shōgakukan's largest rival—Kōdansha.

Finally, *King of Editors* is a wonderful way to learn about terminology and slang in the giant manga subculture. *Meshisutanto*, a contraction of *meshi* (meal) and "assistant," is the employee who prepares the meals for the production team; "tone" refers to the patterned films applied to create instant textured backgrounds or shadows; and *nēmu* (from the English "name") is the word for the dialogue that is printed on paper, cut into strips, and then glued into the word balloons on the final artwork. For more esoteric manga terms, such as *daigen*—which in this case means a substitute work that editors stock in advance in case an artist fails to make his deadline—Tsuchida kindly provides footnotes.

A Declaration of Arrogant-ism

『ゴーマニズム宣言』

YOSHINORI KOBAYASHI: AN ARTIST MAKES WAVES

On April 25, 1994, the author of a column on literature in the *Asahi* newspaper took the unusual step of recommending not a novel, but a manga series to her readers. Titled *Gōmanizumu Sengen* ("A Declaration of Arrogant-ism"), and authored by Yoshinori Kobayashi, it was the subject of considerable media discussion and controversy.

Known affectionately as *Gō-sen* by its fans, *A Declaration of Arrogant-ism* began serialization in 1991, not in a manga magazine but in a general newsweekly for adults called *Spa!* Compiled into deluxe paperback formats, it can often be found stacked in the book—not manga—sections of bookstores.

What is *Gō-sen*? It is a series of essays in manga format (two to eight pages long), but it is also the author's personal "soapbox," a platform for him to discuss subjects about which he has strong opinions. Political and social satire cartoons—of the sort that grace the editorial pages in European and American newspapers—have tended to be rather insipid and uninspired in Japan (pre- and immediately postwar censorship is partly to blame). Kobayashi, using the longer manga format, is one of the first Japanese artists to deliver the punch of American or European political cartoonists in a Japanese context. Impassioned in expressing his personal beliefs (calling himself an "arrogant-ist" for doing so), he nonetheless always maintains a sense of humor and allows readers to laugh at his inconsistencies.

The range of Kobayashi's subject matter is breathtaking: discrimination against Japan's *burakumin* or former outcastes, censorship in the media, rape, hazing and bullying in schools, drugs, the AUM religious cult, contaminated blood products that infected Japan's hemophiliac population with AIDS, and his own belief that too many Japanese young women are sleeping with foreigners. As he implies in the introduction to his first paperback volume, young people in Japan in the eighties seemed obsessed with merely having a good time. Anything with a serious theme was regarded as "old-fashioned" and depressing. After the Gulf War, however, Kobayashi sensed that the national mood had shifted, that people were finally ready for manga with a strong message, ready for something that would make them think.

Kobayashi stakes out his position in the very first episode in the series; it shows him berating his fellow countrymen for being too passive—for being too willing to follow others' opinions and too unwilling to express their own, for "existing like jellyfish, floating back and forth, left and right, between the waves. . . ." It's time, he declares, for Japanese to speak up and express themselves. Before he states his own opinion in each episode, however, Kobayashi always says, *Gōman kamashite yoka desuka,* or, in Kyushu dialect, "'Mind if I sound off a bit arrogantly?" His conclusions at the end of each story are usually akin to a declaration of war on human ignorance and stupidity.

Kobayashi's brazenness has sometimes gotten him into trouble in Japan, but his run-ins seem only to have energized him. When the Crown Prince of Japan in 1993 married the commoner Masako Owada, the entire nation was transfixed by the event, and for a while the mass media was heavily censoring itself, ignoring anything that might seem disrespectful or frivolous. Kobayashi, reacting to what he saw as media overprotection of the imperial family, drew a series showing a newly married Masako lobbing grenades at crowds from her limousine and shouting anti-emperor-system slogans. The episode, regarded as disrespectful, was pulled from *Spa!* magazine. Kobayashi, unchastened, took it to Japan's premier avant-garde manga magazine, *Garo*, and let them publish it for free. (To his publisher's credit, the episode is included in the paperback compilation.)

In 1995, before its alleged gas attack on the Tokyo subway system, Kobayashi began taking on the AUM religious cult, condemning it for its bizarre behavior at a time when many others in the media were unwilling to do so, and before the true extent of the madness of the cult's leaders was known. Not only was Kobayashi sued for libel by cult lawyers; later in the year, he was allegedly found on a list of public figures the cult had ordered assassinated with deadly VX gas. In what became an anti-AUM crusade for Kobayashi, he began quarreling with Japan's pundits and pointy-headed intellectuals (and his own editors) for having coddled the cult. At the end of the year, in a move almost unprecedented in Japanese media, Kobayashi publicly split with the magazine *Spa!* and moved his popular series to a rival news publication, *Sapio*.

This boldness seems only to have enchanced his reputation among intellectuals and youth. In 1995, one of Japan's top manga critics, Tomofusa Kure, edited a book of essays by Japanese pundits, all analyzing and praising Kobayashi's novel attitude.

Surprisingly, perhaps, Kobayashi was until recently

The artist rages against the news media and their overprotection of the Imperial family. Far right panel: "If the gag on the previous page is published in* SPA!*, Japan has a bright future; if it's a blank page, our future is bleak. . . ." From Yoshinori Kobayashi's* Gōman-izumu Sengen *("A Declaration of Arrogant-ism").

best known for his children's manga. He made his debut in 1976 with *Tōdai Itchokusen* ("Tōdai Bee-line"), a gag strip serialized in the weekly young boys' *Jump*. The story starred an obnoxious, idiotic young student named Tōru Tōdai, who, like many students in Japan, was obsessed with getting into the University of Tokyo (called "Tōdai" for short). Rather crudely drawn and filled with clever puns and the vulgar jokes that naughty children love (often involving scatology and innocent nudity), it was a major hit in the late seventies—a time when people first realized that the proliferation of after-hours cram schools and superheated academic competition among young children was a social problem. In the eighties Kobayashi was better known for *Obotchama-kun* (roughly, "Little Lord Fauntleroy"), which was serialized in *CoroCoro Comic,* a manga magazine for very young boys. Filled with amusing puns and wordplay, it starred a spoiled young boy with an allowance equal to half the annual budget of the Japanese Self-Defense Forces.

Why is *A Declaration of Arrogant-ism* so controversial and popular? I suspect it is because in Japan it is still difficult to reveal one's true feelings, or *honne*, in public. People devote so much of their lives to maintaining public images and an illusion of harmony that Kobayashi's approach is very refreshing. In the Japanese context what he is doing is not only controversial, but "arrogant," because he draws so much attention to himself (hence the title). But this only makes him more interesting. The fact that Kobayashi draws and writes in the tongue-in-cheek, anarchist style of children's gag manga helps keep his excesses funny. Like the little boy who pointed out that the emperor wore no clothes, his boldness is offset by his innocence and honesty. His mission, however, is radical—to destroy intellectual complacency and narrow-mindedness.

AUM Cult Comics

オウム真理教のマンガ

MANGA AS RELIGION

I was determined to locate some manga produced by the AUM Shinrikyō cult, but I couldn't find them anywhere. It was November 1995, and only a few weeks earlier the cult had been ordered to disband by the Japanese government, the first time in postwar history such an action had been taken against a religious group. The order meant all their assets, including buildings, cars, stores, and presumably even manga, would have to be liquidated. The cult lawyers had appealed the decision, but a national shunning process was already in effect. This was, after all, the same group that had allegedly planted nerve gas on Tokyo subways, murdered, then vaporized, opponents in a microwave oven, and plotted to take over society—and whose jailed leader faced the death penalty.

I first inquired at a secondhand manga store. In American fashion, I reasoned that in a few years the manga would be worth a fortune, so the store ought to have some for a price. To my disappointment, the manager looked at me as if I were from another planet and said, "We wouldn't touch them under any conditions."

Nonetheless, another employee kindly told me (to my great surprise) that there was still a cult store selling AUM "goods" (the word Japanese use to refer to souvenir items, licensed merchandise, etc.) near Kōenji Station just west of Shinjuku.

The first thing I saw after exiting the train station at Kōenji was a large banner in the plaza proclaiming, *BANISH THE CULT* and *PROTECT RESIDENTS AND OUR YOUTH FROM AUM*. Sure enough, the same banner was on every telephone pole along the shop-lined street that led for a half mile or so to the store. The closer I got, the more nervous I started to feel. The tension in the neighborhood was palpable.

The store had a bright and airy interior. It was staffed by two polite young women with long hair and the believer-light in their eyes, dressed in the cult's faux Indian garb. Tables displayed cute dolls in the likeness of the guru, copies of his musical recordings, guru-image T-shirts, and religious books and paraphernalia. To my delight, there was also a stack of the cult's manga (as well as used anime cells). I bought as many as I could afford, and before I left, I noted from the open store ledger that I was the only customer who had visited in a long time.

Outside, when I tried to take a photograph of the store for the record, a young policeman materialized out of nowhere and politely motioned me over.

"You just went in that store, didn't you?" he inquired.

"Why, yes, I did," I replied. In the politicized seventies I had often been pulled over by suspicious police in Japan. I knew the routine well, but his next question surprised me.

"Tell me," he asked in an almost plaintive voice. "What are they doing in there? You see, we're not allowed inside."

I told him the boring details as best as I could, which allowed him to then get to the real questions he was obliged to ask—what was *I* doing in there, what was my name, address, nationality, and so forth. I politely explained that I was doing research for a book on manga, and as a member of the manga-saturated generation he eventually seemed to understand. But when I finally asked if I could take my photo, yet another policeman suddenly appeared and sternly remarked: "That would not be a good idea." The entire area, I realized, was staked out by policemen, perhaps fearing that new, even more dastardly deeds were being plotted inside the store or hoping some still-fugitive cult leaders would show up whom they could arrest.

* * * * *

On the walk back to the station—past the banner-bedecked telephone poles and (it being a neighborhood with foreign laborers) an occasional shop with the sign, "Only Japanese allowed"—I had time to reflect on the response of Japanese society to the AUM cult. If there was anything the establishment feared, it was the strange attraction this cult had for some of the nation's best and brightest youth. Two small boys whizzed by me on bicycles, talking to each other in loud voices about how Shōkō Asahara, the cult leader, should be hanged. So apparently the "right" message was getting through.

One secret of the cult's success (it claimed over 10,000 members in Japan and even more in Russia) was its ability to package its twisted message in an attractive fashion. The teachings are a blend of Hinduism and tantric Buddhism, and—other than the fact that they encouraged blind obedience to a nearly blind guru with apocalyptic visions who is paranoid and psychotic—fairly innocuous. Anime and manga—because they are so popular, because they can be used to dramatize and exaggerate information and simplify a complex reality, and because they are often rendered in a cute, "fashionable" style—were the perfect vehicle for the cult to proselytize. Not surprisingly, the group had its own in-house production staff. It is hard to imagine a more sinister abuse of the manga medium.

Perhaps reflecting the cult's proselytization efforts overseas, and its awareness of fashion, all the manga I purchased had English in their cover titles.

After accumulating virtue in the eyes of the cult by creating spiritual "Astral" music for them, a young musician (shaggy hair, 2nd panel from top) is personally asked by Asahara (1st panel from top) to become one of his ordained disciples. The young man accepts gratefully and presumably goes on to renounce society and all his worldly possessions for the cult. From the paperback* Spirit Jump*, vol. 1.

The Buddha describes how, after very ordinary beginnings, cult guru Asahara trained hard, developed his special powers (levitation, prophesy, and so on), and, after visiting various spiritual leaders in India, realized he had to help more people attain salvation through his teachings and thus survive the coming Armageddon. Appropriately, a dramatic male manga style (*gekiga*, or "dramatic pictures") was used, with lots of bold lines in backgrounds emphasizing speed and emotional revelations and making Asahara look exciting and forceful. A subtext of the story, which apparently had great appeal in Japan, was that anyone who follows Asahara's teachings can acquire his same powers.

AUM Comic features several short stories by different cult artists about the experiences of young people joining the group; it also contains personal text-only messages from the guru, ads for cult shops and restaurants illustrated in cute manga style, and, on the back page, an ad for the latest cult publication—a book claiming that all of Japan was under a form of mind-control for believing the cult had used nerve gas and that the opposite was true, that the cult was the victim, presumably of a plot by the government and the U.S. military.

I was most impressed by *Spirit Jump*, a three-volume set of paperback manga filled with true stories of how various disciples had become disillusioned with their humdrum, spiritually empty lives in modern Japan, joined the cult, and found happiness. The stories are rendered in a variety of styles, including the typical *shōjo* (girls') style complete with bug-eyed cute characters and flowers to highlight emotions and sensitivity. All are remarkably high in quality. The paperbacks are indistinguishable from mainstream manga books, and over 180 pages in length, with ISBN codes so they can be sold in regular distribution channels. The artists are all cult disciples who presumably work in the cult's AUM MAT Studio, but the guru is always listed as providing editorial supervision. One volume, I noted to my amusement, was even copyrighted His Holiness the Master, Shōkō Asahara.

The artists may have the last laugh. On January 9, 1996, the *Asahi* newspaper ran an intriguing article on the (unnamed) former head of the AUM MAT anime and manga studio. He had spent over seven years with the cult but had been arrested during the police crackdown—on suspicion of murder and attempted murder for having participated in construction of nerve gas production facilities. While in jail his blind faith in his religion had been shaken by his interrogators. In what is a common pattern in the Japanese legal system, he then began to reflect on the folly of his former ways. Since his actual involvement in the criminal acts turned out to have been minor and unwitting, he was released on probation. Shortly thereafter, the article said, he had begun to create a lengthy exposé manga about his days with the cult, about his guru's mind-control techniques, and about his guru's personal guilt in the subway gas attacks.

5 OSAMU TEZUKA: A TRIBUTE TO THE GOD OF COMICS

マンガの神様ー手塚治虫

THE DEATH OF OSAMU TEZUKA FROM STOMACH CANCER ON February 9, 1989, received only brief mention in a few newspapers outside of Japan. But in his own land he was mourned like a fallen monarch. Tezuka had lived sixty years, almost exactly the length of the Shōwa Emperor's reign, but many people seemed far more shocked by his death than that of the emperor, which had occurred only a few weeks earlier. The emperor had lingered on so long, and was so old, that when his death finally came it was almost anticlimactic. Tezuka's took everyone by surprise. Many young people wept unabashedly, and the media ran seemingly endless retrospectives on his life.

The Human Dream Factory

限りない夢のクリエーター

WHO WAS OSAMU TEZUKA?

Who was Osamu Tezuka, and why was he so famous? In Japan, Tezuka was referred to as the "God of Comics" and even the "God of Animation." When introduced to ignorant foreigners, the appellation the "Walt Disney of Japan" was often tacked on, as if this somehow explained everything. In reality Tezuka was entirely different from Disney. He was largely a failure as a businessman and manager. He was first and foremost a storyteller, a man who generated ideas and plots as easily as some people breathe. And he was a gifted artist.

With these talents he helped pioneer the "story comic"—the long (often thousands of pages), intricate novelistic format that is the mainstay of Japanese manga today and that relies heavily on so-called cinematic techniques. Tezuka was, in a very real sense, the father of Japan's huge contemporary comics and animation culture. As the prestigious *Asahi* newspaper put it in an emotional editorial the day after he died:

> Foreign visitors to Japan often find it difficult to understand why Japanese people like comics so much. Reportedly, they often find it odd to see grown men and women engrossed in weekly comic magazines on the trains during commute hours. . . . One explanation for the popularity of comics in Japan, however, is that Japan had Osamu Tezuka, whereas other nations did not. Without Dr. Tezuka, the postwar explosion in comics in Japan would have been inconceivable.

Tezuka was born in Toyonaka City, in Osaka, on November 3, 1928, but he grew up in nearby Takarazuka, famous for its hot springs, theater, and then-abundant natural beauty. Until World War II intensified, he led what must have been an idyllic childhood. His parents were progressive and upper middle class, with a strong interest in the arts. His mother loved drama. His father, although a "salaryman," was a film buff and even had a projector with which he showed early American animated shorts and Chaplin films. Young Osamu soon exhibited a remarkable ability to draw, and as a schoolboy he doodled profusely. One of his hobbies was collecting insects, and he carefully cataloged them, often painstakingly drawing each one in full-color, photolike detail. Because of his love of insects—particularly a beetle called the "osamushi"—he began adding the character for "insect" 虫 or *mushi* to his given name, Osamu 治, writing it with a cartoon-like flourish of two dots in the character to represent "eyes."

A doodle by Osamu Tezuka using the mushi character of his name.

Osamu Tezuka's cartoon self-portrait, and his signatures in Japanese and English.

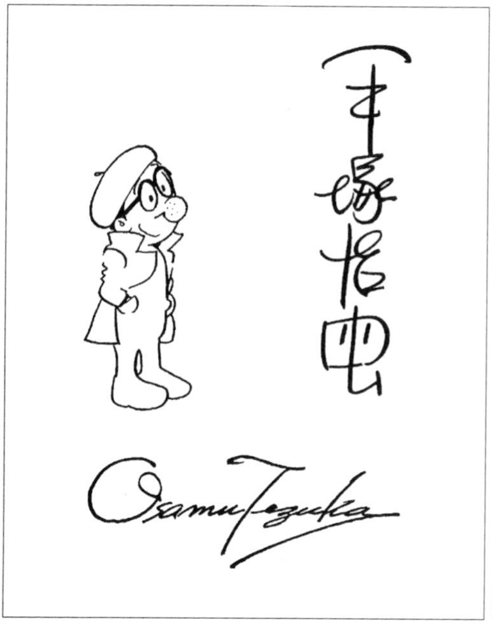

FIRST SUCCESS

Right after the war, at the age of seventeen, Tezuka debuted as a cartoonist in a *Mainichi* newspaper with a serialized cartoon strip titled *Mā-chan no Nikki* ("Mā-chan's Diary." It was a simple four-panel cartoon, similar to others of the time. A year later he created *Shintakarajima* ("New Treasure Island"), based on a story by Shichima Sakai. *New Treasure Island* was a sensation, a manga *book* nearly two hundred pages long and drawn in a style that made it fast-paced, exciting reading. Tezuka, an avid fan of American animation, had incorporated many of that art form's techniques, using different "camera angles" and creating a sense of motion with his page layouts. *New Treasure Island* was so visually oriented that some later said reading it was almost like watching a movie. At a time when many people scarcely had enough money for food, and when manga were still a very minor industry, Tezuka's creation reportedly sold over 400,000 copies.

Drawing in the same style, Tezuka began producing story after story, driving entertainment-starved young readers wild. He created science fiction tales with exotic English titles like *Lost World* and *Metropolis*, and he adapted foreign classics such as *Faust* and *Crime and Punishment* into the comic format.

After Tezuka moved to Tokyo in 1952 and began drawing for major children's magazines, his fame grew exponentially. The rundown apartment building where he lived, named Tokiwasō, became a magnet for young artists who idolized Tezuka and wanted to work as his assistant. Tokiwasō has subsequently become the subject of books and TV documentaries. Many of Tezuka's former assistants are today the reigning veterans of the manga world. (See, for example, the duo Fujiko Fujio discussed in chapter 4.)

In 1951 Tezuka began serializing *Jungle Taitei* ("Jungle Emperor"), a story of animals in Africa learning to live together, and the next year he began drawing *Tetsuwan Atom* ("Mighty Atom"), a story of a robot-child who "fought for peace." Both of these became instant classics and today are among the most beloved of Tezuka's tales; one of the lions of *Jungle Emperor* is currently the mascot for the Seibu Lions baseball team, while Atom advertises securities and telecommunications.

THE MASTER AT WORK

No matter what genre of manga Tezuka dabbled in, he always seemed to discover new possibilities for it. A master of boys' comics, he also pioneered comics for girls. In 1954, he used his "story comic" techniques to create *Ribon no Kishi* (literally, "A Knight in Ribbons," but usually translated as "Princess Knight"). Its enormous popularity helped jumpstart what is now the huge genre of manga exclusively for girls and women. Starting in the sixties, Tezuka also began developing stories with increasingly sophisticated themes for an older audience, trying to do with comics what others have done with literature. In the process he created numerous classic works, many of them thousands of pages long, with intricate plots and characterizations.

Tezuka infused nearly all his stories with what came to be known as "Tezuka humanism." Tezuka respected all people and the sanctity of life. He had an ability to look beyond the superficial actions of people and to view them

DATABOX

THE HUMAN DREAM FACTORY

TYPE OF WORK CREATED	QUANTITY
Pages drawn	150,000
Paperback titles	400
Titles of all works	500
TV animation specials	12
TV animation series	21
Experimental animations works	14
Theatrical animation films	17
Original Video Animation	8
PR animation works	5
Pilot films	13

Source: Tezuka Productions, 1996.

in their totality, to assess them in the context of their environment, history, and even (occasionally) their karma. As a result, Tezuka's heroes were not two-dimensional but complex and flawed: sometimes they did the wrong, not right, thing; sometimes they died. Conversely, Tezuka's villains often had a spark of good in them. Many of his works, like *Hi no Tori* ("Phoenix") and *Buddha*, dealt with religious and philosophical issues like the meaning of life, reincarnation, and the "one-ness" of all things. And because of the destruction he witnessed first hand in World War II, Tezuka was also a passionate believer in peace.

TEZUKA THE ANIMATOR

By the early sixties, Tezuka had become so successful that he could afford to indulge in his other passion—animation. With his own animation company, Mushi Productions, in 1963 he turned *Tetsuwan Atom* into Japan's first black-and-white television animation series; in 1965 he made *Jungle Taitei* into Japan's first color series. Both series were exported to the United States, where they were dubbed and shown on syndicated television under the titles *Astro Boy* and *Kimba, the White Lion*, respectively. Most young American fans had no idea they had originated in Japan.

Tezuka went on to make scores of other animated TV series and theatrical features, including some with adult, erotic themes, such as *Cleopatra* and *Sen'ichiya no Yoru* ("A Thousand and One Nights"). Tezuka was nominally a Buddhist, but at the time of his death his company was creating a series of animated Bible stories for the Vatican and Italian television (initial scripts had highly animistic, almost Shinto-like scenes that had to be edited out). Animation was more than a commercial venture for Tezuka, though. As he often joked, manga were his wife; animation was his mistress. The money he made from manga he often lost on animation projects, which contributed to the bankruptcy of Mushi Productions in 1973. Many of his animated films that won awards were experimental and non-commercial, such as the serious *Mori no Densetsu* ("Legend of the Forest"), with its ecological theme, and the humorous shorts *Broken Down Film* and *Jumping*, which were given wide exposure at animation screenings in the U.S.

On top of all this Tezuka was a skilled pianist and a film critic with a regular column on movies in *Kinema Junpō*, a screen magazine. And he was a national celebrity. Somehow, no matter how busy, he always seemed to find time to make an appearance at a comic- or animation-related event. He even advertised word processors on television.

REMEMBERING TEZUKA

It is easy to list Tezuka's accomplishments as an artist and creator, but what was he like as a man? I had the opportunity to get to know him quite well, and he became my mentor, encouraging and helping me considerably in my career as a writer. Over the years, I also had the honor of working as his interpreter during several trips he made to the United States and Canada. In this position I was with him nearly twenty-four hours a day for extended periods, and thus had ample opportunity to separate the man from the myth.

I was probably one of the few people, other than Tezuka's wife and closest employees, to see him without a beret. He always wore it. Berets were almost *de rigueur*

The author with Osamu Tezuka at Portopia, in Kobe City, in the summer of 1981.

for artists in early postwar Japan, and as Tezuka became more and more famous, and as he began to lose more of his hair, the beret became not only a trademark but a semi-permanent wig-like fixture on his head. It was a little vanity of his, and one of his many endearing, childlike qualities. He only took it off when he went to sleep.

Tezuka was one of the best conversationalists I ever met. He was fascinated by life and learning, and as a comic artist and an animator he was an anomaly; not only was he an intellectual, but a licensed physician (he obtained his medical degree from Osaka University's College of Medicine; his research had been on the sperm of pond snails). Tezuka thus found it easy to hold a discussion on nearly any subject with nearly anyone. And if listening is the art of being a good conversationalist, he perfected it. An information sponge, he constantly asked questions. After all, he was constantly writing three or four stories in his head, and he needed as much information as possible to keep them going. Remarkably, Tezuka not only absorbed information, but retained it. He could quote me things I had casually mentioned years earlier, almost verbatim. And his memory wasn't all aural, either. What he saw, he recorded with a near photographic

In Osamu Tezuka's manga version of **Crime and Punishment,** *first published in 1953, the increasingly paranoid and tormented murderer, Raskolnikov, tries to flee. From the English version issued by* **The Japan Times** *in 1990.*

memory. Often, these remembered scenes would be adapted later in his comics.

Tezuka had a remarkable way of communicating with people, whether they were five years old, or fifty, whether they were construction workers or intellectuals. He threw temper tantrums regularly with his staff and probably with his family, but in public he was always kind and gentle, with an engaging manner and a ready smile. He never talked down to anyone, and if words didn't work, he could always communicate by drawing a picture. In fact, he was such a pushover for fans that he was constantly abused by them. After a public talk or appearance, he was deluged with requests for autographs, and, much to the irritation of those in charge of his schedule, he would oblige, usually drawing a detailed picture of one of his characters as "a special service for the fans." Tezuka might privately grumble and complain when things didn't go right, but he could also be remarkably forgiving. Once, on the way to a film festival in Canada, when I was in charge of his schedule, I became so engrossed in a conversation with him that I didn't notice our airplane had left the gate. Tezuka took it all in stride. He was a Buddhist and a humanist at heart, well aware of the imperfections of his fellow man.

Tezuka's dynamism was legendary. In fact, given his typical schedule, it is remarkable that he lived as long as he did. Doubtless, as a physician he was able to monitor his own health. He slept only four hours a night and still had enough energy and enthusiasm during the day to wear much younger people into the ground. Tezuka did use assistants to help fill in backgrounds and details, but he relied on them far less than many of his peers in the industry. Once, when in Florida for the filming of a TV special, I watched him retreat after an exhaustingly long day to his hotel room with paper, pencils, and ink. Sure enough, early in the morning, he was up and smiling. He probably hadn't slept a wink, but his quota of pages was done—beautifully penciled and inked and ready for shipping to Japan for a final touch-up at his company before going to the printer. In his life, Tezuka is said to have drawn over 150,000 pages of manga and produced over 500 separate works.

TEZUKA AT WORK

Tezuka had such energy and enthusiasm that he tended to take on far more work than he should have, and as a result he was probably the manga artist in Japan that editors feared, or hated, the most. He often neglected deadlines until the last minute, and like many famous Japanese comic artists he came to depend on his own staff and editors to hound him; scrambling to meet the deadline became an essential part of his daily routine. Once, when visiting San Francisco, he began enjoying himself too much, so an editor was flown out from Japan to apply pressure on him. Protocol required that the editor use great tact with an older, famous artist/writer. But the deadline grew nearer and nearer, and the editor became so visibly agitated he looked as though he might hemorrhage internally. Only at the very last minute was he able to corral Tezuka, force him to retreat to his hotel room, and get him to complete the minimum number of pages required to save the magazine from disaster. Sure enough, the editor finally flew back to Tokyo with the work, cursing, but relieved.

For all his humanism and gentleness, Tezuka was an extraordinarily competitive person. Although he rarely faced serious intellectual competition in the manga world, fads in art styles changed regularly, and he constantly had to struggle to remain current. When *gekiga* ("dramatic pictures," equivalent to "graphic novels" in America) became popular among increasingly older readers, and when Tezuka's traditionally rounded, Disney-esque style fell out of favor, he began drawing more realistically. When young artists, such as the French-influenced Katsuhiro Ōtomo (author of *Akira* and other works), became the darling of manga critics in the eighties, Tezuka had a hard time hiding his jealousy, for he had a burning desire to be at the top of the popularity list in all genres for all age groups at all times. It was certainly this competitive spirit, in addition to his talents, that allowed him to so dominate the manga industry for so long.

It was thus no wonder that Tezuka's death sent shock waves through nearly everyone under fifty in Japan. Most had been raised on his comics or animation and many were still enjoying his latest creations for adults. People in their twenties had probably competed at athletic meets in elementary school to the accompaniment of the theme song to the *Astro Boy* animation series (and knew all the words by heart). And Tezuka had always seemed so superhuman and indestructible. Following Japanese medical custom, there was never any public acknowledgement of the gravity of his illness. Of course, as a physician, Tezuka himself was fully aware of what was happening to his body. But he kept up the charade to the end. When he died he was still working on several serialized manga stories, including a semibiographical work about Ludwig van Beethoven and his third adaptation of Goethe's *Faust*, which he had titled *Neo-Faust*.

IN ENGLISH

Eigoban Tsumi to Batsu ("Crime and Punishment"). Translated by Frederik L. Schodt. Tokyo: Japan Times, 1990. Based on Fyodor Dostoyevski's novel.

Adolf. Vols. 1–5. Translated by Yūji Oniki. San Francisco: Cadence Books. Volume 1, *A Tale of the Twentieth Century*, was released in 1995, followed shortly thereafter by Volume 2, *An Exile in Japan*.

A short translated sequence from the *Hō-ō* volume of *Hi no Tori* ("Phoenix") appears in Frederik L. Schodt's *Manga! Manga! The World of Japanese Comics* (Tokyo and New York: Kodansha International, 1983), and in issues 17–19 of *Mangajin* magazine.

TEZUKA OVERSEAS

Given his fame in Japan, why is Tezuka so unknown in other countries? Although his TV animation was widely shown in the United States in the sixties, Tezuka's name was rarely associated with it. Until the end of 1995, when his *Adolf* series was finally published in America, the only original Tezuka manga work to appear in English was a 1990 translation of his 1953 manga version of Dostoyevski's *Crime and Punishment*—but it was issued in Japan for students of English and it came with footnotes.

One problem with publishing some of the best Tezuka material is its length. American and European comics publishers generally balk at the idea of committing to a multivolume manga series that may be thousands of pages long. Another problem is that Tezuka's work was a subculture unto itself. Having drawn for so many years, Tezuka established a dialogue with his readers that made some of his stories seem awkward or unfamiliar to new readers not used to his conventions. His early stories relied on a kind of "star system" wherein the same characters would appear in different roles in different stories. He also had an exasperating habit of inserting gags into his stories at the most serious moments. Finally, some of his stories are rendered in a far more "cartoony" style than is common for serious stories in other countries.

In Japan, Tezuka's popularity and prestige has waxed rather than waned since his death. In 1990 the prestigious National Museum of Modern Art in Tokyo held an extravagant retrospective exhibit of his work—the first such honor granted any cartoonist. In 1994, when the city of Takarazuka opened the Osamu Tezuka Manga Museum, over 400,000 people came in the first six months. And Tezuka's manga books have sold extraordinarily well, especially in reissued deluxe editions. In 1995, his company, Tezuka Productions, estimated that around 50 million copies of his books had been sold in the seven years since his death.

Tezuka was engaged in a lifelong quest to discover the meaning of life. Quite by accident, comics and animation happened to be his medium of expression. The result was an enormous gift to postwar Japan and to an often-overlooked popular art form. He helped increase the number of readers of manga, to raise their expectations, and to set a new standard for quality. By inspiring younger artists and challenging them to surpass him, he in effect set in motion a chain reaction that continues to this day and that has made Japan the comics capital of the world. Still, when Tezuka died it was impossible not to speculate on what he could have produced with a little more time. Until the very end, his mind must have been filled with wonderful stories, just waiting to be put to paper.

Mighty Atom and Astro Boy

『鉄腕アトム』

A JAPANESE SUPERHERO

One of the major icons of Japanese popular culture is a robot. *Tetsuwan Atom*, or "Mighty Atom," was created by Osamu Tezuka as a manga character in 1951 and is today a national and international hero.

Atom evolved somewhat over the years, but in his basic form he was a little boy robot, created by a scientist whose real son was killed in a car crash. Atom eventually wound up living in a very normal family of other robots and went to a normal school with normal human children. Unlike the humans around him, however, he had a nuclear reactor for a heart, a computer brain, searchlight eyes, rockets in his feet and hands, a machine gun in his tail. He could fly through the air and smash walls with his "one hundred thousand horsepower" strength, and he could speak over sixty languages. He wasn't threatening, though. He was cute and almost cuddly, and always helped humans, frequently fighting off assorted monsters and criminals.

Unlike American superheroes who usually fought for justice, Atom fought for the ultimate goal of postwar, defeated Japan—"peace." And instead of having special "superpowers," Atom operated according to pseudoscientific principles. Tezuka, Atom's creator, was a licensed physician and for a cartoonist had an extraordinary interest in science. He wrote that he had created Atom to be a 21st-century reverse Pinocchio, a nearly perfect robot who strove to become more human and emotive and to serve as an interface between the two very different cultures of man and machine.

Although Tezuka could never have known it at the time, in Atom he also laid the groundwork for what may arguably be modern Japan's greatest contribution to world fantasy—the interactive, drivable, transforming giant mecha-robots that have altered children's play habits all over the world. Atom wasn't the first robot character in Japanese manga, and he himself wasn't drivable or transforming, but his enormous popularity familiarized Japanese children with the idea of robot-as-pal rather than robot-as-threat, and made robot characters a staple of children's fantasy worlds.

There are basically two types of robots in Japanese fantasy today: autonomous robots that operate free from human intervention and remote-controlled or human-piloted robots that allow little boys and girls to imagine they can actually "drive" their favorite robot. The drivable robots evolved mainly from works like Mitsuteru Yokoyama's giant remote-controlled *Tetsujin 28-go* ("Ironman No. 28," or "Gigantor" in the United States) in 1956, Gō Nagai's pilotable *Mazinger Z* in 1969, and Yoshiyuki Tomino's realistic exoskeletons in the 1979 blockbuster hit,

Earth is threatened by a typhoon made up of falling space station fragments. As Professor Ochanomizu despairs of finding a solution, Atom arrives! From the **Sūpā Senpū no Maki** ***("The Super Whirlwind Chapter") of Osamu Tezuka's*** **Tetsuwan Atom** ***("Mighty Atom"), 1957.***

Gundam. But as early as 1954 Tezuka had anticipated the popularity of this genre with an Atom series titled *Kasei Tanken* ("Mars Exploration"), in which he showed people inside giant robots on Mars, "driving" them.

Atom's international popularity came not through manga but animation. In 1963, Tezuka turned his Atom story into Japan's first black-and-white animated series for television, and it proved so successful that it caught the eye of America's National Broadcasting Company. NBC asked veteran animation producer Fred Ladd to turn a couple episodes of the Japanese series into pilots for the U.S. market. Retitled *Astro Boy*, these were so well received that Ladd went on to direct and supervise the production of 104 episodes for the U.S. market, rewriting many of the scripts, dubbing the dialogue with American voice talent, and creating a product that would win the hearts of young people in the English-speaking world, just as it had with young Japanese. He did an especially superb job with many of the character names. The huge-nosed Professor Ochanomizu, for example, became Dr. Packadermus J. Elefun. But names were clearly one of the easier aspects of the show to change.

"The hardest part in the production," Ladd said in an interview I did with him in 1993, "was downplaying the violence of the action, explaining and justifying it in terms American kids could understand, and rationalizing cultural differences in general. Long before any episode reached the recording studio, the English version had to pass NBC's 'standards and practices' for show content."

The year 1993 marked the thirtieth anniversary of Atom's animation debut in Japan, and it was interesting to note how popular he still was there. This can partly be explained by the heavy exposure Atom continued to receive—a new color series was broadcast on television in the eighties, and Atom himself has always been visible in toy and stationery shops. He has even been seen in national advertising campaigns for stocks and securities and telecommunications.

In the United States, where Atom/Astro Boy never received anywhere near as much attention, the robot-boy's continued popularity was even more surprising. Trendy urban gift shops retailed colorful children's masks, as well as Astro Boy T-shirts and toys. On MTV and on the radio, a popular jazz-rap group called "Digable Planets" had a hit single in which they referred to "Astro Boy" in the lyrics. Despite some copyright questions, one American firm had issued an awkwardly redrawn *Astro Boy* series of comic books, and another company had released the original dubbed animation series on video cassettes that were widely available in rental shops across the nation.

In the United States *Astro Boy* seemed to have a special "kitsch" quality, a kind of quirky, campy appeal. One suspects that this was partly due to the uniqueness of a robot fantasy character like Atom, but it was clearly more than that. Of the original *Astro Boy* series, producer Fred

Ladd said, "it succeeded for many of the same reasons *Pinocchio* succeeded and *Home Alone* succeeded—there's an empowered youngster outperforming the adult bad guys. Also, in the 1960s, the program was unique on TV; there was nothing else like it on the air. Tezuka was a true visionary, who correctly perceived that robots would displace many human beings in our society and that this would lead to a strained relationship between man and robot. And the man had, and understood, humor. Today, the ten year olds who watched *Astro Boy* thirty years ago are forty year olds with their own ten-year-old children. For them the program has dear, nostalgia values. They watch the videos together, and each generation derives its own values out of the experience."

The Three Adolfs

『アドルフに告ぐ』

A DIFFERENT VIEW OF WORLD WAR II

I once knew a half-German young Japanese man in Los Angeles who was from the city of Kobe. He spoke in the Kansai dialect of the Kobe-Osaka region, and the story, as I recall, was that his mother, a German Jew, had been married to an officer in the German army, but when the Nazis came to power she had had to flee both her country and her husband. Arriving in Shanghai, as a surprising number of Jewish refugees did, she met and married a Japanese army officer and then later moved to Japan, where my friend was born.

Whenever I read Tezuka's classic, *Adorufu ni Tsugu* ("Tell Adolf," but titled simply "Adolf" in the English version), I think of my friend. And I think of how World War II twisted people's fates in strange and mysterious ways all over the world.

Adolf, serialized in the newsmagazine *Shūkan Bunshun* from 1983 to 1985, is widely regarded as one of Tezuka's finest works. Nearly 1,300 pages long and the recipient of the prestigious Kōdansha Manga Award in 1986, it was one of the first manga to be sold in the litera-

Young Adolf Kaufmann is congratulated by the Führer, while Goebbels and other Nazi officials look on. From* Adorufu ni Tsugu *("Tell Adolf").

ture—not the manga section—of bookstores when it was compiled into four deluxe hardcover volumes. It is drawn in a very "realistic" style for Tezuka, and it is a story clearly close to his own heart, written not for children, but adults. Unlike most of his manga stories, it was serialized in ten-page segments, which forced him to employ more conventional page layouts, thus making it easier for non-Japanese to read.

Adolf is the story of three "Adolfs": Adolf Kaufmann, born in Kobe of a German consular official and his Japanese wife; Adolf Kamille, the son of a Jewish-German refugee couple who run a bakery in Kobe; and Adolf Hitler himself. It spans several decades and continents, involves dozens of characters, and weaves history and fiction together into a rip-roaring adventure with the richness and sophistication of a Russian novel.

The tale is told from the viewpoint of Sōhei Tōge, a

former marathon runner turned newspaper reporter who is sent from Japan to cover the 1936 Berlin Olympics. Tōge receives a call from his younger brother, who has been studying as an exchange student at a German university but is secretly involved with the Communist underground. His brother wants to give him some terribly important papers that he says could cause the collapse of Hitler and the Nazis. But when Tōge goes to meet him, he finds his brother murdered and the papers gone. Thus Tōge begins a search for the missing papers, which, as we learn later, his brother had managed to send to someone in Kobe. The Gestapo, alas, are also on the trail of the papers.

Meanwhile, in Kobe, young Adolf Kamille and Adolf Kaufmann are best friends. Adolf Kamille is street smart and speaks fluent Kobe dialect, and looks after his younger pal, who idolizes him. But Adolf Kaufmann's father, a dedicated Nazi, forbids his son to play with his Jewish friend and instead decides to send him against his will to Germany, to the Adolf Hitler school to be indoctrinated in Nazi ideology. Before this happens, however, both Adolf Kamille and Adolf Kaufmann learn the secret of the missing papers—documents that prove Adolf Hitler is really part Jewish.

From this point on the story explodes into a complex mix of plots and subplots, mysterious murders, intrigues, and strange twists of fate that involve the main characters and the missing papers. The war engulfs continents and tears apart everyone's life. Adolf Kaufmann grows up to become a brainwashed member of the S.S. and the Gestapo, favored by Hitler himself, but his character becomes more and more distorted by internal conflicts over his loyalty to his friend in Kobe and his confusion over his own half-Japanese, non-Aryan identity. When Adolf Kamille's father is sent from Kobe to help rescue some Jewish refugees stranded in Lithuania, he is caught by the Nazis, and Adolf Kaufmann is forced to execute him. By the time Adolf Kaufmann himself is sent to Japan toward the end of the war to find and destroy anyone who knows about the missing documents, his old affection for Adolf Kamille has turned to hatred.

Eventually Adolf Hitler meets his end in his Berlin bunker, and Germany and Japan are defeated, but for the remaining two Adolfs the story doesn't end there. Adolf Kamille emigrates to Israel and becomes a member of the Israeli military. Adolf Kaufmann works for the PLO and the Black September organization. In the end, Adolf Kamille winds up killing his childhood friend.

Although *Adolf* is a work of fiction, it incorporates many well-known and not-so-well-known aspects of actual history. To many non-Japanese readers, *Adolf* will provide a perspective on World War II that is unusual and indeed provocative. The underground resistance in wartime Japan is introduced, for example, as is the famous Sorge spy incident, when a German journalist was tried and executed as a Soviet agent. Time lines are included as an aid to the readers. Ultimately, however, *Adolf* is not merely a Japanese view of what was a truly global war; it is Osamu Tezuka's.

Tezuka was bitterly opposed to war in all forms. As a teenager during World War II he was heavily indoctrinated in nationalistic propaganda. Too young to be drafted, he was mobilized to work in factories to support the war effort. Yet he doodled constantly, and he was eminently unsuited to a militaristic environment and the spartan discipline it required. Worse yet, he was exposed to some of the worst fire-bombings of World War II, when the city of Osaka (and much of its population) was torched by American bombers. From this Tezuka developed a permanent loathing of militarism (that he was once struck by an inebriated U.S. soldier during the Occupation only reinforced his beliefs). And he became a convinced internationalist. Before his death he wrote that one of his favorite themes was the concept of "justice" and how justice is usually interpreted in a way that ultimately leads to the "egotism" of the state. In *Adolf*, he says, he was finally able to develop this theme the way he wanted.

To those unfamiliar with Japanese history, one of the central constructs of the *Adolf* story—that a Jewish boy and a half-Japanese, half-German boy lived near each other in the city of Kobe before World War II and were pals—may seem forced. But it is an entirely plausible scenario, and easy to imagine how Tezuka might have conceived it. As a youth, Tezuka lived only a short distance from the port city of Kobe, which has long had a diverse population of foreign residents. During World War II, moreover, although Japan was one of the Axis powers it never fully adopted the anti-Semitic ideology of its Nazi German ally. In fact, Japanese nationals in Lithuania and Shanghai assisted and gave shelter to a fairly large number of Jewish refugees. There were thus both Germans and Jews living in the Kobe area at the same time, some of whom Tezuka certainly knew or knew about.

Tezuka was primarily interested in telling a good story, but by making *Adolf* relatively historical and realistic, he also created an important counterpoint to one of the oddest trends in modern Japan publishing. Despite Japan's lack of overt anti-Semitism, and indeed, of permanent Jewish residents, in recent years books with bizarre, fantastic theories about Jews have been extremely popular. With subject matter ranging from recycled American and European anti-Semitic tracts, to claims that Jews are a superior race and (guess what?) that Japanese—not Europeans—are actually the true Jews, such books may really be a metaphor-mirror of Japan's often twisted relationship with all foreigners; either way, one would hope that their readers are also exposed to something like *Adolf*.

Although Tezuka drew *Adolf* in what was for him a very sober, realistic style, his insertion of occasional gags and sometimes "cartoony" drawings may nonetheless puzzle some readers. Yet when the story is read in its entirety, it becomes clear that Tezuka has done nothing less than use the manga medium to create a complex Dostoyevskian novel with a truly global perspective.

In the spring of 1993 *Adolf* was produced in Japan as an acclaimed three-hour radio drama broadcast on TBS radio. At the end of 1995 it became the first of Tezuka's manga stories to be published in the United States.

Princess Knight and Takarazuka

『リボンの騎士』

THE ROOTS OF GIRLS' MANGA

When I first read Osamu Tezuka's *Ribon no Kishi*, I finally realized where many of the elements of girl's manga—the emphasis on bug eyes, gender-bending plots, and romanticized foreign settings—came from. But it was not until I visited the city of Takarazuka and watched a performance of the local theater group that I finally understood the source of much of Tezuka's inspiration.

Ribon no Kishi literally means "A Knight in Ribbons" yet it is often cleverly translated as "Princess Knight" to preserve the androgynous nuance of the Japanese. Tezuka first serialized it from 1953 to 1956 in the girls' magazine *Shōjo Club*. In so doing he captivated girl readers with his new "story comic" format that emphasized narrative structure and cinematic techniques, just as he had early captivated boys. *Princess Knight* is widely regarded as the progenitor of the modern girls' manga format; it opened the door first for other male artists to draw girls' story manga and then for women artists to take over the genre and develop it to its enormous size today.

Princess Knight stars a girl named Sapphire, who—through an error on the part of the deities and a mischievous cherub named Tink—is born into a European royal family that needs a male heir. She is thus raised as a male, but evil forces in the kingdom constantly try to expose her female identity and disqualify her for the throne. After numerous swordfights and adventures, she grows quite befuddled as to her true gender. So Tink finally arranges for her to become a "total woman" and finds her the perfect partner—a Prince Charming named, coincidentally, Franz Charming.

It's a sweet story with romance and adventure and a hodgepodge of elements from medieval pageantry, Christianity, and Greek mythology—and it thrilled the hearts of young girls in Japan at the time. With good reason, it also has elements reminiscent of a musical revue—the well-known Takarazuka Revue.

During a duel, the cherub Tink fires a feminine arrow into Princess Knight, weakening her temporarily. From* Ribon no Kishi *("Princess Knight") in Kōdansha's collected works of Osamu Tezuka, 1977, based on the* Nakayoshi *edition.

Tezuka was born in Japan's second-largest city, Osaka, but he spent his most formative years between five and twenty-four in the town of Takarazuka, which lies between Osaka and Kobe. Straddling the Mukogawa River between two forested mountain ranges, Takarazuka is best known today for its hot springs, its amusement park, and—above all—the revue company that bears its name. Even before World War II, it was a uniquely modern and cosmopolitan area.

The Takarazuka Revue was founded in 1914 by Ishizō Kobayashi, a railway magnate with a passion for theater. After he saw Western-style opera for the first time in Tokyo he decided to combine it with traditional Japanese plays. What resulted is today a charming sort of cultural goulash that upends many of the assumptions Westerners have about theater and about Japan.

Some Takarazuka performances have traditional Japanese themes, but more often they are modern and "Western"; in the past the group has successfully staged Japanese adaptations of Broadway musicals such as *Oklahoma* or *Show Boat*. Takarazuka is known for its elaborate stage productions reminiscent of Paris, Broadway, or even 1930s MGM-style lavish musical films. More distinctive, however, is that—unlike traditional Japanese Kabuki and Noh theater, which use only male actors—Takarazuka is entirely female, with young women specially chosen and trained to play the parts of men. There is nothing racy about the performances; whether playing males or females, the young single women present a perfect picture of innocence and are trained for years in an almost militaristic environment under the motto "Modesty, Fairness, and Grace." Fans are also almost all women, and the best male-impersonator-actors have a fanatical following. To the Westerner accustomed to boxing people into categories of "gay" and "straight," Takarazuka thus appears to be a lavish lesbian-gay fantasy world, but it is not; it is merely modern Japan. Like today's girls' manga, however, the productions offer an exaggerated female view of a male world and, when foreign in theme, an exaggerated Japanese view of the outside world. And they offer girls in a still largely male-oriented society the chance to vicariously fulfill their dreams.

Tezuka's mother was a fan of the Takarazuka Revue, so from early childhood he regularly attended performances with her and also became a fan. He had Takarazuka stars among his neighbors, and after the war he drew cartoons for several Takarazuka Revue fan publications. Takarazuka stimulated in Tezuka an early interest in theater, and in late 1946, while a medical student, he joined a college drama group. A 1947 photograph of a production of Fyodor Dostoyevski's *Crime and Punishment* shows Tezuka standing with the cast on the set; its stairway-like construction looks extraordinarily similar to scenes he later drew in his 1953 manga version of the

Poster from the 1994 Takarazuka production of Osamu Tezuka's* Black Jack *and* Hi no Tori *("Phoenix").

same classic. Although Tezuka later left the drama group, his exposure both to it and Takarazuka clearly influenced the way he approached storytelling (incorporating a wide variety of sources, including mythology and literature), designed scenery, and later developed a "star" system by which his manga characters functioned as a repertory group, playing different roles in different stories. As he wrote in an afterword to a 1970s version of *Princess Knight*, "the works I have created for girls, especially, often reflect a deep nostalgia for Takarazuka."

Princess Knight became so successful that in addition to inspiring other girls' manga in the same format it was also adapted as a girl's ballet, a radio dramatization (in 1956), and a successful animated television series (in 1967). Tezuka, as he did occasionally with his stories, also later redrew parts of the manga to modernize it. Haruyuki Nakano, author of the authoritative *Tezuka Osamu no Takarazuka* ("Osamu Tezuka's Takarazuka"), notes that *Princess Knight* appeared in four different publications over a period of a quarter-century, changing slightly each time. Tezuka retained the scenario, but as he developed a more film-influenced art style he gradually reduced many Takarazuka-style details such as stage-like crowd scenes.

Princess Knight later provided the storytelling foundation for the most famous girls' manga of all, Riyoko

Ikeda's *Versailles no Bara* ("The Rose of Versailles"), a tale of a young woman raised as a man in the family of the captain of Marie Antoinette's palace guard. With its blurred gender roles, fancy uniforms, and romantic European setting, *Berubara*, as the work is affectionately known in Japan today, fit so well in the Takarazuka scheme of things that in 1974 it became one of the theater group's most successful productions ever.

Princess Knight has not yet been performed by the Takarazuka Revue, but when I visited the theater in the spring of 1994, it gave Tezuka the ultimate tribute and staged two of his works—*Black Jack* and *Phoenix*. Tezuka, were he still alive, would undoubtedly have been thrilled. Certainly, his spirit was watching. Only a short stroll from the theater, the city of Takarazuka has proudly erected the Osamu Tezuka Manga Museum.

Black Jack

『ブラックジャック』

A PHYSICIAN'S MANGA

Modern medicine is sometimes referred to in Japan as *seiyō igaku*, or "Western medicine," to distinguish it from more traditional Japanese and Chinese styles of healing. It was embraced in the mid-19th century when Japan's long isolation from the rest of the world ended, and it quickly shoved the older styles of healing aside. Japanese were particularly dazzled by the advances in anatomy and surgery that the more "scientific" Western medicine had achieved. Since Tezuka was a licensed physician in the Western tradition, he naturally created many manga with medical themes, and even several with doctor heroes. One of his most beloved manga in Japan—*Black Jack*—stars an unlicensed surgeon who is a genius with a scalpel.

Black Jack was serialized in the boys' weekly manga magazine *Shōnen Champion* from January 1973 to September 1978 for a total of nearly 4,000 pages. Unlike most of Tezuka's serialized stories, each twenty- to twenty-four-page episode is a complete story.

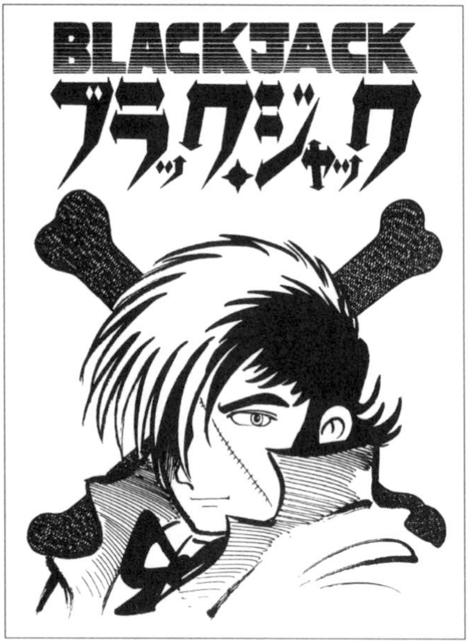

©1975 TEZUKA PRODUCTIONS / AKITA SHOTEN

***Frontispiece illustration to the* Shōnen Champion Comics *paperback edition of Osamu Tezuka's* Black Jack.**

Black Jack, the hero, is mysterious and melodramatic. He dresses in a striking black cape and wears a ribbon bow tie. His hair is part white and part black, and a large shock of it covers half of his face. The exposed other half is crisscrossed by a huge scar; some patches of skin are darker than others. Readers are given little information about his past, but in episode 71 ("In Search of a Friend") we learn that Black Jack was horribly burned and disfigured as a little boy, and saved only when a half-Japanese, half-black friend volunteered for a skin graft. In gratitude, Black Jack resolved to become a surgeon, make lots of money, and somehow repay his pal. In a world of discrimination against people of different colors, he wears his two-tone, scarred face as a badge of pride.

As Tezuka later wrote in a foreword to the *Sunday Comics* paperback edition of his stories:

> Not many manga have doctors for heroes. But the work of doctors is extremely important, for doctors hold people's lives in their hands. I felt an infinite number of dramatic stories could be created around such a doctor character. A "black jack" is actually a metal (once leather) cup, but it also signifies the flag

of pirates—the skull and crossbones. Because the hero of this story slashes away with his scalpel, I've made him into a pirate-like figure. There is no connection to the card game of the same name.

Black Jack lives in a house on top of a lonely windswept hill somewhere in Japan. Unlicensed, and treated like a pariah by the medical establishment, he charges enormous fees for his services, but because of his reputation he is also the doctor people with the most difficult problems come to see. His cold, almost mercenary appearance hides a compassionate heart, for at times he discounts his fees dramatically and may even work for free.

There is a strong moral theme and a fablelike quality to many of the *Black Jack* episodes. Episode 52, "The Chosen Face," reveals more of Black Jack's secrets. His long-missing lout of a father (who had abandoned his wife and run off to Macao with a younger woman when Black Jack was a child) appears, and there is no love lost between him and his son. The father's new wife, however, has contracted leprosy and developed a gross deformity of the face, so he begs Black Jack to perform plastic surgery on her and turn her into "the most beautiful woman in the world." After being assured of a small fortune if he succeeds, Black Jack gets out his scalpel and goes to work. When the bandages are finally removed from the poor woman, she is truly beautiful—the spitting image of Black Jack's mother.

It would be unthinkable in an American comic book for children to have scenes of operations as graphic as those depicted in *Black Jack*. Blood flies. People die. Naked bodies and internal organs are in full view. Like the famous author-neurologist Oliver Sacks, Tezuka often indulges his curiosity by making odd illnesses the centerpiece of his stories; Black Jack cures ectopic pregnancies and hydrocephalus and separates Siamese twins. He's a two-fisted sort of doctor, though, so when he encounters a hysterical, hypochondriac patient who's faking an illness, he's not above slapping the patient around. In another episode, when he's attacked by evil gangster types, he quickly dispatches them with scalpels thrown like ninja knives.

Black Jack performs some extraordinarily difficult open-heart surgery. From Osamu Tezuka's Black Jack.

Although *Black Jack* was originally serialized in a weekly manga magazine for boys, it has a surprising number of female fans. One reason may be the mascot-character Pinoko, who provides the comic relief and "cuteness" that are prerequisites for so many Japanese children's comics. Pinoko (à la Pinocchio) was created by Black Jack himself. In episode 10, when operating on a woman with a huge cyst he discovers that the growth contains remnants of an old unborn and incomplete identical twin. After removing the parts, Black Jack reassembles them in a synthetic skin body to produce Pinoko. Pinoko, who always looks like a three- or four-year-old girl, becomes a surrogate "daughter" and "wife" for Black Jack, caring for him, helping him in surgery, and cheering him up. She can't pronounce r's or d's, and talks like the Elmer Fudd character in *Bugs Bunny*. She frequently does things wrong and throws fits, but she is always devoted to Black Jack.

Black Jack was reportedly one of Tezuka's favorite works.. It is certainly one of his most representative. It bridges his early "cartoony" years with his later, more realistic styles, and it employs his famous "star system" of having familiar characters from his other manga appear in different roles. It incorporates comedy, visual gags, pathos, tragedy, and adventure, but just before it becomes a complete hodgepodge, it is saved by Tezuka's underlying intellectual curiosity and his relentless pursuit of higher philosophical issues—in a comic designed for children, he even explores the ethical dilemma of mercy killings.

Tezuka went on to create other manga with physician protagonists, including a much more serious historical series in 1981 for an older audience, titled *Hidamari no Ki* ("A Tree in the Sun"), about his great-grandfather, one of the first Western-style physicians in Japan. But *Black Jack* was never surpassed in popularity. Since Tezuka's death it has been made into a theatrical feature and Original Video Animation (OVA), attracted a new generation of fans, and been rediscovered by former readers. It is even sold as audio cassettes. The publisher, Akita Shōten, began reissuing a smaller, deluxe paperback edition of *Black Jack* in 1993, and by mid-1995 thirteen volumes had reportedly sold over 9 million copies.

Phoenix

『火の鳥』

ALL IN A LIFE'S WORK

I first encountered Tezuka's *Phoenix* when I was in university in Japan. I could tell it was something very special just by the way a fellow student gave me a volume of it to read. At the time, adults weren't reading manga the way they do today, but to university students manga were already an important form of expression, fulfilling much the same role rock and roll did in the American counter-culture in the sixties and seventies. Among those in the know about manga, *Phoenix* was a universal favorite, and it remains so today.

Of all the stories that Tezuka created in his lifetime, *Phoenix* is the only one he always referred to as his *raifu waaku*, or his "life work." He began drawing it in 1954, and he was still drawing it thirty-five years later when he died, in 1989.

In *Phoenix*, more than any other work, Tezuka experiments with comics as a medium of expression and tries to examine the meaning of life. He obviously needed a great deal of creative room, so his story takes up a vast amount of physical and temporal space. Although referred to as a single work, *Phoenix* is actually twelve separate stories, each one independent yet linked to the rest, with the titles *Dawn*, *Future*, *Yamato*, *Universe*, *Hō-ō*, *Resurrection*, *Robe of Feathers*, *Nostalgia*, *Civil War*, *Life*, *Strange Beings*, and *Sun*. They feature men, women, other life forms, and robots, and they are set in this world and in outer space, in both the past and the future. The overall tale jumps from the future to the past, and vice-versa, and sometimes it slowly seems to be converging on the present. Often, through a form of reincarnation, similar characters appear in different times in different stories, and only the reader is aware of their former (or future) existences.

What links all the eras and characters together is mankind's foolish quest for some sort of immortality, as symbolized by the pursuit of the semi-mythical phoenix. Immortality can supposedly be obtained by catching the bird and drinking its blood, but the bird only reveals itself rarely. The phoenix is a supernatural force, an immortal observer, an occasional protector of mankind and life in the universe, and the main unifying element in the construct of Tezuka's long saga.

In all, *Phoenix* is over 3,000 pages long. It is sold in a variety of formats, the most common being ten paperback or deluxe hardback volumes. Over the years the story went through nearly as many incarnations, editions, and different publishers as the characters in the story. Sometimes Tezuka had to stop drawing *Phoenix* for years at a time. Sometimes he had to change the magazine in which it was being serialized, and the style and readership of the new magazine affected the style of his work. But he always returned to it. The story had its ups and downs, yet it became his most intellectually challenging work.

Although Tezuka began drawing *Phoenix* in 1954 for the boys' monthly *Manga Shōnen*, he did not immerse himself in it until 1967. In 1956 and 1957 he serialized a version of the story in the girls' monthly *Shōjo Club*, and this version was quite different from the later tale, for it was set in ancient Egypt, Greece, and Rome, and it was basically a romance. Tezuka, writing in 1980, blamed what he called the "sappiness" of this version on the fact that at the time he had been watching a lot of American "spectacle" films set in Greece and Egypt and had just finished work on "Princess Knight."

The best part of *Phoenix* was created between 1967 and 1972, in the legendary, and now defunct, monthly manga magazine *COM*. *COM* was issued by Tezuka's own company, Mushi Productions, and it was designed to provide him and other artists a forum to create more experimental, less commercial manga. *COM* obviously gave Tezuka free rein, but this was also a period when he was making a transition from manga for children to more adult, sophisticated themes for a more mature audience. In *COM*, he serialized the sections *Dawn*, *Future*, *Yamato*, *Universe*, *Hō-ō*, and *Resurrection*. From 1976 to 1980 he serialized *Robe of Feathers*, *Nostalgia*, *Civil War*, *Life*, and *Strange Beings* in the boys' monthly, *Manga Shōnen*, and from 1986 to 1988 he serialized *Sun* in *Yasei no Jidai* ("Age of Wildness"), a non-manga magazine for adult males.

RESURRECTION

Two of the stories—my personal favorites—give a glimpse of the direction Tezuka was taking the "story comic." The first is *Resurrection*, which was serialized between 1970 and 1972. Set in the far future, *Resurrection* is about a young man named Leona who falls from his air-car one day and is killed on impact when he hits the ground. Modern medical technology restores him with prosthetic parts and a partially artificial brain, but when he regains consciousness there is something

Leona begs his doctor to turn him into a robot. From the Resurrection *volume of Osamu Tezuka's* Hi no Tori *("Phoenix").*

wrong—the world looks normal to him, but people appear as inorganic forms. Then one day, suffering from terrible loneliness, he spots a beautiful, normal-looking young woman and falls desperately in love with her—only to be told later that she is really a very inorganic, non-android, metal-skinned robot named Chihiro. Leona thus begins a quest to become a true robot.

The story shifts backward and forward in time, from earth to outer space and back again, and Leona eventually gets his wish. His mind, or "soul," is combined with that of Chihiro into a clumsy new robot form called Robita, and his memory of his former identity gradually fades. Robita, however, becomes an extremely popular robot because of its erratic, humanlike qualities, and is mass produced by the millions. When some of the robots are falsely accused of causing the death of a child and sentenced to be melted down, all the Robitas commit mass suicide, saying, "All of us are one, and one of us is all; if one of us is killed, all of us will die." One Robita survives, however, on a moon colony. It recalls a faint memory of having been human, declares itself so, and kills its master to prove it. Hundreds of years later, when a complicated character named Saruta (who appears in several reincarnations in *Phoenix*) visits the moon, he discovers the Robita lying on its exposed surface, having cut off its power by itself in a humanlike gesture of suicide. The revived robot and Saruta, both outcasts from human society, bond together and take off into outer space. . . .

In *Resurrection* Tezuka still draws in his cartoony style and uses plenty of visual gags, but the story is so compelling one is quickly drawn into it. Stylistically, the story is notable for the way Tezuka experiments heavily with panel breakdowns and page designs to create a very artistic layout.

HŌŌ

Hō-ō, the name of the section that was serialized from 1969 to 1970 is another, older word for *Phoenix*, but in English the story would be better titled "Karma." In terms of quality and theme, I believe it best represents the entire *Phoenix* series.

Hō-ō is set in the 8th century, when Japan was still being consolidated as a nation-state. It stars two men: Gao (an incarnation of Saruta from *Resurrection*) and Akanemaru. Gao, crippled as a child, lacks an eye and an arm and later develops a hideously deformed nose. After being persecuted by his fellow villagers, he develops a violent, cruel streak and becomes a mass murderer. But in occasional acts of compassion, such as when he spares a ladybug from being crushed, he exhibits the potential for redemption. Akanemaru is everything Gao is not. He is healthy, handsome, and a gifted woodcarver. But one day he accidentally runs into Gao, who cruelly stabs him in the right arm, rendering him a semi-cripple, too.

The two men's paths then diverge, but their destinies are inextricably linked. Gao continues in his murderous ways, until he meets a priest who inspires him to enter the priesthood. Ironically, he discovers that he, too, has an enormous talent for carving and sculpting, despite his handicap. Akanemaru also meets up with a priest, who helps him recover and encourages him to continue carving with his one good arm. But rather than pursuing a purely spiritual path, Akanemaru becomes wrapped up in the religious politics of the time, and in his search for fame and fortune he begins to lose his artistic soul.

After many twists of plot, and twists of fate, when the Tōdaiji temple is being built in Nara, Gao and Akanemaru are paired in a competition to see who can create the best gargoyle tiles for the building's roof. Gao's creation, it turns out, is far more powerful and superior to Akanemaru's. But when Akanemaru recognizes his competitor as his assailant from years ago. he exposes him as a former mass murderer. Gao thus not only loses the competition; he has his other arm hacked off in punishment and is banished to wander the wilderness. Not all goes well for Akanemaru, however. His spiritual hypocrisy is exposed, and he dies during a fire that later sweeps part of Tōdaiji temple. Gao, we see, is the greater artist. And through his suffering and dedication, he has also become a more enlightened being.

Like the other volumes in *Phoenix*, *Hō-ō* is a story of birth, death, and the struggle to survive, and it inter-

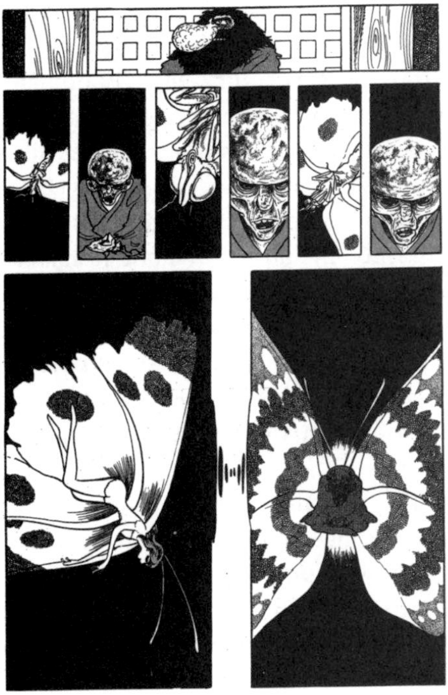

Upon the self-mummification death of his teacher, Gao realizes the Buddhahood of all living things. From the* Karma *volume of Osamu Tezuka's* Hi no Tori *("Phoenix").

weaves key Buddhist concepts of karma and transmigration of the soul. But it also incorporates a great deal of Japanese history from the 8th century, when Buddhism was a religion as well as a tool for unifying Japan. The political rivalry and scheming of historical figures like Kibi no Makibi and Lord Tachibana is vividly portrayed.

In the late seventies, some friends and I translated several volumes of *Phoenix*, including *Hō-ō* and *Resurrection*, into English. But commercial considerations and readers' tastes have prevented them from being released in English-speaking countries, except for a small portion of *Hō-ō*, which appeared in *Manga! Manga! The World of Japanese Comics* and also (with a different translation) in *Mangajin*.

As comics culture in the United States slowly changes to become more like that of Japan, and as the audience for manga grows, someday entire volumes of the *Phoenix* will certainly be published in English. But we will never know exactly how Tezuka planned to resolve his huge story. For years, I believed that Tezuka planned to make his saga slowly converge on the present from both the future and the past, and even that he might have an ending secretly created, waiting in a safe somewhere to be revealed posthumously. Alas, when he died in 1989, I learned this was only my overly romantic imagination at work. Yet for a story about life, karma, and rebirth, perhaps it is fitting that there is no ending to *Phoenix*.

Jungle Emperor

『ジャングル大帝』

A TALE OF TWO LIONS

If Osamu Tezuka had been alive in the summer of 1994 he would have been wickedly amused. Just as Disney's latest animated feature *The Lion King* was being heralded as a critical and box-office success in America, rumor exploded in the U.S. manga and anime fan community and on the Internet that Disney animators had relied

Scene from Osamu Tezuka's* Jungaru Taitei *("Jungle Emperor").

upon—perhaps even plagiarized—a television animation series made by Tezuka in the 1960s known as *Kimba, the White Lion*, and the manga on which it is based.

The similarities were striking. Both *The Lion King* and *Kimba, the White Lion* are coming-of-age tales set in Africa starring young lions—"Simba" in the case of *The Lion King* and "Kimba" in the English version of Tezuka's series—who have to regain their thrones after their fathers have been killed. In both works the protagonist lions are aided by comical and hysterical birds (a hornbill in *Lion King* and a parrot in *Kimba*) that act as messengers and by a wise and elderly baboon-like mentor. In both films the heroes have to confront and defeat an evil usurper lion with a scar over the left eye, who is supported by a band of comical hyena henchmen. Furthermore, in both films there are remarkably similar scenes of lions perched on jutting outcrops of rock, and—most suspicious of all—scenes of young lions looking up at either the clouds or the starry sky and seeing images of their beloved parents.

When Charles Burress, a reporter for the *San Francisco Chronicle* wrote an article on July 11, 1994, titled "Uproar Over 'The Lion King,'" the story broke into the mainstream U.S. media, generating considerable coverage in major newspapers and on national television. The official Disney company response, as first reported in the *Chronicle* on July 14, was that *The Lion King* was an original work, and that none of the people involved in creating *The Lion King* "were aware of *Kimba* or Tezuka."

In Japan, understandably, the story was even bigger news, and Disney's response was like oil tossed on a fire of already inflamed national passions and wounded pride. An editorial in the prestigious *Asahi* newspaper on August 27 took the form of a "letter" to the late Walt Disney in heaven, appealing to his sense of justice. Led by manga artist Machiko Satonaka, a protest petition was signed by hundreds of Japanese fans and prominent manga artists and delivered to the Disney distribution company on Earth. In both America and Japan, emotions were exacerbated by the fact that the Disney company has often taken extremely hard-line legal positions toward what it views as infringements of its copyrights. Since Japanese have often been accused of being copycats by Americans, there was also a delicious irony in the idea that the Disney company might have copied the work of Tezuka, who is often called the "Walt Disney of Japan."

I was quoted in the July 14 edition of *USA Today* as saying that the Disney assertion was "preposterous." I said this not only because of the obvious similarities in the works, but because I knew how the animation industry operates. It takes hundreds of people to make a feature-length animation, and many of Disney's animators certainly grew up watching Tezuka's work. I wasn't the only one to make this observation. As animation historian Fred Patten would document in a 1995 report titled "Simba vs. Kimba: Parallels between *Kimba, the White Lion* and *The Lion King*," the *Kimba* animated series was syndicated by NBC in 1966 and shown widely throughout

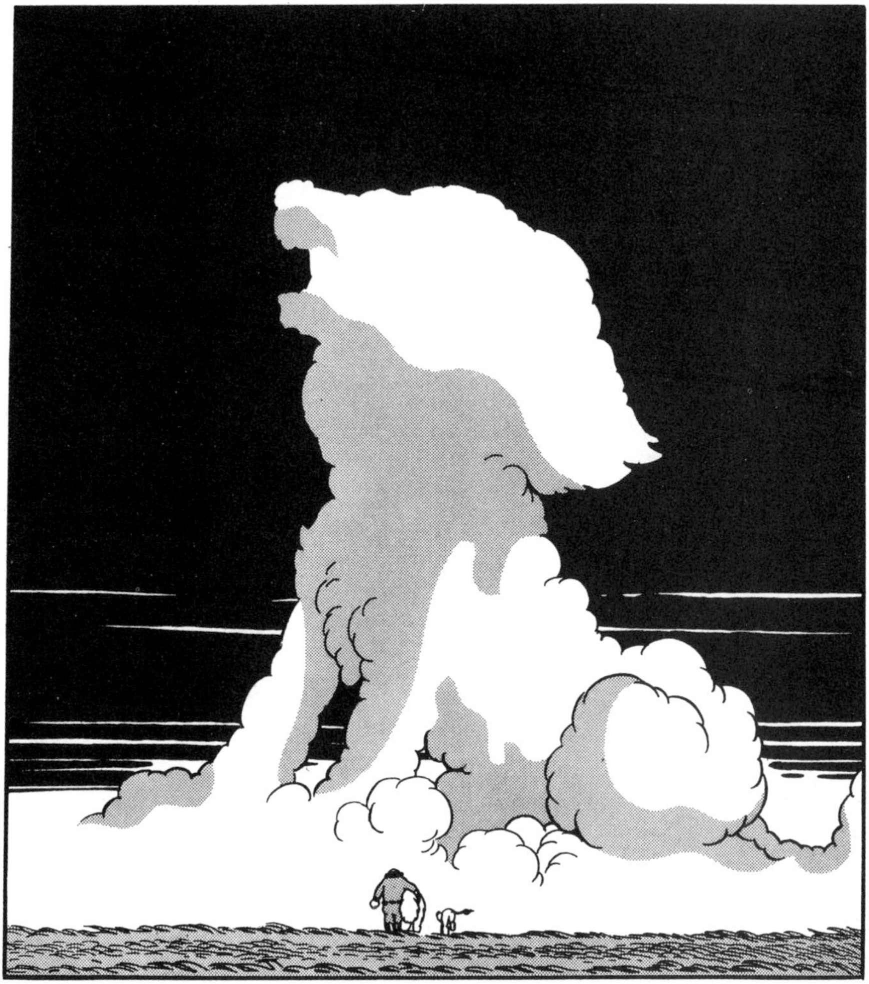

©1977 TEZUKA PRODUCTIONS / KŌDANSHA

The lion in the clouds. From Osamu Tezuka's **Jangaru Taitei** ***("Jungle Emperor").***

the United States until the late 1970s. Furthermore, the nature of animation is such that artists rely heavily on any visual reference materials they can get their hands on, especially when trying to depict the movements of animals such as lions. It would be hard to imagine that they did *not* refer to documentaries of lions, and—especially since it was one of the few animation films with a lion star—to Tezuka's *Kimba, the White Lion*.

Moreover, although Tezuka was virtually unknown in most circles in the United States, this was certainly not true in the animation industry. In the late 1980s and early 1990s, Tezuka's short experimental films, *Broken Down Film* and *Jumping*, were widely shown at animation festivals around the U.S. Tezuka had also won awards in both the U.S. animation and comics industries. And because of Disney's huge presence in Japan (merchandise, Tokyo Disneyland), Disney company higher-ups regularly visit Tokyo, where Tezuka's legacy and his lion characters are impossible to ignore. The giant Seibu Corporation, which owns train lines and buses and one of Japan's most popular baseball teams (the Seibu Lions), licenses one of Tezuka's lions and plasters its image on baseball caps and advertisements throughout Japan.

Tezuka visited the United States regularly while he was alive. I personally accompanied him in the 1980s to Disney World in Florida, to the Disney animation studios in Burbank, California, and to the house of Disney animation luminary Ward Kimball. In 1964, at the New York World's Fair, Tezuka had even met Walt Disney, whom he considered his idol. As the story Tezuka loved to recount goes, he spotted Mr. Disney, ran up to him excitedly like an ordinary fan and introduced himself. To Tezuka's never-ending delight, Mr. Disney reportedly said that he was well aware of Tezuka and *Astro Boy*, and someday "hoped to make something like it."

How the late Walt Disney would have handled the 1994 "Kimba vs. Simba" dispute is anyone's guess, but one suspects he might have been more sensitive to the underlying emotions than was his company. When the controversy first erupted, opinion in the fan community was highly polarized between Disney loyalists who rejected outright any resemblance between the two films, and Japanimation fans who overemphasized the resemblance and hoped Tezuka Productions would "stick it to Disney." Lost in the heated exchange of charges and countercharges was the fact that homages and references to other works are quite common in the animation industry. Moreover, if one accepts that Disney company animators who worked on *The Lion King* referred to Tezuka's creation and that the similarities in concept, character designs, and certain specific situations are more than coincidence, it must also be noted that Tezuka's *Kimba* and Disney's *The Lion King* also have fundamental differences, especially in their storylines.

Kimba, the White Lion is an English remake of the 1965 Japanese animated series *Jungle Taitei*, or "Jungle Emperor," which is in turn based on an over-530-page manga of the same name that Tezuka serialized between 1950 and 1954 in the monthly boys' *Manga Shōnen*. Although humans never appear in Disney's *The Lion King*, the original *Jungle Emperor* manga is a tale of three generations of lions who fight to protect the animal kingdom from humans. Leo, (who became Kimba in the English animation) is raised by humans and at one point wears pants. He learns human speech and tries to organize and civilize the animal kingdom to compete with humans. In a gripping finale, Leo dramatically sacrifices himself to save a dear human friend. As Tezuka wrote in an afterword to a 1977 edition, all in all there were eight book editions of the manga published, and for each edition there were considerable changes made to target audiences of different ages and to cater to reader expectations in different eras. Further changes were made for the animation, and for the English version of it.

Jungle Emperor became one of Japan's most beloved manga and animated works, but in both formats it displays Tezuka's weakness—an excessive desire to please his fans and to satisfy his own intellectual curiosity, the result occasionally verging on a narrative goulash. The printed manga story has gags, comedy, tragedy, allusions to ancient tectonic plates and "supercontinents," and exotic medical conditions. Since the young Tezuka was a great fan of American animation, his animals look like Disney animals. His depictions of African natives, moreover, drew upon images from Tarzan movies and now politically incorrect depictions in American comic strips. As for the animation, despite *Kimba's* great charm, it was made as a long-running television series with 1960s technology; Disney's *Lion King* is clearly better crafted, with a more polished storyline.

Ultimately, the *Lion King* vs. *Kimba* controversy is a case-study in cultural attitudes toward dispute resolution.

Litigation is socially frowned upon except as a last resort in Japan, and the Tezuka family, which still controls Tezuka Productions, was not interested in confronting or suing Disney. Tezuka, after all, had himself been a Disney fan. And there may also have been reluctance over giving too much exposure to the old animation series because of an ongoing lawsuit to reassert rights to the series outside of Japan (ownership of the basic story or manga books was never in dispute), and because the Tezuka people were sensitive to the previous criticism of how African natives were depicted in the manga version.

The Disney company response, on the other hand, was typical of modern American corporate culture, where denials of wrongdoing are automatically issued to stave off potential lawsuits. Ironically, the entire controversy could easily have been resolved by a simple tip of the hat to Tezuka, either in the form of a film credit or a public statement. Instead, one year later, T-shirts were still being sold at American comic conventions that showed Tezuka's Kimba in front of a mirror seeing a reflection of the face of Disney's Simba. Underneath, the caption reads, "The Lyin' King: Mirror mirror, on the wall, who created me after all?"

6

BEYOND MANGA

マンガを超えて

AS A TRULY MASS MEDIUM OF EXPRESSION, MANGA ARE HAVING an ever greater influence on other media, and on culture in general. Conversely, other media and technologies are influencing manga and changing the way artists think and work. As the manga medium matures into the 21st century, pioneering idividuals will increasingly mine this point of convergence and seek to transcend the traditional limits of their field.

Nausicaä and the Manga-Anime Link

マンガとアニメ

HAYAO MIYAZAKI

Financially and artistically, Japan's once-golden film industry has been in the doldrums for the last few decades, except for animation, which has prospered on the back of the manga boom. The output of the animation industry in Japan now dwarfs that of the United States and Europe, and it is increasingly respected abroad. Just as live-action director Akira Kurosawa became the darling of film critics and fans in the early postwar period, today it is animation director Hayao Miyazaki who is lauded around the world. The work for which Miyazaki is arguably best known, and which is often given as an example of the best in Japanese animation, is *Nausicaä of the Valley of Wind. Nausicaä* is based on a manga of the same name, drawn by Miyazaki himself.

After graduating in 1963 from Gakushūin Universi-

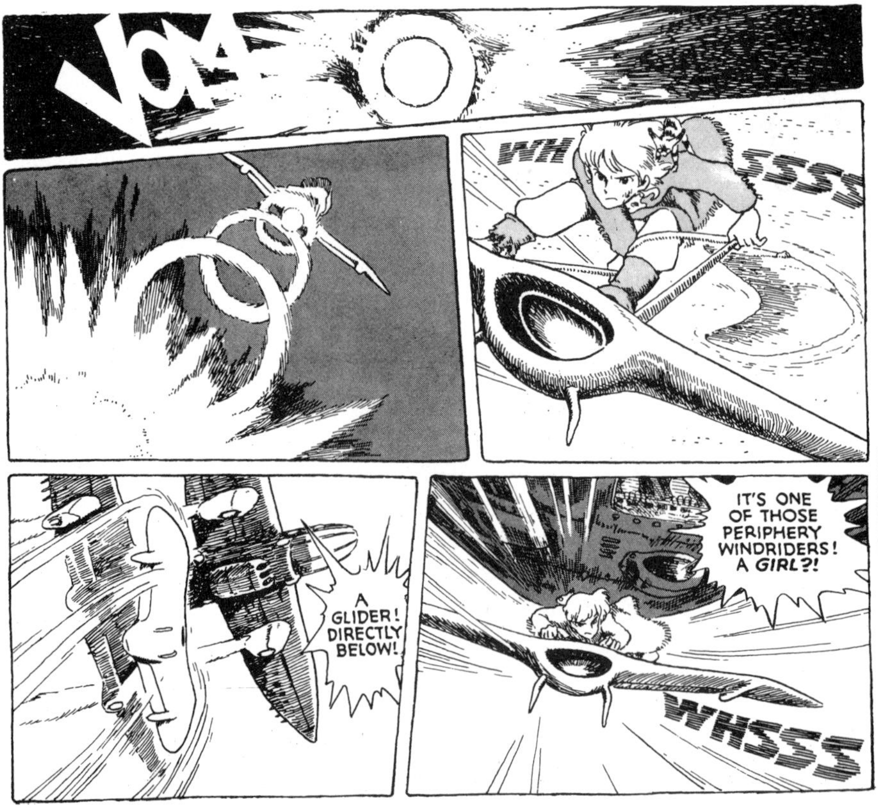
VOM
WHSSSS
A GLIDER! DIRECTLY BELOW!
IT'S ONE OF THOSE PERIPHERY WINDRIDERS! A GIRL?!
WHSSS

Hayao Miyazaki's* Nausicaä of the Valley of Wind. *From the Viz Select Comics English edition.

ty's Department of Politics and Economics, where he was long affiliated with a children's literature study group, Miyazaki worked for many years at Tōei Dōga, one of Japan's premier animation studios. There, he was involved with production on several popular television animated series. In 1979, he directed his first theatrical feature, *Lupin III: Castle of Cagliostro*, based on a delightful manga by a Japanese artist with the tongue-in-cheek pen name of Monkey Punch. This *Lupin* film remains one of the best examples of Japanese animation.

After finishing *Lupin III* Miyazaki was approached by the editor-in-chief of a popular monthly animation review magazine, *Animage*, and asked to draw a manga series. The result, starting in the February 1982 issue and continuing until the end of 1994, was the complex, mysterious, and beautiful manga *Nausicaä*. Instead of a manga drawn by a manga artist being animated by an animation company, as is the usual pattern in Japan, *Nausicaä* thus started as a manga drawn by an animator, which was then animated.

Nausicaä is set in the distant future in a post-nuclear-apocalypse world. As the text on the jacket of the English version dramatically notes, "What was once an enormous flourishing industrial civilization had disappeared into the dark vastness of time. The earth was covered by forests of enormous fungi which exhaled a poisonous miasma called the Sea of Corruption." Diverse medieval-style nations survive on the periphery of the forests (which in addition to giant poisonous fungi are home to huge, threatening insect-creatures called Ohmu) and regularly war among each other. Only shreds of technology from the previous industrial civilization survive, although giant flying ships (with archaic designs) are common.

In the sheltered Valley of Wind, however, there exists a tiny kingdom of five hundred subjects who have mastered wind power and live in idyllic agrarian conditions. One day this peaceful kingdom suddenly finds itself under attack from a country to the west and threatened by a periodic rapid expansion of the fungi forest and a rampage by the Ohmu insects. Nausicaä, the heroine of the story, is a young princess of the kingdom who soars in the sky with a powered glider called a "mehve" and has a special ability to communicate with all creatures, including the giant insects of the forests. She struggles to save her kingdom, and eventually the entire world, and in the process she reveals herself to be a messianic figure who had long been prophesied to appear and lead her people to the "pure land."

AN UNUSUAL MANGA

From the beginning, *Nausicaä* was an unusual manga. First of all, it was different in format. It was serialized in the large A4 size (8.25" x 11.7") of *Animage* magazine, much larger than the normal size for manga. Also, Miyazaki, a brilliant artist, is primarily an animator and did not draw like most manga artists. He drew much of *Nausicaä* in pencil, with no inking, and rendered backgrounds, characters' costumes, and props in great detail. He apparently used few or no assistants, because his characters and backgrounds have a unity to them rarely found in Japanese manga. Miyazaki also did not use the wild page layouts common to many manga but adhered to a very conventional panel scheme with a heavy reliance on words and storytelling. The resulting appearance is very non-Japanese, reminiscent of French comics (minus the color) and a sensibility that brings to mind the French master Jean "Moebius" Giraud. To most Japanese readers, one would suspect, the visual and narrative pacing of *Nausicaä* is excruciatingly slow, requiring multiple readings, for it is dense with information. In a long interview that appeared in the review magazine *Comic Box* in January 1995, the sharp-tongued Miyazaki simultaneously defended himself and criticized the lightweight quality of most manga by stating, "I was determined not to create a manga that people would read while they were eating *soba* noodles."

Another element that makes *Nausicaä* so unlike other manga is that there are few visible "Japanese" elements in the story and no obvious Japanese characters or settings. Miyazaki prefers a more European style, and indeed his people, props, costumes and locations most closely resemble those of medieval Europe, or sometimes the central Asian steppes. Reflecting his wide reading of mythology, world children's literature, and science fiction, the heroine Nausicaä is named after the woman in Homer's *Odyssey* who saved the shipwrecked Ulysses and led him safely to her father's palace. But there are also traces of the Old and New Testaments, ancient Greek, and even Norse myths. The ecological theme and giant insects bring to mind Frank Herbert's popular science fiction series *Dune*.

Japanese culture appears in *Nausicaä* as subtexts and allusions to ancient myths, mainstream and esoteric Buddhism, and contemporary Japanese concerns. The emphasis on giant insects certainly reflects the fact that, like many Japanese males (and the late Osamu Tezuka), Miyazaki was fascinated by them as a young boy. The heroine, Nausicaä, despite her Homerian name, is said to have been inspired in part by a famous tale from the Heian period (A.D. 794–1185) about an odd princess who loved insects. References to nuclear holocausts, alternative energy and wind power, and advanced ceramics link the story to modern Japan, where cultural memories of Hiroshima and Nagasaki are still vivid, where there is much talk of the need for alternative energy, and where high-tech materials made of advanced ceramics are a source of national pride. The strong ecological theme and the romanticization of feudalistic village society are surely Miyazaki's reaction to rapid modernization and to the industrial excesses of Japan. In interviews over the years Miyazaki has consistently expressed strong doubts about modern life, and about Western-style individualism.

Ultimately, Miyazaki manages to smoothly weave all these diverse elements together into a rich tapestry, to create a story set in the distant future but reminiscent of the Middle Ages, all the while retaining relevance to the modern world in which we live. In its epic scale and complexity, *Nausicaä* is like other classics of Japan's manga world, such as Osamu Tezuka's cosmic *Phoenix*, or Sampei Shirato's Marxist-oriented feudal era epics. In the way *Nausicaä*'s world is self-contained, unique, and universal all at the same time, it resembles J.R.R. Tolkien's trilogy, *Lord of the Rings*, or films such as *Star Wars*, *Brazil*, and *Blade Runner*.

FROM MANGA TO ANIME AND BACK . . .

In 1984, after sixteen episodes of *Nausicaä* had been serialized in *Animage*, Miyazaki temporarily stopped drawing and turned to the medium in which he normally works—animation. With the staff of Top Craft studios, he created a 116-minute theatrical version of his manga series. It is, in fact, the animation upon which *Nausicaä*'s high reputation rests, for it is the form of the story to which the greatest number of people have been exposed. While the film lacks the grace of movement of Disney's animated classics (which had far higher budgets), it skillfully translates the narrative and the unique vision Miyazaki established in his manga, including the retro-future and anti-industrial and ecological themes. The heroine, Nausicaä, is essentially the same, although she has a slightly sweeter, almost sappy personality. Commercial animation in Japan puts a heavy emphasis on "prepubescent female cuteness," and

IN ENGLISH

Nausicaä of the Valley of Wind. San Francisco: Viz Communications, 1995.

A color version of Miyazaki's biplane adventure, *Kurenai no Buta,* was serialized in *Animerica,* vol. 1, nos. 5–7, under the title "Crimson Pig." The story is also sometimes known as "Porco Rosso."

as in the manga version, the animated Nausicaä carries around a cute squirrel-like pet. But she also speaks in a high voice and is increasingly the victim of camera angles that show her short skirt fluttering in the wind as she takes off in her glider (leading to debates on the Internet as to whether or not she wears panties). Enough of the intellectual content of the story is retained, however, for Japanese intellectuals like historian Ryōtarō Shiba and director Akira Kurosawa to gush over it enthusiastically.

It may have been fairly easy for Miyazaki to finish the animated *Nausicaä*, but this was not the case with the manga. Perhaps because he tried too hard to create a "classic" (especially after the reception his animation received), and perhaps because he was working outside the brutal constraints of film (limited time and money), *Nausicaä*, the manga, became ever more complicated, with conflicts among more and more kingdoms and religious and secular groups with odd-sounding names. To read *Nausicaä* in its entirety nearly requires a glossary and a guidebook. That Miyazaki struggled, and nearly drowned in the complexity of his own story is clear, for it was published in fits and starts over the years, with a long hiatus, leading to frequent speculation that it would never be completed. After Miyazaki finally did end it in 1994, he expressed his exhaustion to the *Comic Box* interviewer, saying "It was really hard to continue drawing *Nausicaä* for even a year. I'm not exactly sure why, except that it's hard to draw things you don't really understand."

For those who faithfully followed the manga story for thirteen years and loved the optimistic ending to the animation, Miyazaki's conclusion to the manga was shocking. The "human survivors" on earth had in fact all been genetically reengineered by the pre–nuclear holocaust civilization. Nausicaä thus ultimately saves the world for her people (as in the animation), but she also destroys the genetic stock of the original humans, in a sense becoming not the Christ-like savior of man depicted in the animation, but a Shiva-style destroyer in the Hindu tradition.

NAUSICAÄ WORLDWIDE

Despite these problems, Miyazaki's creation has retained its reputation in Japan and overseas. In 1988, San Francisco–based Viz Communications began publishing an English version of the Japanese manga, with Miyazaki's often tricky "faux old-fashioned Japanese" beautifully translated, first by Dana Lewis and Toren Smith and then by Matt Thorn. Perhaps because *Nausicaä* was never very Japanese in form and story in the first place, it has consistently been lauded by U.S. comics critics, who are often not too charitable toward translated manga. Even more remarkable, considering how American translations of long Japanese manga tend to be discontinued partway through the story, the English *Nausicaä* continued over the years to completion, and it has been reissued in a variety of deluxe editions.

The animated version of *Nausicaä* has had a more tortuous introduction into the English-speaking world. When first dubbed and released in 1985 by New World Video, an American company with little experience in the field, nearly twenty minutes of the film were edited out. Miyazaki's thoughtful masterpiece—with its sophisticated antiwar, pro-ecology, and spiritual themes—thus became *Warriors of the Wind*, an action-oriented story with the stock Judeo-Christian theme of "Good battles evil for the future of mankind." As Toren Smith put it in *Comic Box*'s special *Nausicaä* edition, "I was disgusted when I learned this masterpiece had been destroyed by a Hollywood company without a shred of sensitivity." Smith's feelings were shared by many American fans.

But even a botched editing job has been unable to ruin the reputation of the animated *Nausicaä*; true anime fans watch the original versions in Japanese or read fan-translated synopses, and they proselytize in Miyazaki's behalf. In 1996, Miyazaki's contract with New World Video was rumored to be about to expire, and fans were hoping for a rerelease of the film overseas in uncut form.

After *Nausicaä*, Miyazaki rarely worked in comics, but he has created many more classics of Japanese theatrical animation, such as *Laputa*, *Kiki's Delivery Service*, and *My Neighbor Totoro*, the last of which was critically well received in the United States in 1993. Yet among those in the know, Miyazaki's *Nausicaä*, whether in animated or manga form, remains at the top of the list.

Manga Artist as Film Director

マンガと実写映画

TAKASHI ISHII

I first met Takashi Ishii in late 1994 in a smoke-filled basement jazz bar in the crowded Shinjuku area of western Tokyo. With his wireframe glasses, smooth skin, and hair in a carefully trimmed butch cut, he looked much younger, upbeat, and healthier than I would have expected. His works, after all, are generally bleak and focus relentlessly on self-destructive and doomed male-female relations. Yet Ishii has reason to be feeling good these days, for he has accomplished what most manga artists dream of. From an erotic manga artist with a cult following among intellectuals he has worked his way up to become a respected creator and director of disturbing films with an artsy image.

Manga artists have always felt a close connection to film. Nearly all are film buffs, watching favorite movies over and over again for inspiration about ways to create stories and depict actions. Japanese manga, in fact, have deliberately incorporated nearly every camera technique ever invented, from wide angles to close-ups and montages. Many artists also create their stories as if they were film directors, treating their characters as actors and constructing carefully followed scenarios. Understandably, many artists fantasize about being film directors. Even if their manga are extraordinarily popular, however, most are doomed to seeing them animated only for television or, at best, turned into second-rate live-action films by someone else. "As a kid, I always liked films, and I dreamed of becoming a director," Ishii says, "but I was also good at art, and as a schoolboy I used to paint in oils."

When in college, Ishii obtained a part-time job working at Nikkatsu, a once-proud film studio that by the late sixties and seventies was mainly cranking out what the Japanese call *roman porno*, or "romantic" (heavily dramatized) soft-core erotica. A chronic sufferer from asthma, Ishii collapsed on the dust-filled set one day. This, combined with the tumult of the student movement that was swirling around him at the time and his need to earn a decent living for himself and his new bride, led him to give up on his dream of a career in Japan's impoverished film industry. Instead he began working at a detective-story pulp-fiction manga magazine, and in 1970 he made his debut as a *gekiga* or "graphic novel" artist. Ishii's real first name is Hideki, but since much of his work was highly erotic and sensational he began using the pen name Takashi. "Ideally, I would have debuted as a film director with my real name," he laments today.

In the 1970s there was a boom in *ero gekiga*, or realistic erotic manga magazines. Pubic hair and overt depictions of genitalia and sex were all heavily censored at the time, so for a while *ero gekiga* (also occasionally referred to as *sanryū gekiga*, or "third-rate graphic novels") achieved a sort of cult status. Many of the editors, often burned-out former leftist radicals, played a cat-and-mouse game with the authorities, and this in turn encouraged a segment of young intellectuals to regard the publications somewhat romantically as a focus of opposition to the establishment. For a while the magazines did serve an important function as incubators of idiosyncratic talent.

As for Ishii, shortly after graduating from college he had issued a collection of illustrations of "death scenes," which gave an indication of the eccentric direction in which he would eventually be heading. As an *ero gekiga* artist he became a cult hero, especially with a hard-boiled but very cinematic work titled *Tenshi no Harawata*

("Entrails of the Angel"), which ran in the magazine *Young Comic* in 1977. The magazine of literary criticism *Bessatsu Shinpyō* in the spring of 1979 put out a special edition on "The World of Takashi Ishii," advertising it as "A hot blast of ultra-third-rate *ero-gekiga* now shaking up the depressed world of young men's *gekiga*!" When made into a soft-porn movie by Nikkatsu in 1978, Ishii's film proved so lucrative that the company turned it into an entire series.

And this eventually gave Ishii the opportunity to return to film. For the second movie in the "Entrails of the Angel" series, *Akai Kyōshitsu* ("Red Classroom"), he provided the scenario. Then, in 1988, during the production of yet another film in the series *Akai Memai* ("Red Vertigo"), he finally made his debut as director.

Although Ishii drew manga for nearly twenty-five years, his work was never featured in major magazines because of its charged sexual content. "My work wasn't porn," he says. "It was about male-female relationships and communication, and the hopeless gap that exists between men and women in Japan. To depict this, I had to use sex, because sex is a mirror of modern relations." But although full nudity is now fairly common even in mainstream magazines for young children, and far more "pornographic" material is available in true "erotic" or "porno" comics, Ishii claims his work is stigmatized in the former publications yet regarded as "too tame" in the latter. "It isn't as though I've *stopped* drawing manga," he adds with a grin, "but no one gives me manga work anymore. It's almost all film now."

In film, Ishii's manga and cinema skills overlap. His manga were always known for their cinematic style and urban realism. "I always felt my characters were actors, and that I was directing them," he notes, adding that he used to go out and photograph street scenes, xerox them, and incorporate them directly into his stories. "I felt like I was making a film, and imagined that I was putting the characters that I drew into the pictures, sort of pasting them in. Also, I used to start my manga by writing the story scenario on the top of the page and drawing the panel breakdown on the bottom half, and

Cover of brochure for Takashi Ishii's film Yoru ga Mata Kuru, *or "Alone in the Night," drawn by Takashi Ishii.*

then finalizing the work." Now, he says, "I draw the film in my mind before we start, and then I draw continuity sketches or storyboards that are like manga, to use when I'm directing."

This contributes to one of the characteristics of Ishii films; many scenes are like set pieces, carefully staged. Writing in the program notes to the 1994 film *Yoru ga Mata Kuru*, or "Alone in the Night," the cameraman Norimichi Kasamatsu commented, "Most directors I've worked with never draw storyboards, and perhaps because of this, on location they constantly want to take a peek through the camera lens. Ishii, however, almost never asks to take a look."

What is the main difference between creating manga and films? "It was always easy for me to create the stories for manga, but hard to draw them," Ishii says. Since he never used assistants, and tended to draw in a realistic, non-"cartoony" style, he was never able to crank out more than one or two stories a month and achieve the "volume production" demanded in today's industry. A perfectionist, he also tended to redraw works over and over. "It took me over seven years to figure out how to draw the face of my lead character, Nami," he says. But there was one advantage to manga: "I could put the 'actresses' in my manga in any position I wanted. In the films now they often refuse!"

"When I was drawing manga," he adds, "it was agonizing. It was always a solitary, lonely activity, and I was responsible for everything. With film, I work with dozens of people who are all helping me and pooling their abilities. . . . I feel like I'm communicating with others, and I can see I'm helping their own lives and careers. It makes me feel alive."

* * * * *

By 1995, Ishii had made over eight films. Operating on low budgets, he tries to average two films per year. His films are not to everyone's taste. Like all his manga, they feature a single woman character, Nami, who is usually involved in doomed relationships that end in suicides or murders or rapes, and they all contain a heavy dose of violence, twisted eroticism, and sadomasochism. At a time in Japan when there is a relentless, almost monolithic public emphasis on "cuteness" and being "cheery" in all forms of public and creative life, the dark pessimism of Ishii's works makes them stand out. Although his settings are all modern, his doomed and tragic characters are in a sense very old-fashioned Japanese, an archetype one might have seen years ago in yakuza films or popular tragedies. "I've been told that my films are too bloody, or that there is too much violence against women in them,"

Ishii says in his defense," but I think violence, drugs, and sex are a part of reality. I depict how women are exposed to male violence, and overcome it. I try to show how to find salvation."

Many of Ishii's films have won considerable acclaim, especially from foreign critics. The 1993 *Nūdo no Yoru* ("A Night in Nude") received the Grand Prix Award at the Sun Dance Film Festival in Tokyo; the 1992 *Shinde mo Ii* ("Original Sin") won awards at film festivals in Torino, Italy, and Thessaloníki, Greece. Ironically, the popularity of Ishii's films has triggered a revival of many of his manga that had gone out of print. In 1993, a collection titled *Nami Returns* was issued by Wise Shuppan in deluxe hardback format, complete with the scenario for *Original Sin*.

The Manga-Novel Nexus

マンガと小説

MEDIA FUSION

Creating manga involves both writing and drawing. Sometimes manga artists become illustrators or fine artists and sometimes the reverse happens. What has had a larger impact on Japanese society as a whole is the increasing degree of crossover today between creators of manga and creators of books, between manga and what is normally thought of as "literature."

The crossover tends to fall into distinct categories.

1. *Established writers who in their youth created manga but never became particularly famous or successful and treat that period of their career with humor, nostalgia, and pride, but sometimes also with embarrassment.*

In the 1950s, scores of young Japanese submitted works they created to the magazine *Manga Shōnen* ("Manga Boy") in the hopes of joining the manga boom. Many of them became prominent cameramen, actors, poets, screenplay writers, graphic artists, and writers, including the famous science-fiction author Sakyō

Komatsu, best known for his 1973 novel *Nihon Chinbotsu* ("Japan Sinks"). A more recent example is Hiroshi Aramata, one of Japan's most prolific writers and the author or translator of over a hundred fiction and nonfiction books. In 1994 he published *Manga to Jinsei* ("Manga and Life"), a collection of his essays on manga, and proudly included a manga work he had himself authored years previously, *The Dust Lady*. Aramata, coincidentally, was once married for six months to the famous Edo-genre manga artist, Hinako Sugiura.

"Serious" novelists may not always be eager to publicize the fact that they were once manga artists—even in Japan there can still be a certain stigma attached to manga, especially among the more snobbish literary elite. Amy Yamada, the award-winning writer whose hard-boiled sex-filled novels such as the 1991 *Torasshu* ("Trash") have won her overseas acclaim as an example of "new Japanese fiction," once had a career as an author/artist of syrupy girls' romance comics under her real name Futaba Yamada. In 1994, when I tried to obtain an interview with her about her manga connection, she made it very clear that she had absolutely no interest in talking about that side of her past.

2. *Well-known manga artists who give up creating manga and turn to writing.*

Tatsuhiko Yamagami is certainly the most famous artist in this category. He helped launch a revolution in Japanese humor in the seventies with a gag manga series titled *Gaki Deka* ("Kid Cop"). *Kid Cop* starred an incongruous little boy policeman who lived in a very normal family but created havoc with his anarchic personality, often tearing off his clothes, displaying his little penis, and screaming "I sentence you to death" or other nonsensicals. It was like taking a sledgehammer to the straight-jacket decorum of Japanese society, and it earned Yamagami fortune and fame.

Around 1990, however, Yamagami decided to stop creating manga and to focus on writing short stories and novels, several of which have been published. They retained his barbed sense of humor and his sense of the absurd, and met with a certain success, but the shift nonetheless meant a considerable step down the ladder of fame and fortune for Yamagami. Inevitably, the media at the time was obsessed with wanting to know why anyone would quit being a successful manga artist (by the time I got around to asking Yamagami for an interview he was so sick of the subject that he turned me down flat). In a September 14, 1993, interview in *Aera* magazine he mentioned that while drawing *Kid Cop* he had already begun to lose his passion for expressing himself through drawings. "At one point," he said, "Kid Cop used to move around on the pages himself and almost create the jokes for me, but then I stopped getting any creative stimulation from the pictures themselves." Eventually he developed a loathing for drawing, and when he finally turned to a prose-only medium of expression, he found it liberating.

Yamagami may have simply reached a creative impasse in his career as a manga artist, but he is certainly not the only famous and wealthy manga artist to view his or her less-well-off writer counterparts with some degree of envy. One reason for this is that successful manga artists are on a treadmill that is hard to get off. They are hounded by the press like other celebrities (with their affairs and failed marriages the subject of talk shows and headlines). The system of volume production forced on them means they have to hire managers, assistants, and establish a factorylike work flow, scheduling far into the future. Taking vacations and cutting down on assignments not only affects the artist's own livelihood, but that of dozens of other dependent people.

3. *Manga artists who continue to draw manga while also writing books.*

It is not unusual for famous manga artists to write autobiographical or how-to-draw books. It is less common for working artists to simultaneously aspire to be taken seriously as authors of prose fiction. Like many famous manga artists, Shungicu Uchida writes essays and articles, but in 1993 she published her first novel, a semi-autobiographical work with the provocative title *Father Fucker*, based on her experience of being molested by her stepfather. It was nominated for the prestigious Naoki Prize.* Uchida has continued writing fiction and semifictional works, including the book *Kiomi* in 1995. In his review in the *Asahi Evening News*, alluding to the poor quality of what passes for Japanese "literature" overseas today, John Vacho wrote that if translated *Kiomi* "would make a corrective to the sophomoric stories of people like Banana Yoshimoto and Haruki Murakami." Ironically, in 1994 Uchida did win the Prix Des Deux Magots Bunkamura literary award—not for a novel, but for a manga she authored on child-rearing titled *Watashitachi wa Hanshoku Shite Iru* ("We Are Reproducing").

4. *Serious novelists and nonfiction writers who also work in the manga field.*

Manga depend on stories and dialogue, and in the past many wannabe novelists may have reluctantly "stepped down" to writing manga scenarios. Today there is little such stigma attached to professional manga writers. Some, such as Kazuo Koike (who runs a manga writing school), team up with artists who lack confidence in their own storytelling ability and make more money than a novelist ever would. Established non-manga writers may also dabble in the manga field for fun or profit or both. Natsuo Sekikawa, a well-known award-winning author of fiction and nonfiction books, teamed up with manga artist Jirō Taniguchi in 1986 to produce *Kaikei Shūten* (published in English in 1991 by Viz Communications under the title *Hotel Harbor View*) and has subsequently written several other well-received manga. Naoki Inose, a prolific and well-known nonfiction writer with books on largely historical subjects, teamed up in the mid-nineties with manga artist Kenshi Hirokane, creator of the enormously popular "salaryman drama" *Kachō Shima Kōsaku* ("Section Chief Kōsaku Shima") to create a manga tale on the workings of the media. Titled *Last News*, it ran in the biweekly *Big Comic Original*, where the readership is mainly middle-aged men. Rather than diminish Inose's reputation, if any-

* In 1995 it was also made into a live action feature film starring Mami Nakamura and Kaori Momoi, among others. At the 1996 San Francisco Film Festival it was shown under the title of "The Girl of the Silence."

Part of a cinematic sequence from **Hotel Harbor View.**

thing it elevated it among the audience of serious manga readers, who most certainly far outnumber those who read his text-only books.

5. *Novelists who consciously or unconsciously try to emulate manga styles.*

The phenomenon of novelists admiring manga is not new. Yukio Mishima, who disemboweled himself in a narcissistic samurai-style ritual in 1970 and who is almost never associated with comics, was a great fan of manga. Shortly before his death he wrote a defense of Japan's more lurid manga and declared himself an admirer of Hiroshi Hirata, who drew violent, hyper-realistic samurai stories. Whether Mishima's prose was actually influenced by Hirata's work is doubtful, however.

With younger writers, the manga influence is much more clear. Many were raised on manga, and manga pacing and constructions now inform their literary style. This is especially true of women authors; since the seventies in particular, girls' and women's manga have regularly used introspection and poetic musings on human psychology and relationships to achieve a literary quality. Author Banana Yoshimoto, who wrote the best-selling 1988 novel *Kitchin* ("Kitchen"), which sold well in translation in the United States and has also been made into a charming live-action movie, is a great fan of manga. In a July 1993 issue of the literary magazine *Kaien* (with a special feature titled "Manga Is Literature"), she was both criticized and lauded for being a novelist who "translated" or developed the world of girls' manga into the arena of pure literature. Yoshimoto is often said to have been influenced by the woman manga artist Yumiko Ōshima. In the May 11, 1994, issue of the magazine *Views*, manga-fan psychiatrist Rika Kayama wrote, "When Banana Yoshimoto first appeared there were people who said she was imitating Yumiko Ōshima. Of course, they said this in a pejorative sense, but to someone like me, who had always thought that no writer could even come *close* to Yumiko Ōshima, this seemed like tremendous praise."

In the less serious literary realms and the truly "popular" mass-market books for young people, many writers *deliberately* mine the convergence between novels and comics. Wataru Kusanagi, winner of the Shōsetsu Subaru Award for new writers, demonstrated this in 1992 with a novel titled *Hirugaeru Hitohata* ("Flying the Flag") about a young manga genius. Like so many books in Japan today, it was light and fluffy and read just like a manga. The cover jacket proclaimed the story to be, "A super-interesting novel that depicts what pictures can't, and is filled with youthful dreams, romance, and adventure." In the afterword, the author declared himself a big fan and regular reader of manga and wrote, "I hope that readers will enjoy my novel in the same way I enjoy manga."

* * * * *

The convergence between manga and regular books is not just a result of a crossover between manga artists and book writers, but of industries. In the United States, comic book publishing and book publishing have entirely different organizations, distribution systems, readers, and attitudes. In Japan, however, the two worlds increasingly overlap. Manga are a cash cow, so most literary publishers now issue manga magazines and paperbacks of their own. Magazines that were formerly mostly text, today incorporate more and more manga pages to boost their sales. And as book publishers are discovering, designs that remind young readers of manga sell well.

Novels for young people that previously would have been all text now incorporate manga-style illustrations. And clever publishers have discovered that manga-style dust jackets, in particular, help sell novels, especially to young people. In bookstores it has become hard to distinguish text-based paperback romances for young women from manga-based paperbacks of the same genre—because the covers are often drawn by popular manga and anime artists. Ironically, publishers are also drawing older readers to their manga paperbacks by packaging them in the smaller size of paperback novels (*bunko* versions) and giving them dust jackets drawn not by manga artists but by top-notch book-cover illustrators. Thus grown-ups can presumably feel less self-conscious about reading comic books on the train. After publisher Akita Shoten succeeded with Osamu Tezuka's *Black Jack* in this format, nearly every publisher jumped on the bandwagon. In 1995, according to the Research Institute for Publications, the number of manga-books handled by distributors as "books" (and not "magazines") jumped 54.9 percent over the previous year, mainly fueled by sales of *bunko* format books. In 1995 alone 105 publishers issued 2,076 manga titles as regular "books," including 947 titles of *bunko*-format manga-books; in all, 57 million copies of both were sold. There's still room to grow, of course. Most manga-books are still handled as "magazines" in the distribution system—486 million copies were sold in 1995.

Cover to Jump Novel, *April 1, 1995.*

Finally, there is a very good reason many novels in Japan read like manga—many of them are novelizations of manga stories. Years ago, publishers discovered there is a fairly large market for novelized manga because (for whatever reason) some people simply prefer text to pictures. And this trend extends beyond books to magazines. The largest manga publisher in Japan—Shūeisha—issues a line of novels called "Jump J Books" that it advertises as "New entertainment super visual novels"; many are based on the company's best-selling manga titles. In 1991 Shūeisha also began issuing a 400-page biannual magazine modeled after its enormously popular manga magazine, the weekly *Jump*. Titled *Jump Novel*, it serializes fiction either based on manga stories or in a "manga-style." Heavily illustrated by manga artists, it also happens to contain ads for *Jump J Books* and for Shūeisha manga magazines.

Information Manga

情報マンガ

WE TURN TEXT INTO MANGA!

Mr. Mitsuru Okazaki is the president of a small company called Trend Pro in Tokyo's Shinbashi district. The back of his business card says it all: large characters proclaim "*WE TURN TEXT INTO MANGA,*" followed by "*We can make anything in manga format, including manuals, company guides, reports, marketing tools, project plans, company and personal histories, etc.*"

Tall, youthful, and engaging, Okazaki used to work for the sales department of Yamaha Motor Company. Part of his job was to create a manual for motorcycle shop dealers in Japan, and he did so in the *kami-shibai*, or "paper-play," format that combined manga-style illustrated panels with narration. When making a presentation on the manual, he first realized how effective manga are as an educational tool. Executives who normally snored through meetings stayed awake and seemed genuinely interested. It was "manga power" at work.

In 1988, after leaving Yamaha, Okazaki formed Trend Pro to produce manga for businesses. His company is a pioneer in the business manga field and has attracted considerable media attention in Japan. By 1995 it had a full-time staff of eight people in charge of planning and direction, and a network of nearly a hundred manga artists, illustrators, and scenario writers it could call on for specific projects. Trend Pro was thus able to offer clients a wide range of styles. Most of the company's publications use the Japanese "story comic" format complete with lengthy narrative and identifiable characters. The artists are sometimes well known, but most are less established yet nonetheless skilled artists who can emulate the more popular styles.

According to Okazaki, the company's first big success was a manga "infomercial" insert that appeared in the March 23, 1990 issue of the prestigious *Asahi* newspaper. Titled "1990's Business Trender," it featured a manga-style story of a salaryman in a fictional joint ven-

Four classmates stumble across a bag filled with ¥1 million. From a book on how to save money, with the English title *If You Have ¥1,000,000.* Produced by Trend Pro.

ture and in the process illustrated probable trends in the work environment in the 1990s (such as greater computerization and an increase in the number of women coworkers). Whereas only around 2 percent of the target readers might normally read such inserts, a survey done by the *Asahi* later showed that an astounding 38 percent had looked at Trend Pro's manga presentation. Moreover, nearly 60 percent of this group had read it to the end. And it was people in their thirties and sixties—not their teens or twenties—who were most likely to have read it.

Today, in addition to producing annual manga inserts for the *Asahi*, Trend Pro is involved in a wide variety of manga ventures. According to Okazaki, by 1995 the company had created over 500 products for nearly 200 companies, including many of Japan's top corporations. Sales manuals in manga form are its most popular product, but other items include computer manuals and manga versions of government white papers. For the oil company General Sekiyu, Trend Pro created "A Manual for Lubricating Oil." For a doctor who runs a popular clinic specializing in plastic surgery, it created a manga on "Male Esthetics" to explain such things as vasectomies and an operation increasingly popular among young Japanese males—circumcision. Trend Pro currently manga-izes about two books a year for the Japanese government. In 1994 the company brought out a fifty-page version of a white paper on the environment, timed for Environment Day on June 5. Other government works include a manga version of a booklet showing how to purchase a home and—in reaction to the excesses of the eighties' bubble economy and a rash of personal bankruptcies brought on by easy credit—a manga story for young people illustrating the advantages of saving one's money. In 1996, Trend Pro also began working with the Ministry of Education to create CD-ROMs that used manga characters to discuss reforms in Japan's system of higher education.

Okazaki is a firm believer in the effectiveness of manga-based information, and he puts forth a convincing argument for its increased use. "There is so much information in the world today," he says, "that, as in the case of a newspaper, no one can read it all unless they have lots of time. Manga create the motivation to read. Manga are the hook that pulls people in and gets them to read the text information."

In the future will all publications in Japan become manga? "No, not all" says Okazaki, "but we will see more and more manga-based information. Not only corporate publications, but school texts, for example, will probably use more and more manga. In subjects like math and history, the more interesting and fun sections will probably be rendered in manga, and they will motivate the students to read the rest of the text. Getting people interested in the information—moving them emotionally—is the main role of manga. And," Okazaki points out, correcting any misplaced notions a foreign observer might have about comics and illiteracy, "in Japan today, a rule of thumb is that it is the children who read manga who also tend to read books."

How much does it cost to turn text into manga? Okazaki estimates a 200-page manga-book will cost around ¥6 million, or $60,000, which includes consulting, scripting, and artwork—the whole package. "It's not much different from the cost of a text-only publication," he says, "especially when you consider that it has nearly ten times greater impact."

Manga Artists and Computers

マンガ家とコンピューター

DIGITAL MANGA

Since the early 1980s, computers have steadily infiltrated the arts. And manga—so dependent on idiosyncratic hand work and human creativity that they might once have seemed immune from automation—have been no exception.

In 1984–85, American Mike Saentz drew one of the first comics using a computer. A superhero-type tale titled *Shatter*, it was painfully executed on an eight-bit Commodore 64 and looked like it had been printed on a high-resolution color dot-matrix printer. Since that time, computers have become increasingly common in comics creation, with many American artists and publishers using them as just another production tool for coloring or adding special effects. Unlike Japan, where dialogue in comics has almost always been typeset, in America computers are even being used to replicate the hand lettering traditionally demanded by readers.

In Japan, the diffusion of computers into the general population has considerably lagged behind that in the United States due to language problems and a general unfamiliarity with keyboards. Still, Japan's much larger population of manga artists and their inherently gadget-crazy, inquisitive nature led some of them to begin experimenting with computers quite early on. On November 12, 1983, the *Nikkei Sangyō Shinbun,* one of Japan's major economic-industrial newspapers, did a short article on Kyūsoku Iwamoto, a social-satire cartoonist who was using his personal computer—not to draw—but to help think up new ideas. Around the same time, manga artists like Mitsuru Sugaya—a children's artist and computer buff who of course created an early manga about computers—became an international presence on CompuServe, uploading his drawings for fans to enjoy.

In the late 1980s, the diffusion of Macintosh systems into Japanese graphic design studios had a profound effect on the more technologically progressive manga artists. I first realized this in 1989 when I interviewed Shigeru Tamura and found him using about ¥5 million (around $50,000) worth of computer equipment in his home to generate manga. Tamura, however, is someone who straddles the line between manga artist and illustrator, and in the Japanese context considers himself more of the latter. His beautifully rendered drawings and fantasy stories have a non-Japanese, European feel, and he is much in demand as an illustrator for posters, magazine covers, and *ehon*, or illustrated "picture books." *Ehon* were originally mainly for children but are now popular among adults and young women. Although some resemble manga and may be in "comics" format with panels and word balloons, they have fewer pages. Larger, hard-case deluxe editions, they are also printed on far better paper and carefully colored.

To the untrained eye, there is little about most of Tamura's work that hints it was done on a computer. When I asked Tamura why he was using computers in 1989, the main reason he gave was that "the color comes out closer to the original drawings. With current offset printing, the color tends to change. I like tighter control, and want the colors to be closer to my original drawings. Even if it takes longer, I'm willing to invest the extra time." In the volume- and speed-obsessed manga industry, Tamura on his computer was spending an entire day doing the line drawings for each page, and another whole day coloring each page.

One of the challenges artists who use computer technology face is whether to control it or be manipulated by it. The moment their artwork looks as though it is generated by a computer, or the computer effects become too obvious, it will be too easy for other artists with the same equipment to generate the same effects. And, given the pace of technological innovation, effects in art that are too readily associated with computers will make the drawings look dated in no time.

* * * * *

More and more young artists in Japan—the hip, so-called "digital people"—now use computers. Monkey Punch (aka Kazuhiko Katō) is one artist of the older generation who began using computers at a very early stage. "I try my best to avoid any sort of 'computer-graphics' look," he told me n 1995, "and I ideally want my [color] art to look as though it was done with a brush and paint. In other words, I want to avoid anything that gives the artwork the cold look of a computer drawing. For me, the scanner acts sort of like a pencil; the computer functions as the paper, the brush, and the inks."

Following this eminently practical approach, Monkey (as he likes to be called), uses his system to create a database of images—of characters, backgrounds, and props—that he can then use as needed. It is this database aspect that he considers to be computers' greatest strength. He uses his computer to perform the usual image-processing tricks—creating complex geometric designs or applying special filter effects. In addition, he uses his system for inspiration. "When I'm having difficulty coming up with a good idea for a design, I'll take my digital camera outdoors and photograph patterns in clouds, rocks, water surfaces, or the ground, and then process them in a variety of ways. Computer technology allows me to experiment several times more than if I were drawing by hand; it has become an indispensable tool."

This doesn't mean that computers don't have their drawbacks. Monkey notes the time factor involved in any new technology. "They're no good for work that has to be done in a hurry," he says, "and for rush jobs I still create everything by hand." Speaking with the experience of someone who had lost his work in system "crashes," he adds that when he works on his computer, "I always try to make sure I have everything backed up. . . ."

Monkey is excited about the future of computers and manga. "Computer technology and the world of multimedia have infinite possibilities," he says. "So-called digital manga are limited only by the potential inability of manga artists' imagination to keep up with multimedia technology."

* * * * *

The manga artist who has been the most vocal advocate of computers in manga production is Buichi Terasawa. A former assistant to Osamu Tezuka, Terasawa is best known for his hard-boiled SF adventure stories drawn in a very "American" style and especially for his work *Space Adventure Cobra*. Along with Monkey Punch, Terasawa has been invited to several comics conventions in America and Europe and is today one of the better-known Japanese artists overseas. His *Cobra* has been translated and published in English by Viz Communications. In the early 1990s it was indirectly given wide exposure when MTV ran the video for rock and roll star Matthew Sweet's song "Girlfriend." Sweet is a big fan of Terasawa and Japanese animation in general (he has a tattoo of a favorite character), and he used snippets of the animated version of *Cobra* as imagery in his video.

Always an innovator, as early as 1985 Terasawa used a computer system based on an NEC 9801 PC (it reportedly cost ¥10 million, or $100,000 at 1995 rates) to create the color pages of *Black Knight Bat*, a story that ran in the weekly *Shōnen Jump*. Subsequently, Terasawa aggressively pursued the possibilities of computerized manga, creating video games and CD-ROMs based on his creations. He also has become a major proponent of "digital comics."

In 1992, partly as a result of an earlier visit to California where he saw what George Lucas's people were doing with Macintosh computers, Terasawa began using a Mac-based system to create an innovative manga series called *Takeru*. First he roughed out the story in pencil; then he traced the characters and the backgrounds for the story separately, scanned them into the computer, and touched up the drawings and colorized them with programs such as Photoshop and Illustrator. Next, for each panel of the comic, he composited both the characters and backgrounds in the computer and added a variety of special effects. The end result was a full-color SF fantasy manga published as a paperback book in 1993, with a sequel in 1994. This attracted so much interest that in 1994 the same publisher issued a detailed how-to book titled *Macintosh no Dennō Manga Jutsu: Mac de Hirogaru Terasawa Buichi Wārudo* ("Cyber Manga Techniques with the Macintosh: The World of Buichi Terasawa Expands with the Mac"). Billed as "The World's First Book to Introduce Computer Graphic Comics," it came with a floppy disk containing digitized selections from *Takeru*.

In the spring of 1994 I visited Terasawa at his Tokyo studio and had a chance to better understand his very Japanese view of "digital comics." Since Terasawa likes black in his decor, and almost always wears black clothes, the light-colored computer equipment stood out in the otherwise somber and futuristic environment of his office. It was easy to see why he has a lot of fans among the heavy-metal crowd.

Like Shigeru Tamura and Monkey Punch, Terasawa claims it takes him far longer to create comics by computer than by hand; three times longer, in fact. "I'm a pioneer of a sort," he says with a wry grin. "It'll be a lot easier for those who come after me!" The main advantage he now sees in using computers is that it gives him the ability to experiment with different colors and incorporate special effects, even after compositing the character and background images. Indeed, by carefully applying shadows and special lighting effects, Terasawa can give his drawings a 3D effect and make his characters transparent, or even glowing. In one scene in *Takeru* he does a

Buichi Terasawa's computer screen when creating digital manga.

beautiful job of illustrating the female warrior character Asuka standing on the limb of a giant tree, the sunlight coursing through the leaves and creating a beautiful dappled pattern on her face and body. It's an effect that would be painstakingly difficult by hand.

Like Tamura, Terasawa is particularly attracted to color. "One of the reasons for the growth of the manga industry in Japan," he notes, "is the use of monochrome printing and cheap paper. For someone like me, therefore, one of the biggest problems is the lack of color manga publications, because I'm going in the reverse direction of the whole industry. . . . I want to express myself in a different way. Unlike someone like Shigeru Tamura, I'm also more of a manga artist, and I need more pages to tell my stories than are available in the standard *ehon* [illustrated color "picture books"] or even in American comic books."

When Terasawa talks about the manga industry in Japan, it's clear he has met with considerable resistance. The industry, he notes, is successful and established, averse to change; editors are not comfortable with computers, and many still demand that work be submitted in the old "pre-digital" ways. Eventually, it will be necessary to overturn the system, Terasawa predicts.

There are clearly other advantages to digitizing imagery. Digitization of images makes them easier to use in other media, such as game software and CD-ROM-based manga, as well as in animation production. And Terasawa has his sights set on more than Japan. In the United States, where bookstores rarely carry comics and there are still relatively few comics specialty shops, distribution is always a problem. "It might be possible," he says, "to get around the traditional U.S. comics distribution system with CD-ROM-based manga, because there are so many more stores that now carry computer application software."

As Terasawa's manager, Junco Itō, notes, publishing in English or European languages often requires flipping and tailoring images so stories can be read from left to right instead of the Japanese right-to-left style. With a digitized version of the comic, reversing and revising material is easier than ever.

7 MANGA IN THE ENGLISH-SPEAKING WORLD

英語圏におけるマンガ

I HADN'T BEEN TO ENGLAND FOR A LONG TIME (THIRTY-FIVE YEARS, in fact), so in the summer of 1995 I was delighted when I was invited to speak on manga at a conference held at the University of London. Titled "Hiroshima, The Week," it turned out to be one of the oddest forums where I have ever delivered my manga "message." London was in the midst of a heat wave, there was no air conditioning, and the lecture rooms were sweltering steambaths. Most of the other speakers dealt with such topics as "Asia's Wars Since Hiroshima," "The Japanese Left and the Bomb," and even "Female Circumcision: A Cause for Concern?" My talk, on "The Meaning of Manga," was presumably included for entertainment purposes, and it was packed with polite and attentive people, all intensely interested in Japanese manga, but very different from the normal manga-fan crowd. As I later discovered, most of them (including the sponsors) were affiliated with the Revolutionary Communist Party.

MANGA IN ASIA

Japanese manga are a hot item around the world today, regardless of the political persuasion of those reading them. Often, manga ride on the popularity of anime exports, but they have nonetheless carved out a niche for themselves in the global marketplace. Asia was the first region anime and manga entered in force, starting in the early seventies. Japan's geographical and cultural proximity meant that Japanese manga (both art and publishing styles) were quickly adopted and quickly displaced American-style comics in popularity. In Korea today stores sell

Cover to the July 10, 1995 edition of "New Youth Express Weekly," the Taiwan edition of **Shōnen Magazine.**

1995 © KŌDANSHA/TONG LI

fat omnibus-style manga magazines identical in format and style to those of Japan. In Taiwan, Hong Kong, and Thailand, many manga paperbacks and magazines are issued in translation under license from their original Japanese publishers. In Thailand and other Southeast Asian nations, Japanese manga-icons such as the robot-cat Doraemon and the series *Dragon Ball* are nearly as famous and popular as they are at home. In Taiwan, where Japanese manga culture seems to have made the greatest inroads, all the major Japanese boys' manga magazines are issued, as are several girls' manga magazines and some for young male adults. In 1995, according to the editor-in-chief of Kōdansha's *Shōnen Magazine*, a weekly for boys, his company had set up a system so the stories in the Japanese publication appeared translated in the licensed Taiwanese counterpart with only a three-day delay.

Until the 1990s a huge number of Japanese manga in Asia were pirated, either reprinted or retraced. American researcher Professor John Lent has documented this phenomenon in a paper titled "Manga and Anime in Asia" (based on interviews with more than 200 Asian cartoonists and animators in fifteen countries). In Taiwan, he notes, the Tong Li Publishing Company run by Fang Wennan, the "self-appointed 'king of pirated manga,'" released more than a thousand different titles over a fifteen-year period.

When Japanese publishers finally began asserting control over their properties in Asia through licensing ventures, piracy was only one problem. Manga are so popular that in several nations—particularly the former colonies of Japan—they have created a considerable backlash and are sometimes seen as a source of moral corruption or even of cultural imperialism. Nowhere has this backlash been stronger than in South Korea, with its long-standing and complicated love-hate relationship with Japan. As Lent notes, quoting a member of a Korean Ethics Committee, Japanese manga have long been censored for "deep kissing, nudity, profanity, and portrayals of stabbings, shootings, blood, and amputations." The Korean Cartoonists Association has in the past called for the banning of Japanese manga, and individuals and groups have struggled to "Koreanize" manga.

MANGA IN EUROPE

Manga have made major inroads in Europe, too, with surprisingly little resistance given the cultural differences. As in other regions, manga ride partly on the popularity of Japanese animation, which can be seen regularly on television or rented as videos. In the United Kingdom, the London-based entertainment empire controlled by white Jamaican Chris Blackwell (who introduced reggae into the United States) rolled into the nascent manga market, forming a company called Manga Entertainment in 1991. Issuing dubbed anime (which it confusingly called "manga") and distributing translated manga publications, Manga Entertainment's entry into the market sent shockwaves through the manga subculture on the continent and even in the United States, where it acquired an existing anime importer, opened an office, and exercised its marketing savvy by forming distribution deals for anime videos with national music store chains.

In Italy, anime and manga stories for children, such as Yumiko Iigarashi's melodramatic story of a little waif from Minnesota, *Candy Candy*, were particularly well received at the beginning of the eighties. By the 1990s the range of material published had broadened far beyond giant robots and saccharine love stories to include titles like the "super-violence" martial-arts series *JoJo no Kimyō na Bōken* ("JoJo's Bizarre Adventures") and a slew of adult, erotic works. In France, where *bandes dessinée*s (the beautifully produced indigenous French comic books) have been elevated to a new art form and where a thriving domestic industry exists in comics for grown-ups, manga from Japan have nonetheless exploded in popularity—both in the larger hardback *bande desinée* format and the smaller Japanese format. One publisher, Glénat, issues *Kameha*, a fat "magazine" of mainly manga, bound in hardcover *bande desinée* style. One of the more interesting Parisian trends is for the publishers of translated manga, such as Tonkam or Glénat, to also act as retailers through their own comics specialty stores. Many anime- and manga-related shops are clustered in the colorful Bastille area and boast Japanese names like Madoka, Gaijin, and Katsumi. When I visited Katsumi, I thought the shop name was that of the proprietor and asked to see him, thinking I could communicate in Japanese instead of broken French. Instead, I discovered to my chagrin that the shop was merely named after the French owner's favorite manga character.

Whether in Asia or Europe, each country's approach to manga is slightly different. But in Europe, even if many of the works are translated into local languages, they often come from Japan via the English-speaking world, especially the United States.

English-Language Manga Publishers

英語版マンガの出版社

A SLOW START

In the mid-1980s, several ambitious people came and talked to me about visions they had of publishing translated Japanese comics in America. I tried to be encouraging, but I couldn't hide the fact that I was skeptical of their success. I had seen too many failed attempts, and I knew it would be difficult for manga to take hold in America. Modern comics were invented in the United States, and there is a uniquely American style of reading, publishing format, and even distribution. There was also a personal reason for my pessimism. Around 1977, some friends and I had had a dream of translating Japanese manga and getting them published in English. We had formed a group called Dadakai and translated some of our favorite manga, but had had little luck in getting them published.

By 1980, the only real "story manga" available in English and distributed in the United States was *Barefoot Gen*. A semi-autobiographical manga series about the bombing of Hiroshima, *Gen* was authored by Keiji Nakazawa, himself a survivor of the bombing. *Gen* had such a powerful message that the translation and production of the English edition were done by volunteers—Japanese and American members of a nonprofit organization formed in 1976 called Project Gen (which included members of Dadakai) who were dedicated to spreading Nakazawa's message. The nature of the *Gen* venture made the publishing effort into something of a cause, and this ultimately made it possible to circumvent normal distribution channels and put the English books in the hands of readers around the world. *Gen* was a smashing critical success and it was ultimately translated into many languages, including French, German, Swedish, Norwegian, Indonesian, Portuguese, Russian, Tagalog, and Esperanto. In 1983 a shorter, similar story by Nakazawa, *I Saw It*, became the first Japanese comic published in the U.S. in true American format, complete with color printing, when it was issued by Leonard Rifas's Educomics. But this was a risky endeavor at the time, and nearly destroyed tiny Educomics. Until the English *Gen* books were picked up by New Society Publishers and by Penguin Books nearly fifteen years later, *Gen* could hardly be called a successful commercial venture.

In the wake of *Gen*, in the early eighties, several translations of manga appeared, but these were mostly short stories, works based on anime, "vanity press" efforts by Japanese artists hungry for international atten-

"Here come the robots!" From the Italian edition of Yoshihisa Tagami's Grey. *Published in 1991 by Granata Press, via America.*

tion, or manga translated not for an English-speaking audience but for home consumption by the language-learning market in Japan. Often the translations were poor, or the formats were unconventional and not designed for teachers accustomed to American-style comic books.

Americans had actually been exposed to Japanese comics long before *Gen*. In the early twenties and thirties, when American newspaper comic strips were the model for Japanese manga, several Japanese artists spent time in the United States. Sakō Shishido, the author of the popular 1930 comic strip *Spiido Tarō* ("Speedy") lived in America nine years and took correspondence courses on U.S. comics. Yoshitaka (Henry) Kiyama, who arrived in San Francisco at the turn of the century and experienced the 1906 earthquake, in 1931 published *Yonin Shosei* (Four Students)—an autobiographical comic book for Japanese-American audiences (one had to be fluent in both English and Japanese in order to read the dialogue, which must have severely crimped its sales). During World War II,

Tarō Yashima, an exiled Japanese dissident artist, published a cartoon/comic book titled *New Sun*. Designed for Americans, it was a devastating critique of Japan's militarist government. Still, it is safe to say that these artists had little effect on American artists and readers; they worked in relative isolation, and in any case Japan's manga and anime cultures had not yet assumed the distinctive features they have today.

The 1963 broadcast on American television of Osamu Tezuka's animation series *Tetsuwan Atom*, or *Astro Boy*, was therefore a far more significant event. Tezuka's story of a little boy robot was imported by NBC and syndicated on U.S. television, and it was issued as an American-style comic book drawn by an American artist. The animation was so well edited and dubbed in English by U.S. producer Fred Ladd that most American children had no inkling their hero was Japanese; the comic book also gave no indication of its Japanese roots. The success of the venture paved the way for the import of several other Japanese programs—even though network restrictions on violence and content severely limited the scope of suitable material, and efforts were usually made to downplay or disguise the animation's Japanese origins.

SUCCESS

It took changes in the cultural environment in America for manga and anime to be better received, and these occurred in the early eighties:

First, a few subtitled Japanese animation shows were broadcast on UHF channels in American cities with large Japanese-speaking populations; these were watched by an increasingly broad audience, many of whom were not of Japanese descent but simply curious about Japan.

Second, some dubbed and heavily edited—but nonetheless identifiably Japanese—shows such as *Battle of the Planets*, *Star Blazers* (based on Leiji Matsumoto's "Space Battleship Yamato" manga series), and *Robotech* also appeared on cable and local channels. *Robotech* was cleverly created by producer Carl Macek, who combined three separate Japanese animation series into one original story with an entirely new script. Although among purists Macek would come to be regarded as the equivalent of the Antichrist for altering the original stories, *Robotech* garnered a near-fanatical following and generated huge interest in Japanese animation; it eventually spawned anime-style novels, comic books, and toys.

Third, the Cartoon/Fantasy Organization began aggressively proselytizing Japanese anime. Formed in Los Angeles in 1977 by indefatigable anime publicist and historian Fred Patten with Mark Merlino, Robin Leyden, and other fans to hold regular screenings of Japanese animation, C/FO quickly began branching out nationally.

Fourth, famous Japanese manga artists began attending American comics conventions, starting with a visit by Osamu Tezuka, Gō Nagai, Monkey Punch, and Yumiko Iigarashi to the San Diego Comic-Con in 1980.

The real boost in anime fandom (and by extension manga fandom) in America and the rest of the world came with the advent of inexpensive video cassette recorders. For the first time, fans were able to copy favorite anime shows and share them with friends, shanghaiing acquaintances fluent in Japanese to provide translations of the dialogue or simply making up the dialogue from what they saw on the screen. Given the nature of animation, it was easier to figure out what was going on than with printed manga, which remained much more foreign and required some familiarity with Japanese manga conventions, even in translation. Much later, with inexpensive computer equipment, many fans learned to subtitle the anime themselves. Since most anime were too violent or erotic or culturally "odd" to be shown on mainstream American television, video taping made possible wide exposure throughout the country. In 1995, working under the provocative acronym JAILED (Japanese Animation Industry Legal Enforcement Division), producers and distributors of subtitled and dubbed animation attempted to crack down on piracy of Japanese anime videos, despite the fact that anime (and manga) owe their popularity in no small measure to unlicensed translations, subtitling, and copying.

Part of the reason manga began to enjoy some measure of commercial success in the mid-1980s is that

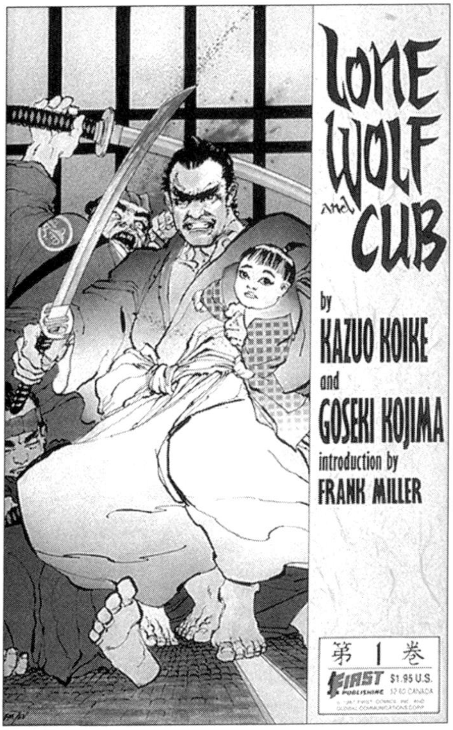

Volume 1 of Kazuo Koike and Gōseki Kojima's* Lone Wolf and Cub*, with cover by Frank Miller. Issued by First Publications, 1987.

many American comics fans and artists were looking for something different from the superhero genre that so dominates American comics. Keiji Nakazawa's *Barefoot Gen*, which had appeared in English in 1978, helped show many Americans how a longer, expanded format of comics could be used to create a more novelistic style. Kazuo Koike and Gōseki Kojima's beautifully rendered twenty-eight-volume samurai classic, *Kozure Ōkami* ("Lone Wolf and Cub"), helped awaken artists such as Frank Miller, the 1980s American comics superstar, to the cinematic potential of the comics medium. Partly as a result of Miller's enthusiasm, an English translation of *Lone Wolf* was published in 1987 by Chicago-based First Comics. With covers by Miller, it was an instant sensation among American comics fans.

Subsequently, nearly every major American comic book publisher has at one time or another issued translated Japanese manga or at least toyed with the idea of doing so. One of the most high-profile experiments has been Marvel Comics' publication (under its Epic Comics imprint) of Katsuhiro Ōtomo's dark sci-fi thriller *Akira*, beginning in 1988. Ōtomo draws in a detailed, realistic style familiar to Americans (he is influenced by French and American art styles and was one of the first postwar Japanese manga artists to draw Japanese with smaller eyes and a more "Asian" look). The dystopian science-fiction theme of his long-running story about a delinquent biker with apocalyptic powers in neo-Tokyo is exactly the type of material modern American readers enjoy. Sales were helped by the legitimacy Marvel's name lent to the project, by Marvel's efforts to make the Japanese work seem as "American" as possible (even colorizing the originally black-and-white artwork), and by the existence in Japan of a highly successful animated feature film version of the manga. When released in art theaters in the United States, the dubbed *Akira* film garnered considerable critical acclaim despite a plot that was too long and muddled. It was violent and graphic, with exquisitely rendered scenes of exploding buildings and transformations, and it was unlike anything Americans accustomed mainly to Disney-style animation had ever seen. But even Marvel's publication of *Akira*—which is regarded as one of the great manga successes in America—ran into problems. Whereas the Japan-side serialization finally concluded in 1992 after ten years, in the United States publication ran into difficulties and went on such a long hiatus that in early 1995 many fans speculated the series would never be completed.

* * * * *

In 1995 the largest publishers of translated manga in America were not the big East Coast comics publishers Marvel and D.C., but Viz Communications and Dark Horse Comics, both on the West Coast. Reflecting the particularly high level of interest in manga in the region, and a once-close-but-now-often-tortured relationship, Viz and the manga production arm of Dark Horse—Studio Proteus—were both located in San Francisco, only a few miles from each other. Further down the list but rapidly growing was Antarctic Press, based in Texas.

VIZ COMICS

Viz began publishing translated Japanese manga in 1987, first in alliance with American comic book publisher Eclipse and then independently in 1988. The brainchild of Seiji Horibuchi—a long-term resident of the San Francisco Bay Area who once lived on a California commune and has his finger on the pulse of pop culture in both Japan and America—Viz went on to become the largest publisher of translated Japanese manga in the U.S. In early 1995 PR materials from Viz claimed it published 90 percent of the black-and-white English-translated manga titles in America. By the end of the year, Viz's competitors said the true figure was closer to 60–65 percent, or even 45 percent, and even Viz admitted an erosion in its share. But the figures nonetheless indicated the company's huge presence in a relatively small field. Viz had issued over fifty manga titles in a variety of formats, including paperbacks and deluxe editions. It published a monthly anthology magazine of translations, *Manga Vizion*. And, it had taken the lead in introducing Japanese women's manga under the title of "Viz Flower Comics," an act of considerable courage in the overwhelmingly male-dominated U.S. comics market,

From the beginning, Viz had some major advantages over other American publishers of translated manga. As a total subsidiary of one of Japan's largest manga publishers, Shōgakukan, Viz could obtain the rights to some of the most popular works in Japan. It also had greater financial security. (The life cycle of publishers outside the Marvel and D.C. oligarchy is rather short; by 1996, two of the original pioneers of translated manga—Eclipse and First—had already vanished from the publishing map. Even Marvel's own Epic Comics, which published *Akira*, was gone.)

Again because of its Japan connections, Viz was able to enter the dubbed anime business and in many cases—such as with the very popular *Ranma 1/2* by Rumiko Takahashi—create a marketing synergy by marketing both anime and manga versions of the same works. By 1995, Viz director and editor-in-chief Satoru Fujii reported that

Issue No. 2 of* Manga Vizion*, with cover by the ever-popular Ryōichi Ikegami.

his company's revenues from sales of anime videos and manga publications were almost equal.

From the beginning, Viz had to struggle to adapt Japanese comics to the U.S. market. The company had to evolve a system of translation, often settling on a team approach, using a translator and a "rewriter" or editor of the translations for natural-sounding dialog. Since Japanese manga are read from right to left, pages also had to be flipped and "sound effects" (the *booms* and *pows*) had to be relettered. When interviewed in 1992, Fujii commented on some of the problems the company initially faced when it first worked with an American publisher before going independent:"We had a lot of disputes over editorial policy," he says. "They were used to American comics, and wanted to adapt and change manga to fit those conventions. For example, they wanted 'thought balloons' (containing a character's thoughts, as opposed to 'speech') to always be bubble-shaped. Also, in manga 'sound effects' are an integral part of the whole drawing, but they wanted more traditional American effects."

And then there was the issue of colorization. Most American comics are in color, whereas most manga are not. This can be a major disadvantage in the mainstream

U.S. marketplace. Coloring manga can be successfully done, as was the case with Marvel's version of *Akira*, but manga are designed in black and white to exploit subtle monochrome nuances and shadings, and these can be ruined by an overlay of color. Like the colorization of old black-and-white movies, colorization of manga is highly controversial. After a year or two of trying to colorize its translated manga, Viz gave up. "Some people like color," Fujii noted in 1992, "and some don't. We've found that color alone doesn't sell a manga, so we're going back to black and white."

Despite the existence in Japan of thousands of manga titles targeted at men, women, and children, the fickleness and narrowness of the male-oriented U.S. market means that selecting titles for translation is always a challenge. "It's a hit and miss process," Fujii lamented in 1992, "because the tastes of the readers keep changing. *Lum* (*Urusei Yatsura*) and *Fist of the North Star* (*Hokutō no Ken*), for example, are tremendously popular in Japan and even among fans here, but in translation the initial sales didn't live up to our expectations."

That other major Japanese manga publishers

Rumiko Takahashi's* Ranma *1/2 (English adaptation by Gerard Jones).

haven't entered the U.S. market the way Shōgakukan has is in itself revealing of the problems involved. "In Japan," Fujii said, "manga are a huge business, but what we're doing here is very small scale. The comic book market in America is much, much smaller than in Japan, and we've carved out our niche with a share of around 1 percent. For most Japanese publishers, this simply wouldn't be a very profitable business. Ironically, one of our most profitable areas now is the sale of rights of our English translations to European publishers, who then work them into their own languages. We've licensed nearly all our titles in Italy, and we've done very well in Spain and Sweden, and recently Germany. We've even sold rights to Indonesia and Brazil, and we've been approached by Turkey. Once manga are translated into English, it seems to open a door to the rest of the world."

STUDIO PROTEUS

The second biggest source of translated manga in the United States in 1995 was Studio Proteus, a "manga packaging" company run by Toren Smith in San Francisco. Studio Proteus has close ties to Dark Horse, one of the largest independent comics publishers (i.e., not part of the Marvel-DC oligarchy), and it also produces erotic comics for *Eros Comix* magazine. Smith, a long time aficionado of Japanese manga, once worked with Viz when they were just entering the U.S. market. Along with translator Dana Lewis, he "English-ized" for them some of the manga that have been best received in America, such as Hayao Miyazaki's *Nausicaä* and Sampei Shirato's *Legend of Kamui*. After a falling out with Viz, however, Smith became their competitor. As a "packager," he explains, his company "finds a Japanese manga we're interested in, locates a U.S. publisher who's interested in publishing it, and then handles the contracts and the production—including the translation, retouching, and lettering—and delivers a camera-ready copy." By 1995 he and his company had worked on over 16,000 pages of manga and handled over 35 titles.

One characteristic of many Studio Proteus manga is that Smith concentrates heavily on locating works by Jap-

Major Motoko Kusanagi jacks into a robot she has just destroyed. From Masamune Shirow's **Ghost in the Shell.**

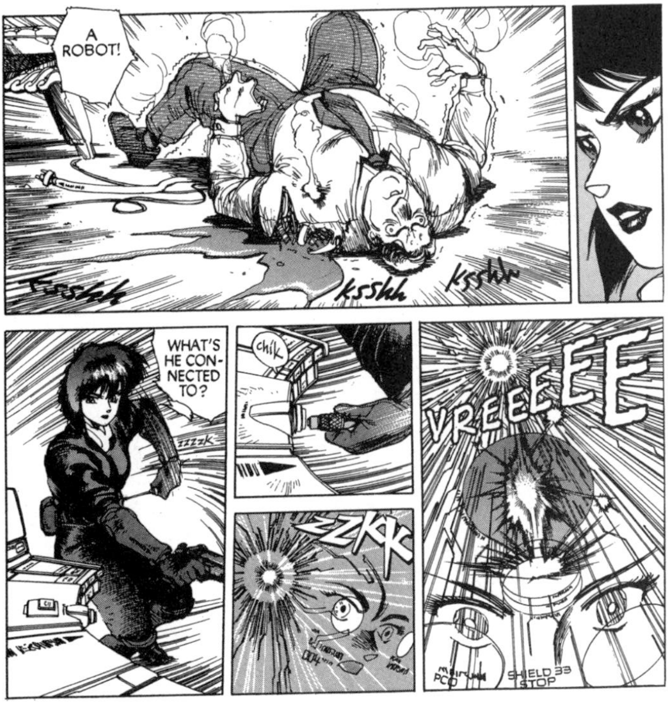

anese artists who draw in a rather non-Japanese style. This, combined with Smith's talent for writing the uniquely snappy dialogue preferred by American readers, has helped the firm's survival. In addition to Katsuhiro Ōtomo's *Domu* (arguably one of the finest Japanese manga rendered into English), Studio Proteus has produced many stories by Masamune Shirow, a brilliant artist with an opaque and mysterious style of storytelling who, thanks to Studio Proteus, may have achieved cult status among U.S. fans before he did in Japan. The Shirow works issued by Studio Proteus and Dark Horse include *Dominion*, *Orion*, *Ghost in the Shell*, and the well-received *Appleseed*. In 1992, when I asked Smith why he thought *Appleseed* was so popular, he commented, "One, the artwork is very accepted in the U.S.—it's detailed and more realistic than most manga. Two, the story is told in a more dense fashion than the average manga—you can't read it in two seconds per page. American readers are accustomed to pages with lots of information, and they feel

The beautiful young Seska gets serious in Masamune Shirow's supernatural spoof,* Orion, *a powerful stew of Buddhism, Shinto, Taoism, and quantum physics.

cheated if they can skip over the pages too fast. Three, the story—a post-apocalyptic vision of the future after World War III—is very suited to the U.S. market."

Producing manga hasn't been any easier for Studio Proteus than it has for Viz Communications. "Other than getting paid for our work," Smith says, "the biggest problem is finding manga that are both good and suitable for the U.S. market. There are lots of manga in Japan that are superb but wouldn't sell 1,000 copies here because of the nature of the U.S. market. One difficulty is that U.S. readers prefer detailed artwork. When we reverse the pages and have to change the sound effects or remove them, if there is a panel with lots of screen tone [which artists use for shading], it's difficult to retouch. *Appleseed* was a real nightmare in that regard. There's also a certain resistance in the U.S. market to black-and-white comics, so probably 40 percent of the stores in the U.S. don't even order manga. But translated manga have nonetheless been very successful. The average black-and-white American comic sells 3,000 copies, while the average translated manga sells around 13,000."

Smith is not overly optimistic about the future of translated manga,. "Barring unforeseen circumstances," he said in 1992, "I don't think Japanese manga are going to carve more of a niche in the direct sales market. They've maxed out. I think the average issue will continue to sell 10,000 or 13,000 copies. There's still room for hits, such as our upcoming *Ghost in the Shell* by Masamune Shirow, which has the potential to sell 30–40,000 copies, possibly more, because it's right up the American reader's alley and has a color section at the beginning of every issue."

In 1995, the year anime started to put down roots in mainstream America, Smith was slightly more positive; buoyed by the anime boom, sales of all his titles were rising. But he warned that "The worst thing that could possibly happen is for a large company to become involved in the translated manga business. They'd pour a lot of money into it, make bad choices in material, then pull out, having thoroughly peed in the pool; and in the meantime they'd have wiped out me and the smaller companies."

THE ANIME CONNECTION TAKES HOLD

As the anime industry began to explode into the North American mainstream in the mid-nineties, acquiring an increasingly hip aura on MTV and among Generation Xers, manga publishing became as linked to anime as it is in Japan, if not more so. Companies that had been issuing translated manga, such as Viz, began issuing "Englishized" anime videos directly tied in to the manga. Firms like Central Park Media, primarily an anime video importer/localizer firm, also branched out into publishing, issuing manga titles of their video releases under the logo CPM Comics. In England, the giant Manga Entertainment began English-izing anime, distributing translated manga, and even participating in the financing of the production of anime in Japan. In 1995, in an industry first, the animated theatrical feature *Ghost in the Shell*, based on Masamune Shirow's manga and jointly financed by Manga Entertainment and a Japanese production company, was simultaneously released in English and Japanese versions for mainstream distribution networks in both markets.

By the mid-nineties, manga were thus available in English both as individual titles on subjects from sex to cyber-wars and as serializations in magazines. Except for Viz's informative all-manga monthly, *Manga Vizion*, most of these magazines were anime-oriented, running manga as a bonus feature. These included Viz's monthly *Animerica* (edited by Trish Ledoux, a veteran of anime-oriented fan publications and co-author of *The Complete Anime Guide*) and, in the U.K., Manga Entertainment's *Manga Mania*. But even anime-oriented magazines that did not typically serialize manga stories included a great deal of information on manga (how could they not, when the anime are often derived from manga?). The London-based *Anime UK* (later renamed *Anime FX*), headed by tireless manga/anime booster Helen McCarthy, author of *The Anime Movie Guide*, ran historical and introductory articles on manga as well as anime, targeting an increasingly global audience. In Montreal, a delightful magazine with the intriguing title *Protoculture Addicts* (published by a group of French Canadians in English, originally for fans of the *Robotech* anime series), also featured regular articles on manga. Finally, there was Texas-based Antarctic Press's *Mangazine*, whose ten-year off-and-on history makes it one of the oldest manga-inspired publications in the U.S.

MANGAJIN

In 1995 one of the best sources of information on non-anime related manga, and of translated manga in general, was a magazine that did not specifically target the usual manga/anime "fan" market. Titled *Mangajin* (of no relation to *Mangazine*), it was published in Atlanta, Georgia, for students of Japanese language and culture. Formed in 1990 by former translator and ex–rock and roller Vaughan Simmons, *Mangajin* took the novel approach of serializing excerpts from popular and non-popular manga to teach living language usage. Reflecting his own investment in learning the language, Simmons says, "I thought Americans deserved a break, that they needed something a little more fun than the standard language textbook." This approach permitted two things not possi-

***April 1994 cover to* Mangajin.**

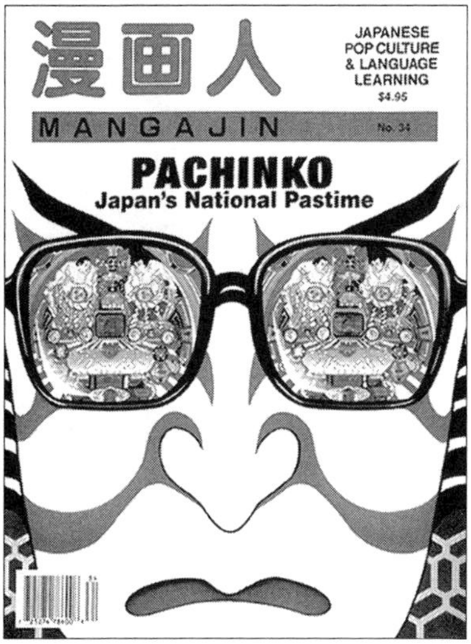

漫画人
JAPANESE POP CULTURE & LANGUAGE LEARNING
$4.95
MANGAJIN
No. 34
PACHINKO
Japan's National Pastime

©1994 MANGAJIN, INC.

ble in other publications. First it allowed reproduction of the Japanese pages in their original form—in Japanese order, with Japanese dialogue—accompanied by pages of literal translations and explanations (including cultural explanations). And it allowed reproduction of manga that had no anime-link or any hope of ever being commercially published in English. Thus, while *Mangajin*'s focus was on language-learning, it was also the best place to read and learn about the manga that most closely reflected Japanese culture and true Japanese reading tastes. In 1995, the company also began issuing manga books, such as the anthology *Bringing Home the Sushi: An Inside Look at Japanese Business through Japanese Comics.*

* * * * *

The vast majority of translated manga material in America remains skewed to the idiosyncrasies of the marketplace, which is still overwhelmingly dominated by young males. Science fiction stories, with their more universal themes, are popular, and so are stories with an erotic theme. There is also a great deal of pressure on publishers to issue manga with an animation tie-in. Thus, there are lots of panty-clad girls with guns, monsters, cyber-

NEW
OVER 90,000 SOLD IN JAPAN
LANCHESTER STRATEGY
by
SHINICHI YANO
A MOUNTED SWORDSMAN HAS A BIG ADVANTAGE OVER A FOOT-SOLDIER
WE CAN ALSO APPLY THIS STRATEGY TO BASEBALL
OH NO!!.. DOWN ANOTHER 10%
VOLUME 1

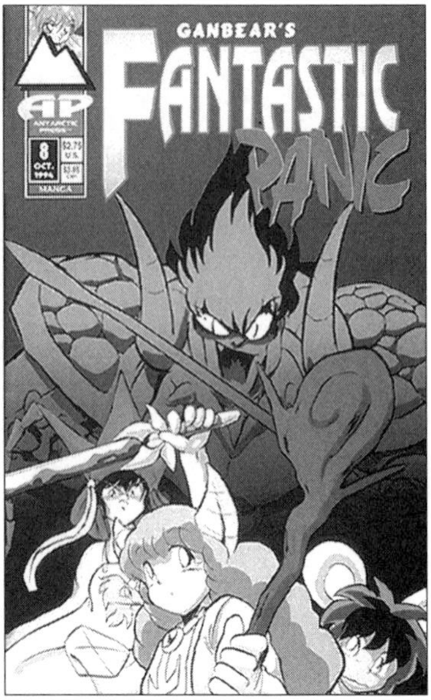

LEFT:* Volume 1 of New Lanchester Strategy *by Shinichi Yano.* *RIGHT:* Ganbear's Fantastic Panic, *No. 8. A "Comic Market"* dōjinshi *in America, from Antarctic Press.

robots, and apocalyptic visions. But if one searches, there is much more. Viz Communications issues women's manga. Blast Books in New York has published a volume of the decadent avant-garde work of Suehiro Maruo. The University of California Press has issued the best-selling economic primer *Japan Inc.* Lanchester Press, also in California, has issued translated manga books on the strategy of market-share domination developed by Frederick William Lanchester, a Britisher (1868–1946) whose theories are (not surprisingly!) enormously popular in Japan. Texas-based Antarctic Press and other firms have issued several *dōjinshi*, or Japanese manga fanzines, as well as a wide variety of the ever-popular Japanese erotic manga.

One of the biggest problems for readers of translated manga is that it is often difficult to find stories that have been published in their entirety. Smaller comics publishers in America, outside of the Marvel-DC orbit, have always led a precarious existence, so if they undertake to translate and publish a lengthy Japanese manga, which may be thousands of pages long, they may well not be around to complete the work. A manga story 2,000 pages long in Japan may be serialized in a weekly maga-

Cover to Hiroyuki Utatane's* Temptation, *from Mangerotica.

zine and be finished in a little over a year. In the United States, where all "comic books" are monthlies, the same story would take nearly five years. Also, the early issues of stories invariably sell far better than later issues due to initial curiosity among readers as well as hoarding by collectors; unless the publisher takes this pattern into account it may not be financially possible to continue publication. Some unconscionable American publishers hungry for up-front profits may undertake the serialization of a story knowing full well at the outset that they will never complete it.

Manga Made in America

まんが「メード・イン・USA」

THE INFLUENCE OF MANGA ON AMERICAN COMICS

In the English-speaking world, manga are not only read, but—increasingly—emulated. Fred Patten, in an article titled "1977–1992: Fifteen Years of North American Fandom," notes one of the first "brash" examples of Japanese anime/manga influences on an American comic book: in 1983, a character in issue 79 of Marvel Comics' *Star Wars* (scripted and drawn by Tom Palmer and manga fan Jo Duffy) was drawn as a pastiche of Leiji Matsumoto's famous Captain Harlock space-pirate character.

Today, the manga influence on American comics is far more obvious. Although American artists generally have far fewer pages to work with than their Japanese counterparts, American page layouts have become much more cinematic and dramatic and are now quite similar to those of Japanese male manga (the distinctively different layouts of women's manga make them much more difficult to emulate). In 1992, Toren Smith claimed that "the Japanese use of screen tone (for shading) is influencing American artists. Some, such as Adam Hughes, are very interested in working in black and white now because they want to try new toning techniques. . . . I've also noticed that American artists seem to be using more Japanese-style sound effects." Other Americans, such as Art Spiegelman, Pulitzer Prize–winning author of the *Maus* graphic novel series (which was very Japanese in its treatment of a serious subject in a long, narrative manga format), have even claimed that the "eyes" of characters in American comics seem to be getting larger and larger because of the Japanese influence.

So-called American manga—comic books authored by Americans but executed in a Japanese-style—are the most striking example of the manga influence on American comics. Page layouts are more dramatic and fluid, and characters have larger eyes, less muscular physiques, and rounder faces. Stories have many more allusions to Japanese culture and may feature Japanese characters or Japa-

Cover to The Dirty Pair, Book Three: A Plague of Angels.

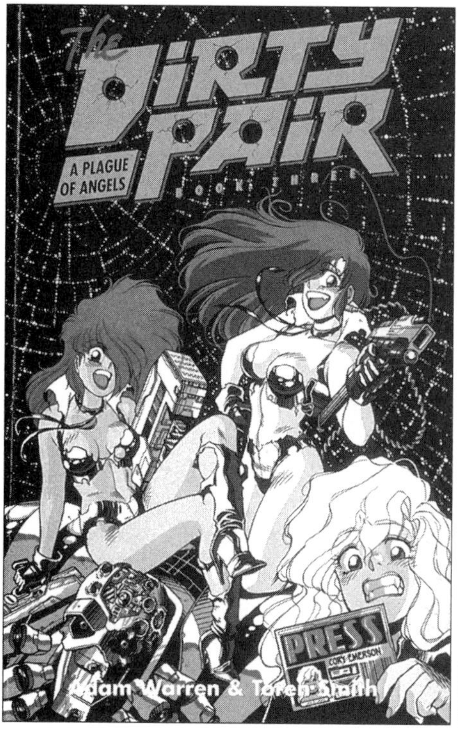

nese subject matter. As one might expect, the artists and writers are enormous fans of manga or anime. Some of the best-known examples in the early 1990s were Ben Dunn's popular parody *Ninja High School* and Adam Warren and Toren Smith's *Dirty Pair*. Dunn, the founder of Antarctic Press, made a minor industry out of *Ninja High School* with paperbacks, a CD-ROM, and special "small-bodied" versions of the story—a take-off on the Japanese fad in the late eighties–early nineties called "super deformation," or "SD," which involved drawing famous characters in a humorous, compressed style. Warren and Smith's *Dirty Pair*, is a particularly interesting example of the American manga genre; the characters were licensed from a popular Japanese novel and animation series and then turned into an "American manga" (in Japan the tale was never a manga). Smith, who scripted the *Dirty Pair* story, is also head of the aforementioned Studio Proteus. Especially intriguing is the case of Studio Go! in Mission Hills, California. It produces the manga-style comic books of Central Park Media and Argo Press, which are in turn based on Japanese animation. Much of the animation, of course, is based on Japanese manga! Finally, in 1993, even Japan-owned Viz began issuing a line of "American manga." It called them "Viz Manga Originals."

Ultimately, in the United States and other countries manga may have had their biggest effect on the publishing system itself. Just as artists have begun to emulate the Japanese style of art, publishers have tried imitating the Japanese system of doing business. Links with animation and movies are being strengthened, as are the rights of creators. Increasingly, thin American-style "comic books" are compiled into paperback book collections and sold through non-traditional channels such as trade book distributors, which gets them into regular bookstores. In an article in the April 1996 edition of *Wizard* magazine, titled "American Manga," writer Carl Gustav Horn even speculated that the growing popularity of Japanese manga might create a renaissance in the otherwise ailing U.S. comics industry.

Fan Power

マニアの力

FAN POWER

Publishers issue manga, but the real driving force behind the spread of manga and anime in the English world is the fans.

Many fans—despite occasionally being viewed by the outside world as members of a highly unusual, if not bizarre, fringe group—have spent enormous amounts of time and energy proselytizing their favorite works and the medium in general. Starting in the late seventies, they began getting together and showing each other anime or trading information on manga. In the early eighties, they began screening works and trading information at comics and science fiction conventions around the U.S. (where dealers had also begun selling untranslated manga). Fans

***Dale Engelhardt (in light suit) and Jeremy Morales (with hat), winners in the masquerade at Anime Expo '92 for best re-creation of anime characters. Characters represented are from Monkey Punch's popular manga-anime* Lupin III.**

didn't have their own conventions, however, and had to borrow meeting space for their activities at the larger sci-fi and comics gatherings. By 1991, their numbers had grown enough so that their wish finally came true; they got their own conventions.

AnimeCon '91—"The First International Conference on Japanese Animation"—was held for four days in San Jose, California. Nearly two thousand *otaku*-fans hobnobbed with each other, bought books, magazines, videotapes, and merchandise, admired each other's costumes, collected autographs, and engaged in marathon sessions of watching Japanese animation.

It didn't matter that some of the main guests of honor didn't come. Superstar manga artists Katsuhiro Ōtomo and Leiji Matsumoto were scheduled to appear but had to cancel. In their stead came animation character designers such as Hideaki Anno, Yoshiyuki Sadamoto, Haruhiko Mikimoto, and Ken'ichi Sonoda, and the manga artist for the popular series *Outlanders*, Johji Manabe. They must have been surprised to learn how popular they were outside of Japan—autograph sessions resulted in lines of over a hundred fans, some of whom waited patiently for hours.

The four days were filled with panel discussions devoted to topics like "Cross-Cultural Issues in Animation and Comics" and "Comics Production" and what most

Yoshiyuki Tomino, the creator of the* Gundam *anime-manga-toy-novel-game-music universe, with two of his fans at Anime Expo 1992. Dressed in* Gundam *costumes are Dawn Therese Gordon of Texas (left, dressed as Haman Kahn) and Jeff Okamoto of California (right, dressed as Brite Noa, aka "Bright Noah").

people would probably view as pathologically obsessive analyses of popular Japanese animation shows (How many beam bazookas can a robot exoskeleton really carry in outer space?). On the second night, fans masquerading as their favorite anime and manga characters put on amusing skits. One fan was dressed as a villain from the evil Zeon empire in Yoshiyuki Tomino's popular outerspace robot epic *Gundam*. When he appeared the audience roared "Zeek Zeon!" ("Hail, Zeon!") in approval, just like in the animated film. Everyone knew the story backward and forward.

Needless to say, organizing an event of this size is no easy matter, especially when those attending are mostly American fans. As a group, American fantasy fans tend to be somewhat anarchic, slightly dislocated from reality, and proud of it. Nonetheless, preparations were carried out very professionally by dedicated volunteers. A contingent of interpreters eased communication problems for the guests of honor from Japan. Conference security personnel politely reminded visitors in full costume that realistic weaponry (swords, pistols, machine guns, laser cannons) had to be inspected and cleared.

The organizers also displayed considerable mastery of modern technology. Computers were used to handle registrations, generate daily announcements with desktop publishing, and program animation shows. Using the hotel's cable television system, Japanese animation was beamed into guests' hotel rooms around the clock on three channels. After staying up day and night for four days, subsisting on diets of liquid stimulants and junk food, and continuously watching three channels of animation simultaneously–while also reading manga—it is a miracle that most convention-goers remained functional. For those who tired of watching TV, several of the same programs could be seen twenty-four hours a day projected in sixteen-millimeter format on a big screen in a large hall. And the conference was truly international. Fans came from the United States and Japan, and from France, England, and Australia. Two French Canadians drove nearly 3,000 miles from Montreal.

AnimeCon '91 became the prototype for subsequent anime and manga conventions, and like Godzilla the manga-anime fan scene in America kept getting bigger and bigger. By 1995 large conventions spanning several days were being held in California, New York, Texas, Pennsylvania, and Virginia. Usually organized and run by amateurs, they had a pool of willing volunteers and an increasingly sophisticated body of experience to draw upon. Nearly all large universities and major cities in the U.S. now have anime or manga fan clubs, many of which publish their own fanzines.

One of the hallmarks of fans at anime-manga conventions in the United States is their diversity and the broad range in their ages. There are few children. The participants are generally in their late teens, twenties, thirties, or older, and—as also seems to be true at comic book and SF conventions in the United States—most are males. Most appear to be gainfully employed; it is not unusual to meet computer programmers, lawyers, truck drivers, and even active-duty U.S. military personnel. In a refreshing change from other white-male-dominated fan conventions, the anime-manga conventions draw from a cross-section of races, with a particularly large contingent of Asian Americans on the West Coast. Even among non-Asians, Japan—since it is the source of favorite anime and manga—is regarded as a sort of a cultural mecca. Japanese *otaku*-fan Toshio Okada's article on this phenomenon—"Anime Culture Is Ultra-Cool! American *Otakus* in Love with Japan"—appeared in the Japanese newsmagazine *Aera* on October 2, 1995: "Why wasn't I born in Japan?" was the reported lament of one U.S. high school student (who claimed to have parents who were members of a white supremacist group). "Americans aren't cool. I wish I was Japanese."

Networking

ネットワーク

FAN POWER

As time passes, fan communities tend to organize themselves, and the manga-anime scene is no exception. Sometimes business and other professionals become fans, bringing with them important skills. Two of the early organizers of manga-anime conferences held in California, I discovered to my amusement, were active-duty servicemen; one an officer in the U.S. Navy with a specialty in oceanography (stationed in Japan for several years as liaison with the Japanese Maritime Self-Defense Forces) and the other an officer in the Air Force with a specialty in command and control. Often, however, amateurs hone their skills at manga-anime conferences or through publishing fanzines and then go on to work in the comics industry as professionals, publishing or translating manga or working in sales. The human network that therefore develops allows greater and greater exchange of information, particularly when some of the fans go on to work in Japan and feed more and more information back to the United States. Like the U.S. and Japanese economies, the fan communities are increasingly intertwined, and friendships continue to grow across oceans and language barriers.

From early on, one of the most important tools in

holding the manga-anime fan community together has been computer networks. There are two main reasons for this. First, the community draws heavily from people in the computer and telecommunications industries and from students of these subjects in universities, where network access has long been available for free. Second, information on favorite works has until recently been extremely hard to come by (most of it located in Japan and in a foreign language to boot), and in many areas the mere admission of interest in a field as obscure as "Japanese comic books" has drawn arched eyebrows from classmates or fellow workers. For fans spread-out across the U.S., therefore, computers and networking have helped overcome great geographical and psychological isolation.

On the commercial CompuServe network, the Anime/Manga (Japan) section was formed under the umbrella of the Comics and Animation Forum around 1986. It has been a place for fans around the world to trade information on anime and manga and to swap digitized imagery of their favorite works. Japanese fans, and even Japanese artists such as Mitsuru Sugaya, have often contributed. On Genie, another commercial network, a similar group called JaMo (Japan and Manga On-line) has existed since mid-1989. In 1996, *Wizard* magazine also had a section on manga on America Online. And finally, there are scores, if not hundreds, of small computer bulletin boards manned by individuals that are at least partly devoted to anime and manga.

The most popular gathering spot for manga fans in the U.S., however, is not the expensive commercial networks but the "Mother of all networks"—the global Internet—and its offspring, the interactive, graphics-intensive World Wide Web. As of 1995 scores of individual fans had their own, self-decorated "home pages" on the Web, filled with information and "appropriated" images from favorite anime and manga works. Publishers were present, too. Steve Pearl, a moderator of an anime-manga forum, noted in 1995 that the Net was already playing a big part in influencing the English-language anime and manga industries, and that due to fan pressure some pub-

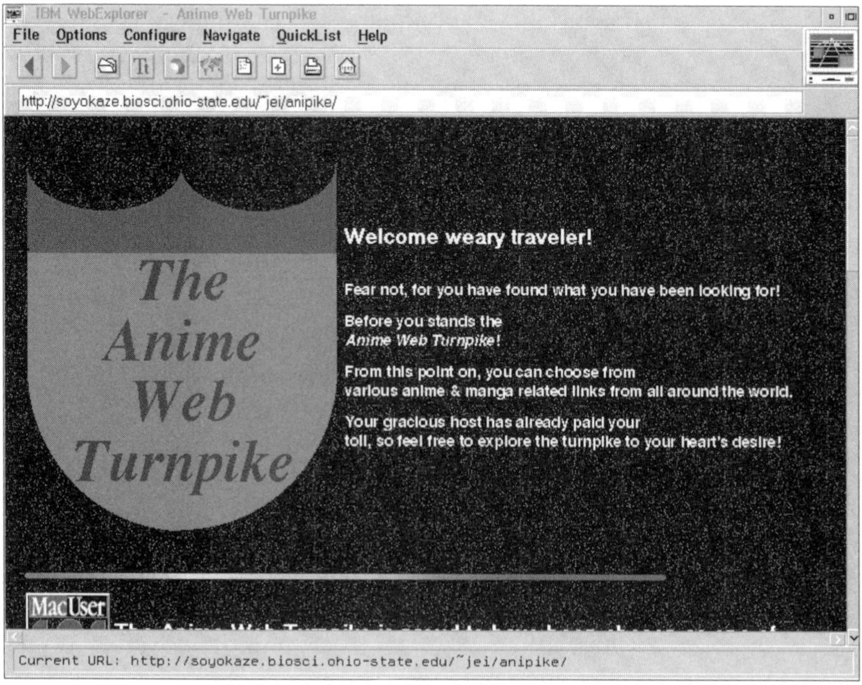

IBM WebExplorer - Anime Web Turnpike
File Options Configure Navigate QuickList Help
http://soyokaze.biosci.ohio-state.edu/~jei/anipike/
The Anime Web Turnpike
Welcome weary traveler!
Fear not, for you have found what you have been looking for!
Before you stands the Anime Web Turnpike!
From this point on, you can choose from various anime & manga related links from all around the world.
Your gracious host has already paid your toll, so feel free to explore the turnpike to your heart's desire!
MacUser
Current URL: http://soyokaze.biosci.ohio-state.edu/~jei/anipike/

Opening page of Jay Fublar Harvey's "The Anime Web Turnpike."

lishers and distributors had even changed their subtitling and sequencing of episodes on laserdisks. "Most of the companies," he said, "are very aware of Electronic Fandom and they maintain websites and have e-mail addresses. But with instantaneous communication between fans all over the world now possible, the Net is also responsible for the explosive growth in underground fandom, such as fan subtitlers, translators, *dōjinshi* artists, and so on."

Meanwhile, on the older text-based USENET portion of the Internet, where some 20,000 "forums" of different interests were represented, information on Japanese manga or anime was available in over twelve different groups, only two of which were in Japanese and frequented mainly by Japanese nationals. The most popular commodity of trade on USENET is information, primarily about favorite works. For newcomers, there are FAQs, or lists of "Frequently Asked Questions" with detailed answers. A thorough reading of these lists gives visitors to the forums the particular "netiquette" (network etiquette) of the group, as well as the arcana necessary to understand the debates and interchanges that take place between fans. Traffic is high. Statistics provided by Steve Pearl, moderator of rec.arts.anime and rec.arts.manga, show that the latter group had a nearly tenfold increase in messages between 1992 and 1995. One fan who frequents both manga and anime forums posted 321 anime-related messages in June 1995, for an *average* of over 10 per day (presumably not on company time).

As on other computer network forums, discussions tend to become heated, passionate, and vituperative, so much so that to an outsider they can seem obsessive, and sick—there is, in other words, what is referred to as a very poor "signal to noise ratio." In 1993–94 a frenzied disagreement took place over the correct translation of the title of the popular manga-anime work, *Aa, Megami-sama*, with one faction insisting it should be "Aah, My Goddess" and the other insisting on "Oh My Goddess!" (in the published English version, the latter won out). Factionalism is a hallmark of the *otaku*-fan community and has been exacerbated by the freewheeling, anarchic nature of the Internet, which itself is often a giant rumor mill and disinformation factory.

Opinions are not the only thing exchanged on USENET forums. One group is devoted entirely to anime/manga-inspired stories by fans. It also has synopses and translations of manga-anime for those who do not read or speak Japanese. These well-intentioned translations are done by fans, for fans. As with the exchange of images they involve serious copyright issues, even though, like the trade in pirated videos, they have helped nurture and grow the fan community, thereby creating the very market that today allows the legitimate publishers and producers to thrive.

Manga and video cassettes of anime are also sold and traded, as are digitized images of favorite characters and works, some of which reflect a darker side of the fan scene. (One popular forum on USENET is named "alt.binaries.pictures.erotica.anime," or in plain-speak, "alternative digitized pictures of anime erotica.")

The vast majority of American manga and anime fans are young males. One Viz survey of readers of its translated manga showed that they are nearly 90 percent male, between the ages of 18 and 36, with incomes between $25,000 and $30,000. One would, therefore, expect a healthy interest in erotica among anime and manga fans, and that the industry would respond to this demand. And it has. In March, 1992, Joe Bob Briggs, the humorous "drive-in movie critic of Grapevine, Texas," wrote a timely column about such material, titled "Japan's 'Annie Maes': Nekkid Women in Children's Cartoons." These "Japaheeno guns-and-hooters cartoon movies," he said, were about "nekkid women flying through space with rockets strapped to their back, lasering enemy aliens so they can travel through time to save their lesbo lovers." As he noted, the anime—to the horror of parents—had often been stocked in the children's sections of video rental shops in America.

In talking with people in the anime and manga industries, and with fans, it becomes clear that the erotica to which fans are attracted is slightly different from that found in many other fantasy-oriented communities. American male fans seem particularly attracted to the big-eyed, young, almost prepubescent characters that cavort in panty-like costumes or shed their clothes on every other page (or video frame). On one level this attraction is easily explainable. To shy, retiring, and still maturing young males, the erotic women characters idealized in American mainstream comics and films may sometimes seem too adult, too threatening. The modern Japanese fantasy ideal—younger, slightly softer, rarely possessing an in-your-face aggressive feminism—may be a type of refuge. But it is hard to escape the conclusion that some of the less healthy minds on the fringe of English manga/anime fandom have pedophilic tendencies that are stimulated, and in their minds even legitimized, by the Japanese "Lolita" erotic ideal. Inevitably, as anime and manga become more and more mainstream, this dark side of the phenomenon will invite more and more criticism.

Beyond Fandom

マニアの世界を超える

MANGA CULTURE

Whatever prurient interest a fringe element of fans has developed is offset by an increasingly serious interest in manga and anime in the English world. Beginning in the early 1990s, both manga and anime have been the theme of several museum exhibits in the English-speaking world. In 1991, the Pomeroy Purdy Gallery in London hosted an exhibit titled "Manga, Comic Strip Books from Japan." In 1992, manga were featured in the Boston Children's Museum and at the Cartoon Art Museum in San Francisco, where an exhibit was held titled "Visions of the Floating World: The Cartoon Art of Japan." In 1995, an international conference on anime and manga was held at the University of Sydney, Australia, and a symposium on manga was hosted at Georgetown University in Washington, D.C.

Manga and anime are increasingly popular subjects for research by academic professionals and by undergraduate and graduate students. Among the topics: Hart Larrabee wrote his 1989 senior thesis at Carleton University on the manga of Sampei Shirato; Jonathan Clements, a British translator of both anime and manga, did his 1995 Master of Philosophy at the University of Stirling on Japan's manga and anime exports; Sharon Kinsella, as part of her doctorate at Oxford University, studied boys' and men's manga; Matthew Thorn, a cultural anthropologist at Columbia University who also translates many manga for Viz Communications, has done extensive research on sexuality and gender in *shōjo* (girls') manga and is writing a book on the subject; David Vernal did an intriguing study for his 1994 senior thesis at Harvard titled "The Power to Command: Society, Authority, and the Individual in Japanese Science Fiction Comic Books and Animation."

* * * * *

Manga artist and A-bomb survivor Keiji Nakazawa in front of one of his* Barefoot Gen *paintings, displayed at the Cartoon Art Museum in San Francisco during the "Visions of the Floating World" exhibit, 1992.

In a September 17, 1995 *New York Times* article, Ty Ahmad-Taylor estimated that sales of Japanese comic books in America in the previous year amounted to $10 million and that home video sales had reached $50 million. Although many people in the industry with whom I talked seemed to feel the figure for translated manga sales was highly inflated (with the real number around $5 to $6 million), there was a general consensus that sales were growing rapidly, mainly because of the popularity of anime. Toren Smith of Studio Proteus estimates that 80 percent of his readers start out as anime fans. "A rising tide lifts all boats," he says. "Anime are becoming part of the American entertainment mainstream, and manga are becoming part of that, too."

Nonetheless, the total share of translated manga in the overall comics market remains small. In 1992, when I asked Satoru Fujii of Viz why he thought young Americans liked Japanese manga, he was quite blunt. "Most don't," he said. "To 90 percent of comics fans, manga are a foreign medium, with different artwork, different sequences, and different stories. But those who like them, *really* like them." Three years later, in 1995, he was still cautious about the future. He saw the growth of translated manga as slow, but noted that if anime truly became mainstream in the U.S. there could be quite a large fan base in ten years, when many of the small children raised on anime would begin buying manga. "If we have a large fan base," he noted hopefully, "we can start publishing the really great Japanese comics, which don't have a market now."

* * * * *

In Japan, anime shows are like commercials for manga, and they are still watched mainly by younger people and *otaku*. Unlike manga, which have permeated mainstream, adult society, anime shows are not something your average office manager spends time watching. In the English-speaking world, however, anime programs are the entry point into a new universe for fans who are often adults. Manga—with their different "vocabulary" and "grammar" and much closer connection to the Japanese "id"—are the inner chamber for initiates. Given Rudyard Kipling's famous lines about East and West never meeting, perhaps the most remarkable aspect of translated manga is that they are popular at all. Especially interesting in America, in light of Kipling's opinion, is that there is no "Western" French or Italian or even British comics subculture.

* * * * *

Ultimately, the popularity of both anime and manga outside of Japan is emblematic of something much larger—perhaps a postwar "mind-meld" among the peoples of industrialized nations, who all inhabit a similar (but steadily shrinking) physical world of cars, computers, buildings, and other manmade objects and systems. Patterns of thinking are still different among cultures, and different enough for people to be fascinated by each other, but the areas of commonality have increased to the point where it is easier than ever before to reach out and understand each other on the deepest levels of human experience and emotion.

During the panel discussion on manga that I attended in London in 1995, sociologist Sharon Kinsella remarked that manga were on the verge of becoming the equivalent of "tea ceremony" to the Japanese government. It was an apt observation. When propagandizing

Japanese culture to Western nations, the government has until recently preferred to stress "safe culture"—refined arts and crafts, Zen, tea ceremony, and so forth. Popular culture, long regarded as too "lowbrow," has rarely been promoted, and the result overseas has been a very dislocated view of modern Japan. According to the January 7, 1996 edition of the *Asahi* newspaper, however, the Overseas Public Relations Division of the Ministry of Foreign Affairs now sends copies of *Mangajin* to its embassies and consulates in 180 nations around the world; at a recent international conference it also handed out copies of a translated "business manga" anthology to 500 foreign reporters.

There is an element of risk in promoting manga, as there is no guarantee foreigners will get a better impression of Japan from reading them. The material foreigners prefer, moreover, may not be what is preferred in Japan, and it may be interpreted differently. In a worst-case scenario, the "Lolita complex virus" might even be inadvertently exported.

More likely, however, manga will give a far truer picture of Japan, warts and all, than "highbrow" tea ceremony or Zen ever could. As a form of popular culture, comics of all nations tend to be tightly woven with local culture and thought. In translation, manga—especially—can be both a medium of entertainment and a Rosetta stone for mutual understanding.

付録—英語のマンガ情報

APPENDIX: MANGA IN ENGLISH

THE LISTINGS HERE REPRESENT ONLY A SNAPSHOT OF THE ENORmous activity taking place in the burgeoning English-language manga industry. Many of the sites and resources listed also provide anime-related information and contacts. Addresses and site URLs constantly change; corrections and additions will be greatly appreciated.

SELECTED PUBLISHERS OF MANGA TRANSLATED INTO ENGLISH (2002)

Antarctic Press
7272 Wurzbach, #204
San Antonio, Texas 78240
TEL: 210-614-0396 • FAX: 210-614-5029
E-MAIL: apcog@hotmail.com
WEB: http://www.antarctic-press.com/

- *Publishes a wide range of translated manga, including dōjinshi, erotica, and "American manga"*

Blast Books
P.O. Box 51
Cooper Station
New York, New York 10276-0051

- *Publishes "edgy" works by Suehiro Maruo, Hideshi Hino, etc., and the anthology* Comics Underground Japan

Bloomsbury Children's Books
38 Soho Square
London W1V 5DF, United Kingdom
E-MAIL: enquiries@bloomsbury.com
WEB: http://www.bloomsbury.com/

- *Publishes Takeshi Maekawa's Tekken Chinmi ("Ironfist Chinmi") in right-to-left style*

Central Park Media
CPM Comics/ U.S. Manga Corps.

250 West 57th Street, Suite 317
New York, New York 10107
TEL: (800-833-7456) • FAX: 212-977-8709
E-MAIL: cpm@centralparkmedia.com
WEB: http://www.centralparkmedia.com;
http://www.animeone.com

- *Publishes "American manga" and translated manga*

ComicsOne

48531 Warm Springs Boulevard, Suite 408
Fremont, CA 94539
TEL: 510-687-1388 • FAX: 510-252-1388
EMAIL: info@comicsone.com
WEB: http://www.comicsone.com

* *Publishes wide variety of manga, including classics and even one with a pachinko theme*

Dark Horse Comics/Studio Proteus

Department DG
10956 SE Main Street
Milwaukie, Oregon 97222
TEL: 800-862-0052 • FAX: 503-654-3218
E-MAIL: mailorder@dhorse.com
WEB: http://www.dhorse.com/; http: //www.studioproteus.com

- *One of the largest publishers of translated manga*

DC Comics

1700 Broadway
New York, New York 10019
WEB: http://www.dccomics.com

- *Known best for superhero comics, DC recently has been publishing some Japanese manga artists and their works*

Educomics

P.O. Box 45831
Seattle, Washington 98145-0831
TEL: 206-985-9483
E-MAIL: rifas@qwest.net

- *Publisher of American comic book versions of Keiji Nakazawa's* I Saw It *and* Gen of Hiroshima

Eros Comics

P.O. Box 25070
Seattle, Washington 98125-1970
TEL: 800-657-1100 (U.S.); 206-524-1967 (outside U.S.)
FAX: 206-524-2104
WEB: http://www.eroscomix.com/

- *A subsidiary of Fantagraphics; publishes* MangErotica, *etc.*

Fantagraphics
7563 Lake City Way NE
Seattle, Washington, 98115
TEL: 800-657-1100
WEB: http://www.fantagraphics.com

- *Publishes an anthology of avant garde manga titled* Sake Jock

Kodansha International
1-17-14 Otowa
Bunkyo-ku
Tokyo, Japan 112-8652
TEL: 03-3944-6493 • FAX: 03-3944-6942

- *Publishes increasing number of classic manga in bilingual format, often obtainable outside of Japan in bookstores that cater to Japanese readers*

Lanchester Press
P.O. Box 60621
Sunnyvale, California 94086
TEL/FAX: 408-732-7723
ORDERS: 800-247-6553
E-MAIL: js@lanchester.com
WEB: http://www.lanchester.com

- *Publishes business and management manga*

Last Gasp
777 Florida Street
San Francisco, California 94110
TEL: 415-824-6636 • FAX: 415-824-1836
E-MAIL: lastgasp@pacbell.net; gasp@lastgasp.com
WEB: http://www.lastgasp.com/

- *Distributor that has published some translated manga erotica; currently provides an extremely important service by publishing Keiji Nakazawa's* Barefoot Gen *in the U.S.*

Marvel Comics
Marvel Entertainment Group, Inc.
387 Park Avenue South
New York, New York 10016
WEB: http://marvelcomics.com

- *Occasionally publishes Japanese artists and their works, such as Katsuhiro Otomo's* Akira

Radio Comix
11765 West Avenue, #117
San Antonio, Texas 78216
TEL/FAX: 210-348-7195
E-MAIL: radiocomix@aol.com

WEB: http://radiocomix.com
- *Publishes translated manga and "American manga"*

Studio Ironcat L.L.C.
607 William Street, Suite #213
Fredericksburg, Virginia 22401
WEB: http://www.ironcat.com
- *Publishes translated manga and "American manga"*

Tokyo Pop
5900 Wilshire Boulevard, Suite 2000
Los Angeles, CA 90036-5020
TEL: 323-692-6700 • FAX: 323-692-6701
E-MAIL: info@tokyopop.com
WEB: http://www.tokyopop.com
- *One of the largest manga publishers in the U.S., issuing manga in magazine and paperback format, often Kodansha titles; manga use Japanese layouts and are read from right-to-left*

University of California Press
2120 Berkeley Way
Berkeley, California 94720
TEL: 510-642-4247 • ORDERS: 800-822-6657
E-MAIL: ucpress@ucop.edu
- *Publishes Shōtarō Ishinomori's* Japan Inc. *(vol. 1)*

Verotik Publishing
P.O. Box No. 64859
Los Angeles, California 90064
WEB: http://www.danzig-verotik.com
- *Publishes Gō Nagai's* Devilman

Viz Comics
Viz Communications Inc.
655 Bryant Street
San Francisco, California 94107
TEL: 800-394-3042 • FAX: 415-546-7086
WEB: http://www.viz.com; http://www.j-pop.com
- *Pioneering and largest U.S. publisher of manga translated into English; issues many titles of parent company, Shōgakukan.*

SELECTED MAGAZINES WITH TRANSLATED JAPANESE MANGA AND REVIEWS

ANIMERICA ("Anime & Manga Monthly")
WEB: http://www.animerica-mag.com
- *Runs articles and features on animation, and serializes select manga in translation; see "Viz Comics" under list of publishers for contact information*

ANIMERICA EXTRA ("The Anime Fans' Comic Magazine")

- *Primarily a manga anthology magazine; see "Viz Comics" under list of publishers for contact information*

COMIC BOX

Fusion Product
2-12-19-1F Asagaya-kita
Suginami-ku
Tokyo 166-0001, Japan
TEL: 03-5373-5780 • FAX: 03-5327-7655
E-MAIL: info@comicbox.co.jp
WEB: http://www.comicbox.co.jp

- *Primarily Japanese, but often has excellent articles in English*

PROTOCULTURE ADDICTS ("The Anime & Manga Magazine")

Protoculture Enr.
P.O. Box 1433, Station B
Montreal, Quebec H3B 3L2, Canada
FAX: 514-527-0347
E-MAIL: info@protoculture.qc.ca
WEB: http://www.protoculture.qc.ca

- *Eclectic magazine of manga/anime criticism and reviews*

SMILE

* *A manga anthology magazine featuring shōjō manga stories, a long-ignored market in the English-language world; see Tokyo Pop for contact information*

SUPER MANGA BLAST!

- *An omnibus or anthology magazine of manga, it represents a collaboration between Dark Horse, Studio Proteus, and Radio Comix; see Dark Horse under list of publishers for contact information*

TOKION MAGAZINE

Knee High Media Japan Inc.
Tokion #101 Wood House
1-11-3 Higashi, Shibuya-ku
Tokyo 150-0011, Japan
TEL/FAX: 03-5469-9318
E-MAIL: tokion@ari.bekkoame.or.jp
WEB: http://www.tokion.com

- *Primarily an alternative arts/fashion magazine,* Tokion *also includes avant-garde manga from* Garo *magazine*

USEFUL INTERNET NEWSGROUPS

alt.manga	Alternative manga topics in English
fj.rec.animation	Anime topics in Japanese
fj.rec.animation.oldies	Info on popular old anime, in Japanese
fj.rec.comics	Manga topics in Japanese
japan.anime	Anime topics, in Japanese
japan.comike.info	Information on *dōjinshi* market, in Japanese
japan.manga	Information on manga, in Japanese
rec.arts.anime.creative	Fan-authored stories based on anime/manga
rec.arts.anime.fandom	Important issues concerning Japanese animation fans
rec.arts.anime.games	Videogames, card games, and Role Playing Games based on anime
rec.arts.anime.info	General anime/manga information in English
rec.arts.anime. marketplace	Anime item trading etc. in English
rec.arts.anime.misc	Japanese animation fan discussion
rec.arts.anime.models	Models designed after Japanese animation characters
rec.arts.anime.music	Music as it pertains to Japanese animation
rec.arts.manga	All aspects of manga in English

- *NOTE: The Internet is one of the best sources of English information on manga and anime. There are scores of individual and corporate manga and anime-related homepages on the World Wide Web, with a vast amount of constantly updated information. Since Web sites and URLs change fairly regularly they are not listed here. Point your browser to YAHOO or other search services and enter the words "manga" or "anime" to find current sites. Two excellent jumping-off points are* **http://www.anipike.com** *and Gilles Poitras's site at* **http://www.koyagi.com**. *Also, many USENET groups can now be accessed through* **http://www.google.com**.

  Many Internet mailing lists cover a wide variety of specific artists, genres, and works. See the extensive "Welcome to rec.arts.manga" FAQ compiled by Steve Pearl and Iain Sinclair with the help of scores of Net manga devotees and authorities; it is regularly posted on **rec.arts.manga** *and* **rec.arts.anime.info** *on USENET.*

COMMERCIAL NETWORKS WITH MANGA-ANIME INFORMATION

America Online

Use "manga" or "anime" as a keyword to navigate to Wizard section or Japanimation Station

CompuServe

See the Anime/Manga (Japan) forum: GO COMICS

ANIME-THEMED CONVENTIONS WITH A MANGA COMPONENT

Conventions tend to change their venues regularly, so addresses and contact numbers are not listed here. Instead, geographical regions and names are provided for some of the major conventions. For up-to-date, accurate information on convention sites, dates, and prices, check with the on-line information services listed above (especially **rec.arts.anime.info**) aor inquire at local comic book specialty shops and manga/anime clubs. Conventions are rapidly growing in size and number.

Anime Central

- *A midwest con*

Anime Expo

- *Summer, Los Angeles; largest U.S. anime-manga con*

Anime North

- *Held in Toronto, Canada, in the summer*

Anime Weekend

- *Atlanta*

Chibicon

- *A smaller but active con now in the Houston, Texas, area*

Fanime Con

- *San Francisco Bay Area's largest con*

Katsucon

- *Usually held in Virginia in late winter or early spring*

Minamicom/Ayacon

- *Two U.K. conventions, usually held in the south and north of England, in spring and fall, respectively*

Otakon

- *Usually held on East Coast in the summer, in Baltimore–Washington, D.C. area*

Project A-Kon

- *Texas, summer*

参考文献

REFERENCES AND RECOMMENDED READINGS

REFERENCES

Adachi, Noriyuki. *Yōkai to Aruku: Hyōden—Shigeru Mizuki* ("Walking with Goblins: A Critical Biography"). Tokyo: Bungei Shunjū, 1994.

Akita Shoten, ed. *Tezuka Osamu Manga 40-nen* ("Forty Years of Osamu Tezuka Cartoons"). Tokyo: Akita Shoten, 1984.

Aramata, Hiroshi. *Manga to Jinsei* ("Manga and Life"). Tokyo: Shūeisha, 1994.

Bisland, Elizabeth, ed. *The Japanese Letters of Lafcadio Hearn*. Boston: Houghton Mifflin, 1910.

Clements, Jonathan. "The Mechanics of the U.S. Anime and Manga Industry." *Foundation: The Review of Science Fiction*, no. 64 (Summer 1995), pp. 32–44.

Cote, Mark. "Crossed Hairs." *Intersect*, February 1993, pp. 23–26.

Covert, Brian. "Manga, Racism, and Tezuka." *The Japan Times Weekly*, vol. 32, no. 16 (18 April 1992), pp. 1–4.

Eisner, Will. *Comics & Sequential Art*. Tamarac, Florida: Poorhouse Press, 1985.

Fujiko Fujio. *Futari de Shōnen Manga Bakari Kaite Kita* ("All We've Ever Done Is Draw Boys' Comics"). Tokyo: Bungei Shunjū, 1980.

Fujishima, Usaku. *Sengō Manga Minzoku-shi* ("Postwar Manga Cultural History"). Tokyo: Kawai Shuppan, 1990.

Fukushima, Akira. *Manga to Nihonjin: "Yūgai" Komikku Bōkokuron o Kiru* ("Manga and the Japanese: Dissecting the Myth of 'Harmful Comics' Ruining the Nation"). Tokyo: Nihon Bungeisha, 1992.

Fukuya, Inc., ed. *'95 COMIC CATALOG*. Tokyo: Fukuya, 1995.

"Garo Fūunroku: Manga Ōkoku 30-nen no Kiseki" ("A Record of *Garo*'s Stormy Times: The Thirty-Year Miracle of the Manga Kingdom"). *Weekly Asahi Graph*, 21 October 1994, pp. 3–23.

Garo 20-nen-shi Kankō-iinkai, ed. *Mokuzō Morutaru no Ō Garo*

20-nenshi ("The Wooden-Mortared Kingdom: *Garo* 20th Memorial Issue"). Tokyo: Seirindō, 1984.

Garo-shi Henshū-iinkai, ed. *Garo Mandara* ("Garo Mandala"). Tokyo: TBS Britannica, 1991.

Gendai Fūzoku Kenkyūkai, ed. *Manga Kankyō: Gendai Fūzoku '93* ("The Manga Environment: Current Public Morals and Manners, 1993"). Tokyo: Riburopōto, 1993.

Groensteen, Thierry. *L'Universe des Mangas: Une introduction à la bande dessinée Japonaise*. Belgium, Tournai: Casterman, 1991.

Horn, Carl Gustav. "American Manga: Why Many American Comic Artists Are 'Turning Japanese.'" *Wizard*, no. 56 (April 1996), pp. 52–57.

Ichinoe, Tadashi. *Mangaka no Seikatsu* ("The Life of Manga Artists"). Tokyo: Hamano Shuppan, 1989.

Ihara, Keiko. "Kyōtsūgo wa SF Anime Da: Ōmu-shiki Hassō no Kagi" ("Sci-Fi Animation Is Their Common Language: The Key to AUM-style Thinking"). *Aera*, no. 19 (24 April 1995), pp.19–21.

Ishigami, Mitsutoshi. *Tezuka Osamu no Jidai* ("The Age of Osamu Tezuka"). Tokyo: Tairiku Shobō, 1989.

———. *Tezuka Osamu no Kimyō na Sekai*. ("The Strange World of Osamu Tezuka"). Tokyo: Kisōtengaisha, 1977.

Ishiko, Jun. *Nihon Mangashi* ("History of Japanese Manga"). Vols. 1 and 2. Tokyo: Ōtsuki Shoten, 1979.

Ishinomori, Shōtarō. *Manga Chō Shinkaron* ("Comic Evolution"). Tokyo: Kawade Shobō Shinsha, 1989.

———. *Shōsetsu: Tokiwasō, Haru* ("The Chapter: Tokiwasō, Spring"). Tokyo: Sukora, 1981.

Ishizu, Arashi. *Mushi Puro no Samurai-tachi* ("The Samurai of Mushi Productions"). Tokyo: Futabasha, 1980.

Japan Cartoonists Association, ed. *Nihon Mangaka Katarogu* ("Catalog of Japan's Manga Artists"). Tokyo: Japan Cartoonists Association, 1992.

Kobayashi, Yoshinori, and Yoshikazu Takeuchi. *Ōmu-teki!* ("AUM-ish!"). Tokyo: Fangs, 1995.

Koike, Masaharu. "Genki na Take Shobō, Seme no Keiei wa Mi o Musubuka" ("Healthy Take Shobō: Will the Aggressive Strategy Bear Fruit?"). *Tsukuru*, November 1994, pp. 44–51.

Komikku Hyōgen no Jiyū o Mamorukai, ed. *Shigaisen* ("Undeclared War on Publications"). Tokyo: Tsukuru Shuppan, 1992.

Kondō, Kōtarō. "Manga Sangyō Tasogare no Hajimari: 5,500-oku En Shijō no Kyodai Media" ("The Beginning of the Twilight of the Manga Industry: A Giant Medium Now Worth 550 Billion Yen"), *Aera*, 27 March 1995, pp. 32–33.

Kure, Tomofusa. *Gendai Manga no Zentaizō: Zōhoban.* ("The Totality of Modern Manga: The Expanded Version"). Tokyo: Shiki Shuppan, 1990.

———, ed. *Kobayashi Yoshinori Ronjōsetsu: Gōmanizumu to wa Nanika* ("Debating Yoshinori Kobayashi: What is 'Arrogantism'?"). Tokyo: Shuppō Shinsha, 1995.

Ledoux, Trish, and Doug Ranney. *The Complete Anime Guide: Japanese Animation Video Directory and Resource Guide.* Edited by Fred Patten. Issaquah, Wash.: Tiger Mountain Press, 1995.

Lent, John A. "Manga and Anime in Asia." *Anime UK*, May 1995, pp. 8–10.

Lowell, Percival. *The Soul of the Far East.* Boston: Houghton, Mifflin, 1888.

Manga Kisō Tekunikku Kōza ("Seminar on Basic Manga Techniques"). Tokyo: Bijutsu Shuppansha, 1989.

Manga Ōyō Tekunikku Kōza ("Seminar on Manga Application Techniques"). Tokyo: Bijitsu Shuppansha, 1990.

Manga Supā Tekunikku Kōza ("Seminar on Manga Super Techniques"). Tokyo: Bijutsu Shuppansha, 1988.

McCarthy, Helen. *The Anime Movie Guide: 1983–1995, The OAV Years.* London: Titan Books, 1996.

McCloud, Scott. *Understanding Comics.* Northampton, Mass.: Kitchen Sink Press, 1993.

———. "Understanding Manga." *Wizard,* no. 56 (April 1996), pp. 52–58.

McPherson, Darwin. "Inside Studio Proteus: A Talk with Toren Smith." *Amazing Heroes,* no. 181 (July 1990), pp. 27–38.

Miller, Jackson. "State of the Industry 1995: The Year Everything Changed." *Comics Buyer's Guide 1996 Annual*, pp. 51–69.

Murakami, Tomohiko, and Osamu Takeuchi, ed. *Manga Hihyō Taikei* ("An Organized System of Manga Criticism"). Vols. 1–4. Tokyo: Heibonsha, 1989.

Nakano, Haruyuki. *Tezuka Osamu no Takarazuka* ("Tezuka Osamu's Takarazuka"). Tokyo: Chikuma Shobō, 1994.

Natsume, Fusanosuke. *Natsume Fusanosuke no Mangagaku* ("Fusanosuke Natsume's School of Manga"). Tokyo: Chikuma Shobō, 1992.

———. *Tezuka Osamu wa Doko ni Iru* ("Where is Osamu Tezuka?"). Tokyo: Chikuma Shobō, 1995.

Nagai, Katsuichi. *Garo Henshūchō: Watashi no Sengo Manga Shuppanshi* ("The Editor-in-Chief of *Garo*: My Postwar Comics Publishing History"). Tokyo: Chikuma Shobō, 1982.

Newitz, Annalee. "Magical Girls and Atomic Bomb Sperm: Japanese Animation in America." *Film Quarterly*, vol. 49, no. 1 (Fall 1995).

Nihon Manga Gakuin and Tadao Kimura, ed. *Mangaka Meikan* ("A Directory of Manga Artists"). Tokyo: Kusanone Shuppankai, 1989.

Nihon Mangaka Meikan 500 Committee, ed. *Nihon Mangaka Meikan 500* ("Directory of 500 Japanese Manga Artists"). Tokyo: Aqua Planning, 1992.

Nishimura, Shigeo. *Saraba Waga Seishun no "Shōnen Jampu"* ("Farewell to the *Shōnen Jump* of My Youth"). Tokyo: Asuka Shinsha, 1994.

Okada, Toshio. "Anime Bunka wa Chō Kakkoii!!: Nihon ni Koi Suru Beikoku no Otaku" (Anime Culture is Ultra-Cool! American *Otakus* in Love with Japan"). *Aera,* 2 October 1995, pp. 43–44.

Ōtsuka, Eiji, et al. *Emu no Sedai: Bokura to Miyazaki-kun* ("The M-Generation: Young Miyazaki and Us"). Tokyo: Ōta Shuppan, 1989.

Patten, Fred. "Simba vs. Kimba: Parallels between *Kimba, the White Lion* and *The Lion King*." Paper submitted at "The Life of Illusion: Australia's Second International Conference on Animation," Museum of Contemporary Art, Sydney, N.S.W., Australia, 3–5 March 1995.

———. "1977–1992: Fifteen Years of North American Fandom" (Parts 1 and 2). *Anime UK Magazine* (12), vol 3, no. 1 (February–March 1994), pp. 12–17; (13), vol 3, no. 2 (April–May 1994), pp. 34–39.

Pollack, Andrew. "Japan: A Superpower Among Superheroes." *New York Times*, 17 September 1995, p. 32.

Saitani, Ryō. "Miyazaki Hayao Rongu Intabyū: Mae Yori mo Naushikā no Koto ga Sukoshi Wakaru Yō ni Natta." ("The Long Interview with Hayao Miyazaki: I Now Understand Nausicaä a Little Better Than Before"). *Comic Box*, vol. 98 (January 1995), pp. 6–37.

Sakuma, Akira. *Dakara Manga Daisuki!* ("That's Why I Love Manga!"). Tokyo: Shūeisha, 1982.

Sakura, Tetsuo. *Tezuka Osamu: Jidai to Kirimusubu Hyōgensha.* ("Osamu Tezuka: A Man Who Took On and Expressed His Era"). Tokyo: Kōdansha, 1990.

Sandē Manga Karedji, ed. *Tsukurō! Dōjinshi* ("Let's Make Dōjinshi!"). Tokyo: Shōgakukan, 1983.

Schodt, Frederik L. *America and the Four Japans: Friend, Foe, Model, Mirror.* Berkeley: Stone Bridge Press, 1994.

———. *Inside the Robot Kingdom: Japan, Mechatronics, and the Coming Robotopia*. Tokyo: Kodansha International, 1988.

———. *Manga! Manga! The World of Japanese Comics*. Tokyo: Kodansha International, 1983.

———.. "Comics and Social Change," *PHP*, April 1984, pp. 15–25.

———. "Manga Honyaku wa Doko Made Kanōka" ("What Are the Limits on Translating Comics and Cartoons?"). *Honyaku Jiten*, November 1984.

Sekikawa, Natsuo. *Chishikiteki Taishū Shokun: Kore mo Manga Da* ("Ah, Yee Intelligent Masses: These, Too, Are Manga"). Tokyo: Bungei Shunjū, 1991.

Setagaya Doraemon Kenkyūkai. *Doraemon no Himitsu* ("The Secrets of Doraemon"). Tokyo: Data House, 1993.

Seward, Jack, ed. *Japanese Eroticism: A Language Guide to Current Comics*. Houston, Texas: Yugen Press, 1993.

Shimizu, Isao. *Nihon Manga no Jiten* ("Dictionary of Japanese Manga"). Tokyo: Sanseidō, 1985.

Shuppan Shihyō Nenpō: 1995-nenban ("Annual Indices of Publishing: The 1995 Edition"). Tokyo: Zenkoku Shuppan Kyōkai / Shuppan Kagaku Kenkyū Sentā, 1995.

Sischy, Ingrid. "Onward and Upward with the Arts: Selling Dreams." *New Yorker*, 28 September 1992, pp. 84–103.

Smith, Toren. "Sex in Manga." *Comics Journal*, no. 143 (July 1991).

Takahashi, Keiichi. "Byakuya Shobō no 'Soredemo Erobon wa Fumetsu Desu'" ("Byakuya Shobō's Philosophy of 'Despite All This, We Think Erotic Publications Will Last Forever'"). *Tsukuru*, November 1994, pp. 80–86.

Takeuchi, Natsuki. *Manga no Tatsujin: Manga to Dōjinshi no Subete ga Wakaru!* ("The Manga Experts: Everything You Need to Know about Manga and Dōjinshi"). Tokyo: KK Best Sellers, 1993.

Takeuchi, Osamu. *Sengō Manga 50-nenshi* ("Fifty-Year History of Postwar Manga"). Tokyo: Chikuma Shobō, 1995.

Terada, Hirō, ed. *Manga Shōnen-shi* ("A History of Boys' Manga"). Tokyo: Shōnan Shuppansha, 1981.

Terasawa, Buichi, Junco Itō, Scholar editorial staff, et al. *Macintosh no Dennō Manga Jutsu: Mac de Hirogaru Terasawa Buichi Wārudo* ("Cyber Manga Techniques with the Macintosh: The World of Buichi Terasawa Expands with the Mac"). Tokyo: Scholar, 1994.

Tezuka, Osamu. *Boku wa Mangaka: Tezuka Osamu Jiden 1* ("I Am a Cartoonist: Osamu Tezuka's Autobiography 1"). Tokyo: Daiwa Shobō, 1979.

———. *Mitari, Tottari, Utsushitari* ("Viewing, Shooting, Screening"). Tokyo: Kinema Junpōsha, 1987.

———. *Mushirareppanashi* ("Plucked and Nibbled Talks"). Tokyo: Shinchōsha, 1981.

———. *Tezuka Osamu no Subete.* ("A Collection of the Works of Osamu Tezuka"). Tokyo: Daitōsha, 1981.

———. *Tezuka Osamu Rando* ("Osamu Tezuka Land"). Tokyo: Daiwa Shobō, 1977.

———. *Tezuka Osamu Rando 2* ("Osamu Tezuka Land 2"). Tokyo: Daiwa Shobō, 1978.

Tezuka Productions, ed. *Tezuka Osamu Gekijō* ("The Animation Filmography of Osamu Tezuka"). Tokyo: Tezuka Productions, 1991.

———. *Tezuka Osamu Kinenkan* ("The Osamu Tezuka Manga Museum"). Takarazuka: Takarazuka City Osamu Tezuka Manga Museum, 1994.

Tokio, Teruhiko, ed. *Chinmoku no Kantai: Kaitai Shinsho* ("Silent Service: A New Book of Analysis"). Tokyo: Kōdansha, 1995.

Tsuge, Yoshiharu. *Tsuge Yoshiharu to Boku* ("Me and Yoshiharu Tsuge"). Tokyo: Shōbunsha, 1977.

———. *Hinkonryokōki* ("Journal of Impoverished Travel"). Tokyo: Shōbunsha, 1991.

Tsukuru editorial staff, ed. *"Yūgai" Komikku Mondai o Kangaeru* ("Thinking About the Issue of 'Harmful' Comics"). Tokyo: Tsukuru Shuppan, 1991.

Uchida, Shungicu. *Fuazā Fakkā* ("Father Fucker"). Tokyo: Bungei Shunjū, 1993.

Yamamoto, Eiichi. *Mushi Puro Kōbōki: Animēta no Seishun* ("The Rise and Fall of Mushi Productions: My Youth as an Animator"). Tokyo: Shinchōsha, 1989.

Yonezawa, Yoshihiro. *Sengō Gyaggu Mangashi* ("A History of Postwar Gag Manga"). Tokyo: Shinpyōsha, 1981.

———. *Sengō SF Mangashi* ("A History of Postwar Sci-Fi Manga"). Tokyo: Shinpyōsha, 1980.

———. *Sengō Shōjō Mangashi* ("A History of Postwar Girls' Manga"). Tokyo: Shinpyōsha, 1980.

Zasshi Shinbun Sōkatarogu ("Japan's Periodicals in Print"). Tokyo: Media Research Center, 1979.

"Zenryaku W. Dizunisama." ("Dear Mr. Walt Disney"). *Asahi Shinbun*, 27 August 1994, p. 5.

SPECIAL FEATURES IN MAGAZINES

(Regularly issued magazines with multiple articles at least partially dedicated to a specific feature subject)

"Banana Fishu to Yoshida Akimi Gurafiti" ("*Banana Fish* and Akimi Yoshida Graffiti"). *Comic Box*, September 1990, pp. 23–49.

"Chinmoku no Kantai" ("Silent Service"). *Comic Box*, July 1991, pp. 15–30.

"Dēta de Miru Komikkusu Shijō '95" ("The 1995 Comics' Market According to the Data"). *Shuppan Geppō*, March 1995, pp. 4–9.

"Dokyumento: Haru no Komikku Māketto" ("Document of the Spring Comic Market"). *Comic Box*, June 1989, pp. 20–34.

"Ebisu Yoshikazu Tokushū" ("Special Yoshikazu Ebisu Feature"). *Garo*, May 1993, pp. 3–42.

"Hanawa Kazuichi no Sekai" ("The World of Kazuichi Hanawa"). *Garo*, May 1992, pp. 3–47.

Manga Bakari Yome! Komikku Dorankā no Tame no Manga Gaido ("Read Only Manga! Manga Guide for Comics Drunkards!"). *03 Tokyo Calling*. September 1991, pp.18–71.

"Manga wa Bungaku" ("Manga Are Literature"). *Kaien*, July 1993, pp. 3–114.

"Manga Zasshi Dai Kenkyū!" *Comic Box*, vol. 44 (November 1987), pp. 92–106.

"Maruo Suehiro" ("Suehiro Maruo"). *Garo*, May 1993, pp. 3–40.

"Mizuki Shigeru no Sekai" ("The World of Shigeru Mizuki"). Expanded edition of *Asahi Graph*, no. 3735 (10 December 1993), pp. 3–22.

"Mizuki Shigeru Tokushū 2" ("Shigeru Mizuki Special 2"). *Garo*, January 1993, pp. 3–58.

"Mizuki Shigeru Tokushūgo" ("The Shigeru Mizuki Special Edition"). *Garo*, September 1991, pp. 3–80.

"Poruno na Kibun" ("A Porn Feeling"). *CREA*, June 1994, pp. 59–107.

"Sabetsu to Hyōgen 1" ("Discrimination and Expression 1"). *Comic Box*, January 1991, pp. 22–33.

"Sabetsu to Hyōgen 3" ("Discrimination and Expression 3"). *Comic Box*, March/ April 1991, pp. 134–44.

"Susume Manga Seinen!" ("Onward, Manga Youths!"). *Marco Polo*, May 1993, pp. 3–108.

"THE Shōjo Manga!" ("THE Girls' Manga!"). *CREA*, September 1992, pp. 71–132.

"'Tsuge Yoshiharu' suru!" ("Doing Yoshiharu Tsuge!"). *Garo*, August 1993, pp. 3–59.

"Uchida Shungicu Intābyū: 'The Life of UltraDeep'" ("Shungicu Uchida Interview: The Life of UltraDeep"). *Garo,* November 1992, pp. 11–32.

"Umi o Koeru Doraemon" ("Doraemon Goes Overseas"). *Yom,* June 1993, pp. 2–23.

"Yamada Murasaki Tokushū" ("Special Murasaki Yamada Feature Issue"). *Garo,* February–March 1993, pp. 4–67.

SPECIAL FEATURE EDITIONS OF MAGAZINES

(Regular editions usually entirely devoted to a specific feature subject)

"Comic Box: Manga 1993–1994" ("Manga 1993-1994"). Expanded June/July edition of *Comic Box Jr.*, July 1994.

"Kaze no Tani no Naushika" ("Nausicaä, of the Valley of Wind"). *Comic Box*, vol. 98 (January 1995).

"Manga Ōkoku no Kageri?" ("Shadows on the Manga Kingdom?"). *The Tsukuru*, no. 10 (1995), pp. 16–105.

"Manga Sōkessan: 1988" ("Settling of Accounts for Manga: 1988"). *Comic Box*, March/ April 1989).

"Manga Sōkessan: 1989" ("Settling of Accounts for Manga: 1989"). *Comic Box*, May 1990.

"Manga Sōkessan: 1992" ("Settling of Accounts for Manga: 1992"). *Comic Box*, vol. 95 (August 1993).

"Manga Sōkessan: 1994–95" ("Settling of Accounts for Manga: 1994–95"). *Comic Box*. vol. 99 (July 1995).

"Manga Taikoku Nippon" ("Manga Superpower Japan"). *The Tsukuru*, no. 8 (1994), pp. 18–109.

"Miyazaki Hayao to Manga Eiga" ("Hayao Miyazaki and Manga Movies"). *Comic Box*, September 1989.

MAGAZINE *BESSATSU* ("SUPPLEMENT") EDITIONS

(Similar to books, but published as special supplement editions of regular magazines and usually dedicated to a specific subject)

Bessatsu Shinpyō: Sanryūgekiga no Sekai ("The World of Third-Rate Graphic Novels"). Spring 1979. Shinpyōsha.

Bessatsu Takarajima 196; Media de Yokujō Suru Hon: Nippon wa Dennō Etchi no Jikkenjō Da! ("Takarajima Supplement 196; The Book of Media-Inflamed Passions: Japan Is a Testing Site for Cyber Eroticism"). Tokyo: Takarajima-sha, 1994.

Bessatsu Takarajima 104: Otaku no Hon ("Takarajima Supplement 104: The Otaku Book"). Tokyo: Takarajima-sha, 1989.

Gendai Manga no Techō ("Handbook of Modern Manga"). Special supplement of *Kokubungaku: Kaishaku to Kyōzai no Kenkyū*. April 1981.

Kodomo no Shōwashi—Shōjo Manga no Sekai: Shōwa 20–37-nen ("Children's History of the Shōwa Era—The World of Girls'

Manga: 1945–62"). Special supplement issue of *Taiheiyō*. Tokyo: Heibonsha, 1991.

Kodomo no Shōwashi—Shōjo Manga no Sekai II: Shōwa 38–64-nen ("Children's History of the Shōwa Era: The World of Girls' Manga II, 1962–89). Special supplement issue of *Taiheiyō*. Tokyo: Heibonsha, 1991.

MT Manga Tekunikku ("MT Manga Techniques"). Special supplement of *Bessatsu BT Bijutsu Techō*. May 1994.

MT Manga Tekunikku ("MT Manga Techniques"). Special supplement of *Bessatsu BT Bijutsu Techō*. 2nd quarter, August 1995.

MT Manga Tekunikku: Bokutachi no Komikku Bishōjō Densetsu ("MT Manga Techniques: The Legendary Beautiful Girls of Our Comics"). Special supplement of *Bessatsu BT Bijutsu Techō*. 3rd quarter, November 1994.

Tezuka Osamu no Sekai ("The World of Osamu Tezuka"). Special supplement edition of *Asahi Journal*. 20 April 1989.

Viva Comic: Mangaka Daishūgō ("Viva Comic: A Grand Gathering of Manga Artists"). Special edition of *Shūkan Taishū*. 27 December 1984.

EXHIBITION CATALOGS AND PUBLICATIONS

Manga Hanseikiten: Kakareta Nippon no Shakai ("What's What in This 50 Years in Japanese Comic Books"). Special exhibition catalog. Tokyo Shinbun, 1995.

Museum of Contemporary Art, Sydney, ed. *KABOOM! Explosive Animation from America and Japan*. Sydney: Museum of Contemporary Art, 1994.

Tezuka Osamu-ten ("The Osamu Tezuka Exhibition"). Tokyo: National Museum of Modern Art / Asahi Shinbun, 1990.

Tezuka Osamu-ten: Kakō to Mirai no Imēji ("The Osamu Tezuka Exhibition: Images of the Past and Future"). Tokyo: Tezuka Productions / Asahi Shinbun, 1995.

索引

INDEX